PN

Literature (General)

Library of Congress Classification
2004

Prepared by the Cataloging Policy and Support Office
Library Services

LIBRARY OF CONGRESS
Cataloging Distribution Service
Washington, D.C.

This edition cumulates all additions and changes to Subclass PN through Weekly List 2004/18, dated May 5, 2004. Additions and changes made subsequent to that date are published in weekly lists posted on the World Wide Web at

<http://lcweb.loc.gov/catdir/cpso/cpso.html#class>

and are also available in *Classification Web*, the online Web-based edition of the Library of Congress Classification.

Library of Congress Cataloging-in-Publication Data

Library of Congress.
      Library of Congress classification. PN. Literature (General) / prepared by the Cataloging Policy and Support Office, Library Services.—2004 ed.
         p. cm.
      "This edition cumulates all additions and changes to subclass PN through Weekly list 2004/18, dated May 5, 2004. Additions and changes made subsequent to that date are published in weekly lists posted on the World Wide Web ... and are also available in Classification Web, the online Web-based editions of the Library of Congress classification."
      Includes index.
      ISBN 0-8444-1116-7
      1. Classification, Library of Congress. 2. Classification—Books—Literature. I. Title: Literature (general). II. Library of Congress. Cataloging Policy and Support Office. III. Title.

Z696.U5P75 2004
025.4'68—dc22

                                        2004048822

For sale by the Library of Congress Cataloging Distribution Service, 101 Independence Avenue, S.E., Washington, DC 20541-4912. Product catalog available on the Web at <http://www.loc.gov/cds>.

PREFACE

The first edition of *Subclass PN, Literature (General)*, was published in 1915, together with *Subclasses PR, PS*, and *PZ*. That edition was reissued in 1964 with supplementary pages. Subsequent editions were published in 1978 and 1988. In 1997, *Subclass PN* was published separately for the first time. This 2004 edition cumulates changes that have been made since the 1997 edition was published.

In this edition, classification numbers or spans of numbers that appear in parentheses are formerly valid numbers that are now obsolete. Numbers or spans that appear in angle brackets are optional numbers that have never been used at the Library of Congress but are provided for other libraries that wish to use them. In most cases, a parenthesized or angle-bracketed number is accompanied by a "see" reference directing the user to the actual number that the Library of Congress currently uses, or a note explaining Library of Congress practice.

Access to the online version of the full Library of Congress Classification is available on the World Wide Web by subscription to Classification Web. Details about ordering and pricing may be obtained from the Cataloging Distribution Service at:

<http://www.loc.gov/cds/>

New or revised numbers and captions are added to the L.C. Classification schedules as a result of development proposals made by the cataloging staff of the Library of Congress and cooperating institutions. Upon approval of these proposals by the weekly editorial meeting of the Cataloging Policy and Support Office, new classification records are created or existing records are revised in the master classification database. Weekly lists of newly approved or revised classification numbers and captions are posted on the World Wide Web at:

<http://lcweb.loc.gov/catdir/cpso/cpso.html#class>

Milicent Wewerka, senior cataloging policy specialist in the Cataloging Policy and Support Office, is responsible for coordinating the overall intellectual and editorial content of class P and its various subclasses. The Classification Editorial team, consisting of Barry Bellinger, Kent Griffiths, Nancy Jones, and Dorothy Thomas, assistant editors, creates new classification records and their associated index terms, and maintains the master database.

Barbara B. Tillett, Chief
Cataloging Policy and Support Office

May 2004

OUTLINE

PN1-6790   Literature (General)
PN1-9   Periodicals
PN20-30   Societies
PN45-57   Theory. Philosophy. Esthetics
PN59-72   Study and teaching
PN80-99   Criticism
PN101-245   Authorship
PN172-239   Technique. Literary composition, etc.
PN241-241.5   Translating as a literary pursuit
PN441-1009.5   Literary history
PN451-497   Biography
PN500-519   Collections
PN597-605   Special relations, movements, and
                     currents of literature

PN610-779   By period
PN611-649   Ancient
PN661-694   Medieval (to 1500)
PN683-687   Legends
PN688-691   Poetry
PN692-693   Prose. Prose fiction
PN695-779   Modern
PN715-749   Renaissance (1500-1700)
PN801-820   Romance literature
PN821-840   Germanic literature
PN841   Black literature (General)
PN842   Jewish literature in various languages
PN851-(884)   Comparative literature
PN(905)-1008   Folk literature
PN980-995   Fables
PN1008.2-1009.5 Juvenile literature
PN1010-1525   Poetry
PN1031-1049   Theory, philosophy, relations, etc.
PN1065-1085   Relations to, and treatment of,
                     special subjects

PN1110-1279   History and criticism
PN1301-1333   Epic poetry
PN1341-1347   Folk poetry
PN1351-1389   Lyric poetry
PN1530   The monologue
PN1551   The dialogue
PN1560-1590   The performing arts. Show business
PN1585-1589   Centers for the performing arts

OUTLINE

Literature (General) - Continued

PN1600-3307	Drama
PN1635-1650	Relation to, and treatment of, special subjects
PN1660-1693	Technique of dramatic composition
PN1720-1861	History
PN1865-1988	Special types
PN1990-1992.92	Broadcasting
PN1991-1991.9	Radio broadcasts
PN1992-1992.92	Television broadcasts
PN1992.93-19 92.95	Nonbroadcast video recordings
PN1993-1999	Motion pictures
PN1997-1997.85	Plays, scenarios, etc.
PN2000-3307	Dramatic representation. The theater
PN2061-2071	Art of acting
PN2085-2091	The stage and accessories
PN2131-2193	By period
PN2131-2145	Ancient
PN2152-2160	Medieval
PN2171-2179	Renaissance
PN2181-2193	Modern
PN2219.3-3030	Special regions or countries
PN3035	The Jewish theater
PN3151-3171	Amateur theater
PN3175-3191	College and school theatricals
PN3203-3299	Tableaux, pageants, "Happenings," etc.
PN3311-3503	Prose. Prose fiction
PN3329-3352	Philosophy, theory, etc.
PN3355-3383	Technique. Authorship
PN3427-3448	Special kinds of fiction. Fiction genres
PN3451-3503	History
PN4001-4355	Oratory. Elocution, etc.
PN4071-4095	Study and teaching
PN4177-4191	Debating
PN4199-4321	Recitations (in English)
PN4331-4355	Recitations in foreign languages
PN4390	Diaries
PN4400	Letters (Literary history)
PN4500	Essays (Literary history)
PN4699-5650	Journalism. The periodical press, etc.
PN4735-4748	Relation to the state. Government and the press. Liberty of the press
PN4775-4784	Technique. Practical journalism

OUTLINE

Literature (General)

Journalism. The periodical press, etc. - Continued

PN4825-4830	Amateur journalism
PN4832-4836	Magazines and other periodicals
PN4840-5648	By region or country
PN5650	The Jewish press
PN6010-6790	Collections of general literature
PN6066-6069	Special classes of authors
PN6080-6095	Quotations
PN6081-6084	English
PN6086-6089	French
PN6090-6110	German
PN6099-6110	Poetry
PN6110.5-6120	Drama
PN6120.15-6120.95	Fiction
PN6121-6129	Orations
PN6130-6140	Letters
PN6141-6145	Essays
PN6146.5-6231	Wit and humor
PN6157-6222	By region or country
PN6233-6238	Anacreontic literature
PN6244-6246	Literary extracts. Commonplace books
PN6249-6258	Ana
PN6259-6268	Anecdotes. Table talk
PN6269-6278	Aphorisms. Apothegms
PN6279-6288	Epigrams
PN6288.5-6298	Epitaphs
PN6299-6308	Maxims
PN6309-6318	Mottoes
PN6319-6328	Sayings, bon mots, etc.
PN6329-6338	Thoughts
PN6340-6348	Toasts
PN6348.5-6358	Emblems, devices
PN6361	Paradoxes
PN6366-6377	Riddles, acrostics, charades, conundrums, etc.
PN6400-6525	Proverbs
PN6700-6790	Comic books, strips, etc.

Literature (General)
  Periodicals
        Class here periodicals devoted to general
            literary history and criticism with or
            without creative writing
        For purely bibliographical periodicals and
            reviews, see class Z (e.g., Review
            critique); for periodicals on general
            linguistics and special languages and
            literature, see P - PZ
        For general periodicals, magazines, and reviews
            not limited to a specific subject field see
            AP1+

1	International (Polyglot)
2	American and English
3	French
4	German
5	Italian
6	Spanish
9	Other

  Yearbooks

11	International (Polyglot)
12	American and English
13	French
14	German
15	Italian
16	Spanish
19	Other

  Societies
        Class here all literary societies of general
            nature
        Cf. PN121 Authors' associations
        Cf. PR5 Literary societies (English literature)
        Cf. PS5 Literary societies (American literature)

20	Aims, scope, utility, etc.
	Individual societies
21	International (Polyglot)
21.A2	Collective
22	American and English
22.A2	Collective
23	French
23.A2	Collective
24	German
24.A2	Collective
25	Italian
25.A2	Collective
26	Spanish

	Societies
	Individual societies
	Spanish -- Continued
26.A2	Collective
29	Other
30	Literary societies in public schools
33	Congresses
34	Museums. Exhibitions. By author
	Collections
	Cf. PN861+ Comparative literature (Collections)
35	Series. Monographs by different authors
36.A-Z	Studies in honor of a particular person or institution. Festschriften. By honoree, A-Z
37	Collected works, papers, essays, of individual authors
	Cf. PN58 Single essays
	Encyclopedias. Dictionaries
	Cf. PN451+ Biography
41	General
43	Miscellaneous and special
	Including works not in dictionary form, i.e., Notes and queries, Curiosities of literature, Dictionaries of phrase and fable, Allusions, etc.
	Information services
43.5	General works
43.7	Computer network resources
	Including the Internet
44	Digests of literature. Synopses, etc.
	Including Best fifty books condensed
44.5	Terminology
	Theory. Philosophy. Esthetics
	Cf. BH1+ Aesthetics
	Cf. N61+ Visual arts
	Cf. PN80+ Criticism
	Cf. PN101+ Authorship
45	General works. Ideals, content, etc. Plots, motives
45.5	Forms of literature
	Relation to and treatment of special elements, problems, and subjects
46	Inspiration
47	Life

Theory. Philosophy. Esthetics

Relation to and treatment of special elements,
problems, and subjects -- Continued

48	Nature
	Cf. PN56.F5 Fishing
	Cf. PN56.G3 Gardens
	Cf. PQ145.3 French literature
	Cf. PR143 English literature
	Cf. PR508.N3 English poetry, etc.
49	Philosophy, ethics, religion, etc.
	Cf. PN1077 Poetry
	Cf. PN1647 Drama
	Cf. PN3347 Prose
50	Relation to history
51	Relation to sociology, economics, political science, etc. (social ideals, forces, etc. in literature)
52	Relation to education
53	Relation to art
54	Relation to language
55	Relation to science
	Other special
56.A-Z	Topics, A-Z
	Class here works that are not limited to one form, nor to one national literature
56.A23	Abjection
56.A24	Absurdity
56.A3	Adventure
56.A4	Aeronautics
	Aging see PN56.O4
56.A44	Alchemy
56.A45	Alienation (Social psychology)
56.A5	Allegory
56.A55	Ambiguity
	Anagnorisis see PN56.R33
56.A57	Androgyny (Psychology)
56.A59	Angels
56.A6	Anger
56.A64	Animals
56.A67	Antiquities
56.A69	Apocalyptic literature
56.A72	Archetypes
56.A73	Architecture
56.A77	Astrology
56.A8	Astronautics
56.A82	Astronomy
56.A85	Aunts

Theory. Philosophy. Esthetics
Relation to and treatment of special elements,
problems, and subjects
Other special
Topics, A-Z -- Continued

56.A87	Authority
56.A89	Autobiography
56.A9	Automata
56.B23	Babel, Tower of
56.B27	Balloons
56.B3	Baroque literature
56.B5	Bible
56.B56	Birds
56.B6	Blindness
56.B62	Body, Human
56.B64	Books
56.B7	Boredom
56.B74	Boundaries
56.C34	Cannibalism
56.C36	Castration
56.C37	Cats
56.C38	Causation
56.C39	Caves
56.C43	Chance
56.C44	Change
56.C47	Chess
56.C49	Childbirth
56.C53	Chivalry
56.C55	Cities and towns
56.C6	Classicism
56.C612	Climate
56.C614	Cockaigne
56.C63	Colonies
56.C65	Color
56.C66	The comic
56.C662	Communication
56.C663	Concentration camps
56.C67	Confession
56.C674	Conscience
56.C676	Contradiction
56.C68	Cosmology
56.C684	Costume
56.C686	Country life
56.C69	Creation (Artistic, literary, etc.)
56.C7	Crime
56.C72	Criminology
56.C74	Crying

Theory. Philosophy. Esthetics
    Relation to and treatment of special elements,
        problems, and subjects
      Other special
        Topics, A-Z -- Continued

56.C83	Cucurbitaceae
56.D29	Dance
56.D4	Death
56.D45	Decadence (Literary movement)
56.D46	Deception
56.D47	Dependency (Psychology)
56.D477	Deserts
56.D48	Desire
56.D54	Digression (Rhetoric)
56.D56	Diseases
56.D6	Dogs
56.D64	Donkeys
56.D65	Doors
56.D67	Doubles
56.D75	Dreams
56.D8	Drinking
56.D82	Drugs
56.D84	Dueling
56.D94	Dystopias
56.E27	Ecstasy
56.E45	Ekphrasis
56.E57	Emblems
56.E6	Emotions
56.E62	Empathy
56.E63	End of the world
56.E635	Enthusiasm
56.E64	Envy
56.E65	Epic literature
56.E66	Epilepsy
56.E67	Epiphanies
56.E7	Erotic motive
56.E73	Eschatology
56.E74	Etiquette
56.E75	Evil
56.E77	Existentialism
56.E78	Exoticism
56.E785	Expressionism
56.E8	Extortion
56.E9	Eye
56.F27	Failure (Psychology)
56.F29	Fall of man
	Falsehood see PN56.T78

Theory. Philosophy. Esthetics
Relation to and treatment of special elements,
problems, and subjects
Other special
Topics, A-Z -- Continued

56.F297	Fame
56.F3	Family
56.F34	Fantastic literature
56.F35	Fascism
56.F358	Fate and fatalism
56.F36	Father-search
56.F37	Fathers and sons
56.F39	Fear
56.F4	Femininity
56.F46	Feminism
56.F5	Fishing. Piscatory literature
56.F53	Fleas
56.F55	Flowers
	Cf. PN56.R75 Roses
56.F58	Folklore
	Cf. GR41.3 Literature and folklore
56.F59	Food
56.F64	Forests
56.F73	Freemasonry
56.F74	Friendship
56.F76	Fruit
56.F8	Futurism
56.G27	Gambling
56.G3	Gardens
56.G45	Gender identity
56.G46	Genealogy
56.G47	Generations
56.G48	Geography
56.G67	Grail
56.G7	Grotesque
56.G87	Guilt
56.H27	Happiness
56.H3	Harmony (Aesthetics)
56.H35	Healing
56.H37	Health resorts, watering-places, etc.
56.H374	Heart
56.H38	Hell
56.H4	Hellenism
56.H55	Holocaust, Jewish (1939-1945)
56.H557	Home
56.H56	Homeland
56.H57	Homosexuality

Theory. Philosophy. Esthetics
Relation to and treatment of special elements,
problems, and subjects
Other special
Topics, A-Z -- Continued

56.H58	Honor
56.H59	Horizon
56.H6	Horror
56.H63	Horses and horsemen
56.H66	Hospitality
56.H83	Humor
56.H84	Hunting
56.I4	Idealism

> Including realism and idealism, and
> general esthetic discussions of
> idealism, realism, naturalism,
> romanticism, etc.
> For history of movements see PN599
> Cf. PN56.R3 Realism
> Cf. PN56.R7 Romanticism

56.I42	Identity (Psychology)
56.I43	Illusion
	Imaginary voyages see PN56.V59
56.I45	Imagination
56.I46	Imperfection
56.I465	Imperialism
56.I47	Impersonation in literature
56.I48	Implication (Logic)
56.I5	Impressionism
56.I55	Incest
56.I57	Individualism. Individuation
56.I58	Industry
56.I59	Ineffable
56.I593	Influence (Literary, artistic, etc.)
56.I595	Innocence
56.I63	Insects
56.I64	Internet
56.I65	Irony
56.I7	Islands
56.J43	Jealousy
56.J68	Journalism
56.J87	Justice
56.K54	Kissing
56.K62	Knowledge
56.K66	Kosovo, Battle of, 1389
56.L22	Labor. Working classes
56.L223	Labyrinths

Theory. Philosophy. Esthetics
Relation to and treatment of special elements,
problems, and subjects
Other special
Topics, A-Z -- Continued

56.L24	Lakes
56.L25	Lameness
56.L26	Landscape
56.L27	Language and languages
56.L3	Laughter
56.L33	Law
56.L4	Leisure
56.L45	Lesbianism
56.L48	Libraries
56.L52	Life cycle, Human
56.L53	Light and darkness
56.L54	Lists
56.L55	Local color
56.L56	Loneliness
56.L6	Love
56.M2	Machinery
56.M23	Magic
56.M24	Magic realism
56.M25	Man
56.M255	Man-woman relationships
56.M26	Manners and customs
56.M27	Marginality, Social
56.M28	Marriage
56.M3	The Marvelous, miracles, wonders, etc.
56.M316	Masculinity
56.M318	Masks
56.M32	Masochism
56.M33	Masquerades
56.M35	Materialism
56.M37	Meaning (Philosophy)
56.M38	Medicine
56.M4	Melancholy
56.M44	Memory
56.M45	Mental illness
56.M48	Mentoring
56.M52	Mesmerism
56.M53	Metamorphosis
56.M534	Middle Ages

     Class here works on the portrayal of the
      Middle Ages in modern literature
     For literary history of the medieval
      period see PN661+

Theory. Philosophy. Esthetics
Relation to and treatment of special elements,
problems, and subjects
Other special
Topics, A-Z -- Continued

56.M535	Middle classes
56.M536	Mimesis
56.M5363	Miniature dolls
56.M537	Mirrors
56.M538	Misogyny
56.M54	Modernism (Literature)
56.M547	Money
56.M55	Monsters
56.M58	Moon
56.M7	Mountains
56.M8	Multiculturalism
56.M85	Murder
56.M87	Music in literature

For influence of literature on music see
ML3849

56.M94	Myth
56.M95	Mythology
56.N16	Names
56.N18	Narcotics
56.N19	Nationalism
	Naturalism see PN56.R3
56.N36	Negritude
56.N4	Neuroses
56.N5	Night
56.N55	Nihilism
56.N6	"No" as a literary motif
56.N63	Nobility of character
56.N67	Nose
56.N69	Nothingness
56.N83	Nuclear warfare
56.N86	Numbers
56.O33	Occultism. Occult sciences
56.O4	Old age
56.O63	Oracles
56.O66	Order
56.O67	Originality
56.O7	Otherworld
56.P23	Parables

Cf. BL-BX, Religion

56.P25	Paradise
56.P26	Parody
56.P3	Pastoral literature

Theory. Philosophy. Esthetics
Relation to and treatment of special elements,
problems, and subjects
Other special
Topics, A-Z -- Continued

56.P32	Paternity
56.P35	Peace
56.P374	Periodization
56.P377	Personal space
56.P38	Personification
56.P4	Pessimism
56.P46	Photography
56.P5	Plague
56.P52	Plants
56.P53	Play
56.P534	Pleasure
56.P54	Polish Revolution, 1830-1832
56.P547	Popular culture
56.P55	Popular literature
	Press see PN56.J68
56.P6	Pride
56.P7	Primitivism
56.P72	Prisons
56.P74	Progressivism
56.P744	Prophecies
56.P75	Proverbs
56.P9	Psychiatry
56.P92	Psychoanalysis
56.P93	Psychology
56.P95	Public health
56.P97	Punishment
56.P975	Puppets
56.R16	Race
56.R18	Racism
56.R22	Railroads
56.R24	Rape
56.R27	Rats
56.R3	Realism. Naturalism
	Prefer history, e.g. PN760+, Realism in
	the 19th century
56.R32	Reality
56.R33	Recognition. Anagnorisis
56.R34	Reconciliation
56.R35	Refuge
56.R45	Repetition
56.R47	Resurrection
56.R48	Revenge

Theory. Philosophy. Esthetics
Relation to and treatment of special elements,
problems, and subjects
Other special
Topics, A-Z -- Continued

56.R58	Roman charity
56.R6	Romance
56.R7	Romanticism
	Prefer history, e.g., PN750+, Romanticism in the 19th century
56.R73	Rooms
56.R75	Roses
56.R87	Ruins
56.R93	Russo-Turkish War, 1877-1878
56.S34	Salvation
56.S4	Sea
56.S43	Secrecy
56.S45	Seduction
56.S46	Self-knowledge
56.S47	Senses and sensation
56.S475	Sentimentalism
56.S48	Setting
56.S49	Seven (The number)
56.S5	Sex
56.S52	Sex differences
56.S53	Sexual deviation
56.S536	Shades and shadows
56.S54	Shipwrecks
56.S55	Silence
56.S56	Sin
56.S57	Sincerity
56.S574	Sirens (Mythology)
56.S576	Skepticism
56.S577	Sleep
56.S58	Smoking
56.S6	Snobs and snobbishness
56.S64	Social classes
56.S65	Social conflict. Social problems
	Social marginality see PN56.M27
56.S654	Social structure
56.S66	Socialist realism
56.S665	Solitude
56.S666	Soul mates
	Sons and fathers see PN56.F37
56.S667	Space
56.S67	Spanish Civil War
56.S69	Speed

Theory. Philosophy. Esthetics
Relation to and treatment of special elements,
problems, and subjects
Other special
Topics, A-Z -- Continued

56.S697	Spirit possession
56.S7	Spirituality
56.S73	Sports
56.S735	Stars
56.S736	Striptease
56.S737	Stupidity
56.S74	Subconsciousness
56.S7414	Subjectivity
56.S742	Suffering
56.S744	Suicide
56.S747	Sunday
56.S75	Superficiality
56.S8	Supernatural
56.S87	Surrealism
56.S88	Suspense
56.S9	Symbolism
56.S94	Sympathy
56.T34	Tea
56.T37	Technology
56.T4	Teeth
56.T44	Telchines (Greek mythology)
56.T5	Time
56.T62	Torture
56.T64	Totalitarianism
	Tower of Babel see PN56.B23
56.T68	The tragic
56.T7	Travel
56.T73	Trephining
56.T76	Trojan War
56.T77	Trust
56.T78	Truthfulness and falsehood
56.T82	Tuberculosis
56.U54	Universities and colleges
56.U8	Utopias
	Cf. HX806+ Works on Utopia
56.V28	Values
56.V3	Vampires
56.V44	Veils
56.V5	Vienna. Universität
56.V53	Violence
56.V54	Visual literature
56.V543	Visual perception

Theory. Philosophy. Esthetics
Relation to and treatment of special elements,
problems, and subjects
Other special
Topics, A-Z -- Continued

56.V55	Voice
56.V57	Vortex-motion
56.V59	Voyages, Imaginary
56.V6	Voyages, Interplanetary
56.W3	War
56.W34	Water
56.W37	Water spirits
	Watering-places see PN56.H37
56.W4	Wealth
56.W43	Weather
56.W45	Werewolves
56.W47	Windows
56.W49	Winds
56.W5	Wine
56.W54	Wisdom
56.W65	Work
56.W67	Worldliness
56.Z44	Zen Buddhism
56.Z55	Zionism
56.3.A-Z	Countries, cities, ethnic groups, and races, A-Z
56.3.A39	Africa
56.3.A43	Algeria
56.3.A45	America
56.3.A9	Australia
56.3.B3	Basques. Basque provinces
56.3.B4	Berlin
56.3.B55	Blacks
56.3.B84	Bulgaria
56.3.C83	Cuba
56.3.D35	Dagestan (Russia)
56.3.E37	East Asia
56.3.E85	Europe
56.3.F56	Florence
56.3.G3	Georgia (Transcaucasia)
56.3.G6	Goths
56.3.G69	Greece
56.3.I57	India
56.3.I6	Indians
56.3.I74	Istanbul (Turkey)
56.3.J37	Jerusalem
56.3.J4	Jews

Theory. Philosophy. Esthetics
Relation to and treatment of special elements,
problems, and subjects
Other special
Countries, cities, ethnic groups, and races,
A-Z -- Continued

56.3.K3	Karelia
56.3.L4	Leningrad
56.3.L56	Lithuania
56.3.M4	Mediterranean Region
56.3.M45	Mérida (Spain)
56.3.M47	Mexico
	Negroes see PN56.3.B55
56.3.R58	Romanies
56.3.R6	Rome
56.3.S53	Sicily
56.3.S67	Soviet Union
56.3.S7	Spain
56.3.T87	Turkey
56.3.U5	United States
56.3.V4	Venice

Characters
Cf. PN218 Authorship

56.4	General works
56.5.A-Z	Special classes of people, A-Z
	For ethnic groups and races see PN56.3.A+
56.5.A35	Adolescent girls
56.5.A64	Apprentices
56.5.A78	Artists
56.5.A84	Authors
56.5.B74	Brothers and sisters
56.5.B88	Businessmen
56.5.C48	Children
56.5.C5	Clergy
56.5.C65	Comic characters
56.5.D32	Dancers
56.5.D34	Dandies
	Disabilities, People with see PN56.5.H35
56.5.E96	Exiles
56.5.F44	Femmes fatales
56.5.F53	Flaneurs
56.5.F64	Fools and jesters
56.5.G53	Giants
56.5.H35	Handicapped. People with disabilities
56.5.H45	Heroes
56.5.I57	Intellectuals
56.5.K48	Knights

Theory. Philosophy. Esthetics
Relation to and treatment of special elements,
problems, and subjects
Other special
Characters
Special classes of people, A-Z -- Continued

56.5.L3	Lawyers
56.5.M4	Men
56.5.M44	Mentally handicapped. People with mental disabilities
56.5.M46	Merchants
56.5.M5	Miners
56.5.M67	Mothers
56.5.M87	Muslims
56.5.O95	Outsiders
56.5.P35	Parasites (Social sciences)
56.5.P37	Passersby
56.5.P4	Peasants
	People with disabilities see PN56.5.H35
	People with mental disabilities see PN56.5.M44
56.5.P56	Physicians
56.5.P66	Popes
56.5.P7	Printers
56.5.P74	Prostitutes
56.5.P8	Psychologists
56.5.R63	Rogues and vagabonds
56.5.S35	Scientists
	Siblings see PN56.5.B74
56.5.S54	Sibyls
	Sisters and brothers see PN56.5.B74
56.5.S75	Strangers
56.5.S78	Students
56.5.T74	Trickster
56.5.T85	Twins
	Vagabonds see PN56.5.R63
56.5.V5	Villains
56.5.W46	White collar workers
56.5.W5	Wild men
56.5.W56	Witches
56.5.W64	Women
56.5.Y67	Youth
57.A-Z	Individual characters, A-Z
	For individual characters in individual genres or national literatures, see the genre or literature
57.A33	Agamemnon

Theory. Philosophy. Esthetics
Relation to and treatment of special elements,
problems, and subjects
Other special
Characters
Individual characters, A-Z -- Continued

57.A35	Alarcos
57.A37	Alcestis
57.A4	Alexander, the Great
57.A43	Amphitryon
57.A45	Anne of Brittany
57.A47	Antigone
57.A49	Apollo (Greek deity)
57.A5	Apollonius of Tyre
57.A55	Arminius, Prince of the Cherussi
57.A65	Arthur and Arthurian legends
57.A74	Ashurbanipal, King of Assyria, fl. 668-627 B.C.
57.A8	Attila
57.B25	Barlaam and Joasaph
57.B3	Beatrix Sacrista
57.B4	Belisarius, ca.l 505-565
57.B47	Berenice, b. ca. 28
57.B55	Bluebeard
57.C2	Caesar
57.C25	Cain
57.C27	Callisto
57.C3	Carlos, Prince of Asturias, 1545-1568
57.C33	Carmen
57.C38	Cassandra
57.C39	Castro, Ines de, d. 1355
57.C45	Charadrius
57.C48	Charlemagne
57.C5	El Cid Campeador
57.C52	Circe
57.C55	Cleopatra
57.C57	Clytemnestra
57.C6	Columbus, Christopher
57.C64	Cook, James
57.C85	Cupid (Roman deity)
57.D38	David, King of Israel
57.D4	Devil
57.D5	Dido, Queen of Carthage
57.D55	Dietrich von Bern
57.D57	Dionysus (Greek deity)
57.D7	Don Juan
57.E4	Electra

Theory. Philosophy. Esthetics
Relation to and treatment of special elements,
problems, and subjects
Other special
Characters
Individual characters, A-Z -- Continued

57.E68	Erauso, Catalina de, b. ca. 1592
57.E7	Eteocles and Polynices
57.E8	Europa
57.E9	Everyman
57.F3	Faust
57.F6	Flying Dutchman
57.F67	Fortuna (Roman deity)
57.F8	Friedrich II, der Grosse, King of Prussia, 1712-1786
57.G3	Galahad
57.G33	Gandhi, Mohandas Karamchand
57.G35	Garibaldi
57.G4	Geneviève of Brabant
57.G56	Golem
57.G6	The Graces
57.G75	Grendel
57.G8	Griselda
57.G85	Guenevere
57.G9	Gyges
57.H3	Hairy anchorite
57.H32	Hamlet
57.H4	Helen of Troy
57.H42	Hengist
57.H43	Hercules
57.H44	Hero and Leander
57.H45	Herod I, the Great, King of Judea, d. 4 B.C.
57.I3	Icarus
57.I6	Inkle and Yarico
57.I7	Iphigenia
57.J35	Jan III Sobieski, King of Poland, 1629-1696
57.J4	Jeanne d'Arc

> For Jeanne d'Arc in art and literature
> see DC105.9

57.J44	Jephthah, Judge of Israel
57.J47	Jesus Christ

Joan, of Arc, Saint, 1412-1431 see PN57.J4

57.J57	Job, the Patriarch
57.J6	John the Baptist
57.J68	Joseph, the Patriarch
57.J8	Judith

Theory. Philosophy. Esthetics
Relation to and treatment of special elements,
problems, and subjects
Other special
Characters
Individual characters, A-Z -- Continued

57.J84	Jupiter (Roman deity)
57.K27	Karađorđe Petrović
57.K3	Karl XII, King of Sweden
57.K67	Kosciuszko, Tadeusz, 1746-1817
57.K8	Kundrie
57.L3	Lancelot
	Leander see PN57.H44
57.L65	Lorelei
57.L8	Lucretia, Roman matron
57.L9	Luther
57.M24	Marat, Jean Paul, 1743-1793
57.M27	Mary, Virgin
57.M28	Mary Magdalene, Saint
57.M3	Mary Stuart, Queen of the Scots
57.M37	Medea
57.M38	Medici, Lorenzino de'
57.M4	Merlin
57.M44	Merope, wife of Cresphontes
57.M53	Midas
57.M77	Munchausen
57.M8	Mustapha und Zeangir
57.N3	Napoleon I
57.N33	Narcissus
57.O3	Odysseus
57.O35	Oedipus
57.O4	Ogier le Danois
57.O65	Orpheus
57.O7	Oswald, Saint, King of Northumbria
57.P25	Pan (Deity)
57.P255	Pandora
57.P27	Panza, Sancho
57.P3	Parsifal
57.P4	Pedro I, el Cruel, King of Castile and Leon, 1334-1369
57.P43	Penelope (Greek mythology)
57.P45	Persephone (Greek deity)
57.P48	Phaedra
57.P485	Phaeton
57.P487	Philemon and Baucis
57.P4875	Philip II, King of Spain, 1527-1598
57.P488	Philoctetes

Theory. Philosophy. Esthetics
Relation to and treatment of special elements,
problems, and subjects
Other special
Characters
Individual characters, A-Z -- Continued

57.P49	Pierrot
57.P5	Piper of Hamelin
57.P64	Polyphemus
57.P73	Prometheus
(57.P75)	Proserpine
	see PN57.P45
57.P77	Psyche (Greek deity)
57.P79	Punchinello
57.P86	Pygmalion
57.P9	Pyramus and Thisbe
57.R35	Rama (Hindu deity)
57.R48	Reynard the Fox
57.R57	Roberval, Marguerite de
57.R6	Roland or Orlando
57.S27	Saladin, Sultan of Egypt and Syria, 1137-1193
57.S3	Salome
57.S33	Samson, Judge of Israel
	Sancho, Panza see PN57.P27
57.S335	Sappho
57.S34	Saturn (Roman deity)
57.S35	Saul, King of Israel
57.S42	Scheherazade
57.S5	Siegfried
57.S54	Sleeping Beauty
57.S57	Socrates
57.S6	Sohrab and Rustum
57.S82	Stalin, Joseph, 1879-1953
57.S94	The superman
57.T3	Tannhäuser
57.T5	Thais
	Thisbe see PN57.P9
57.T65	Timur, the Great, 1336-1405
57.T8	Tristan and Isolde
	Ulysses see PN57.O3
57.U5	Undine
57.V4	Venus (Goddess)
57.W25	Waldmann, Hans, ca. 1435-1489
57.W257	Walthari, of Aquitaine
57.W3	Wandering Jew
	Cf. GR75.W3 Folklore

Theory. Philosophy. Esthetics
Relation to and treatment of special elements,
problems, and subjects
Other special
Characters
Individual characters, A-Z -- Continued
57.W5   Widow of Ephesus
57.W55   Wild huntsman
Yarico see PN57.I6
Zeangir see PN57.M8
58   Single essays
Books and reading see Z1003+
Study and teaching
Cf. LB1527 Primary education
Cf. LB1575+ Elementary education
Cf. LC1001+ Humanistic education
59   General works
61   General special
61.5   Audiovisual aids
62   Examinations, questions, etc.
By period
63   Ancient
64   Middle ages
65   Renaissance
66   17th-18th centuries
67   19th century
68   20th century
68.2   21st century
By region or country
Prefer subclasses PA - PT
70   United States
71.A-Z   Other regions or countries, A-Z
72.A-Z   By school, A-Z
Prefer subclasses PA - PT
73   Literary research
Methodology see PN441
Biography of literary critics and historians
74   Collective
75.A-Z   Individual, A-Z
Subarrange each by Table P-PZ50
Criticism
80   Periodicals. Societies. Serials
80.5   Congresses
Theory. Canons
Cf. PN1031+ Poetry
Cf. PN3335 Fiction
81   General works

Criticism
    Theory. Canons -- Continued
83   Popular works
                  Including Kerfoot: How to read
85   Addresses, essays, lectures
            History
              Including collections of criticisms
              Cf. PN500+ Literary history
86   General works
87   Ancient
88   Medieval and Renaissance to 1600
89   17th century
90   18th century
92   19th century
94   20th century
94.2   21st century
98.A-Z   Special topics. By subject, A-Z
98.B7   Book reviewing
98.C6   Communists as critics
              For communism and literature see HX531
98.D43   Deconstruction
          Discourse analysis see P302+
98.E36   Ecocriticism
98.E4   Electronic data processing
          Ethical aspects see PN98.M67
98.E93   Existentialism
          Feminist criticism see PN98.W64
98.F6   Formalism
98.H57   Historical criticism
98.H85   Humanistic psychology
98.I54   Information theory
98.I58   Intertextuality
98.L65   Logical positivism
98.M67   Moral and ethical aspects
98.N4   New Criticism
98.P64   Politics
98.P67   Postmodernism
98.P75   Psychoanalytic approach to criticism
98.R38   Reader-response criticism. Reception aesthetics
98.R4   Realism
          Reception aesthetics see PN98.R38
98.R44   Religious approach to criticism
98.S46   Semiotic approach to literature
98.S6   Sociological approach to criticism
98.S7   Structuralism
98.T6   Toposforschung
98.W64   Women critics. Feminist criticism

	Criticism -- Continued
99.A-Z	By region or country, A-Z
	Authorship
	Periodicals
101	American and English
109	Other
111	Yearbooks
121	Associations
	Congresses
131	International
133.A-Z	National (and local). By region or country, A-Z
137	Collections
141	Dictionaries
	Information services
142	General works
142.5	Computer network resources
	Including the Internet
143	Study and teaching. Schools, etc.
	Cf. PN181 Technique (Authorship)
144	Early to 1800
	Treatises
145	General works (Theory and technique)
146	Research work. Historical and scientific authorship
147	Popular works. "Writing for the press"
	Including handbooks, "desk books" (questions of punctuation, capitalization, spelling, etc.)
	Cf. HF5725+ Business correspondence manuals
	Cf. LB1028.6 Programmed instruction authorship
	Cf. PN4775+ Journalism
	Cf. Z253+ Printers' style manuals
147.5	Authorship of children's literature
	Cf. PN3377 Juvenile stories
148	Writing for new literates
149	Addresses, essays, lectures
	Authorship as a profession. Ethics. Relations. Social conditions of authors. etc.
	Biography of literary agents, editors, etc.
	Cf. PN75.A+ Critics and historians
	Cf. PN451+ Authors
149.8	Collective
149.9.A-Z	Individual, A-Z
	Subarrange each by Table P-PZ50
150	Early works
151	General works. Treatises

Authorship
Authorship as a profession. Ethics. Relations.
Social conditions of authors. etc. --
Continued
153   Popular works
154   Literary ethics
Cf. PN49 Literature and ethics
Cf. PN167+ Plagiarism
Cf. PN171.F6+ Forgeries
155   Authors and publishers
Cf. PN173+ Technique
Cf. Z278+ Bookselling and publishing
Copyright
see class K
156   Censorship
Cf. PN2042+ Censorship of the theater
157   Dilettantism
159   Amateur and juvenile writers
160   Preparation of manuscripts, etc.
Preparation of theses, college research papers,
book reports, etc. see LB2369
161   How to sell manuscripts
162   Editing of books and manuscripts
Cf. PN4778 Newspaper editing
163   Literary agents
164   Literary landmarks. Home and haunts of authors
Class here general works only
For national, see PR109+, etc.
165   Miscellany
Including anecdotes, quarrels and amenities
of authors, etc.
166   Imitation (in literature)
Plagiarism
Cf. PA3014.P6 Classical literature
167   General works
168.A-Z   Cases. By the name of the author accused, A-Z
169   Satire. Humor
171.A-Z   Other special topics, A-Z
171.A6   Anonymity
Bibliographical citations see PN171.F56
Bilingualism see PN171.M93
171.C3   Cartoon captions
171.C5   Child authors
171.D37   Data processing
171.D4   Dedications
171.E3   Eccentric literature
171.E8   Errors and blunders

Authorship
  Other special topics, A-Z -- Continued
171.F56   Footnotes. Bibliographical citations
      Including citation of specific forms of
        material, e. g. periodicals, electronic
        information sources
    Literary forgeries, impostures
171.F6   General works
171.F7   Cases. By name, A-Z
171.G47   Ghostwriting
171.G74   Greeting cards
      Cf. NC1860+ Art
171.H67   Housewives as authors
171.I6   Insane authors
      Cf. RC464.A+ Mental patients
171.I66   Interviews
171.I7   Introductions
171.L3   Laboring class authors
171.M93   Multilingualism. Bilingualism
171.O3   Obsequies
171.P4   Pensions
171.P7   Prefaces
    Prisoners as authors see PN494
171.P75   Prizes
      For bibliographies of prize-winning books
        see Z1035.A2
171.P8   Prologues and epilogues
171.P83   Psychological aspects
171.Q6   Quotations
171.S45   Sex differences
171.T5   Titles of books
      Cf. Z242.T6 Printing
    Women writers see PN471+
171.W74   Writer's block
      Cf. RC552.W74 Psychiatry
  Technique. Literary composition, etc.
    For general works on composition and rhetoric
      in a specific language, see the language
      in classes PA - PL
    For rhetoric (General) see P301+
    For rhetoric and composition see PE1401.2+
171.4   Periodicals
171.6   Congresses
172   Dictionaries. Terminology
  Theory. Philosophy
    Cf. BJ42 Relation to ethics
173   Early works

Authorship
Technique. Literary composition, etc.
Theory. Philosophy -- Continued
Later works
175 English
176 French
179 Other
181 Study and teaching
183 History
For ancient Greek and Roman rhetoric, see
subclass PA
Treatises
185 Early works
Later works
187 English
189 Other
191 Compends
193 Elementary manuals
195 Quizzes
Exercises and specimens
197 General works
198 Lists of subjects, outlines
General special
203 Style
Cf. PE1421 Modern English philology
204 Readability
Cf. BF456.R2 Psychology of reading
205 Exposition
207 Argumentation
Cf. P301.5.P47 Linguistics
209 Analysis
212 Narration
Cf. PN3383.N35 Fiction
218 Other
Including inventing of characters
Special elements of style
221 Invention
223 Imitation
225 Amplification
226 Foregrounding
Figures
Cf. PE1445.A2+ Modern English philology
227 General works
228.A-Z Special, A-Z
228.C45 Chiasmus
228.M4 Metaphor
Cf. P301.5.M48 Metaphor (General)

Authorship
Technique. Literary composition, etc.
Special elements of style
Figures
Special, A-Z -- Continued
228.P2   Paradox
                     For collections see PN6361+
228.S5   Simile
228.S95   Synecdoche
229   Use of adjectives, epithets, etc.
229.E9   Expletives
Special kinds of style
           For special forms of literature see PN1010+
           Fiction (Novels, stories) see PN3355+
           History see D13+
           Oratory see PN4142
           Essay writing see PN4500
235   Epistolary
           Dialogue see PN1551
239.A-Z   Other, A-Z
239.P64   Political
               Cf. P301.5.P67 Political rhetoric
                 (General)
Translating as a literary pursuit
         For special subjects, see the subject in
            classes B - Z, e.g. Technology, T11.5
         For general works on translating of a
            specific language, see the language in
            subclasses PA - PL
         For translating and interpreting as a
            linguistic skill and technique see P306+
         Cf. PN885.2+ Literary history of translations
241.A1   Periodicals. Societies. Serials
241.A3-Z   General works
241.5.A-Z   By region or country, A-Z
245   Aids. Scrapbooks, commonplace books
            Cf. PN6244+ Literary extracts
         Indexing see Z695.9+
Literary history
441   Theory and method
Biography
General collections
English
451   Comprehensive
452   Minor
453   Collected memoirs, letters, etc.
French

Literary history
 Biography
  General collections
   French -- Continued
456   Comprehensive
457   Minor
458   Collected memoirs, letters, etc.
   German
461   Comprehensive
462   Minor
463   Collected memoirs, letters, etc.
466   Other
  Women authors
471   English works
472   French works
473   German works
479   Other
481   Feminine influence in literature. Authors'
    relations to women. Love, marriage, etc.
    Class here general works only
    For special countries, see PQ147.5; PR119;
    etc.
  Other classes of authors
485   Catholic authors
490   Black authors
491   Blind authors
491.3   Gay authors
491.5   Minority authors
492   Physicians as authors
494   Prisoners as authors
495   Exiled authors. Expatriates
497   Authors of children's literature
  Collections
   Various authors
500   Early through 1800
    1801-
500.5   Polyglot
501   American and English
502   Dutch
503   French
504   German
505   Italian
506   Scandinavian
507   Slavic
508   Spanish and Portuguese
509.A-Z   Other, A-Z

Literary history
  Collections -- Continued
    Collected essays of individual authors. Essays
      on ancient and modern literature
        For medieval and modern, see PN710; for
          other periods or subjects, see PN630,
          PN681, etc.; subclasses PA - PT

510	Early through 1800
	1801-
510.5	Polyglot
511	American and English
512	Dutch
513	French
514	German
515	Italian
516	Scandinavian
517	Slavic
518	Spanish and Portuguese
519.A-Z	Other, A-Z

  Comprehensive works. Universal histories, etc.
    American and English
      Early works

521	Early through 1800
522	1801-1860
	Recent works
523	Treatises
524	Compends, textbooks, outlines

    Dutch
      Early works

531	Early through 1800
532	1801-1860
	Recent works
533	Treatises
534	Compends, textbooks, outlines

    French
      Early works

541	Early through 1800
542	1801-1860
	Recent works
543	Treatises
544	Compends, textbooks, outlines

    German
      Early works

551	Early through 1800
552	1801-1860
	Recent works
553	Treatises

Literary history
  Comprehensive works. Universal histories, etc.
    German
      Recent works -- Continued
554   Compends, textbooks, outlines
    Italian
      Early works
561   Early through 1800
562   1801-1860
      Recent works
563   Treatises
564   Compends, textbooks, outlines
    Scandinavian
      Early works
571   Early through 1800
572   1801-1860
      Recent works
573   Treatises
574   Compends, textbooks, outlines
    Slavic
      Early works
581   Early through 1800
582   1801-1860
      Recent works
583   Treatises
584   Compends, textbooks, outlines
    Spanish, Portuguese and Spanish American
      Early works
591   Early through 1800
592   1801-1860
      Recent works
593   Treatises
594   Compends, textbooks, outlines
595.A-Z   Other, A-Z
  Special relations, movements, and currents of
    literature
    Class here general works only
    For theory and esthetics see PN45+
    Classical literature in relation to medieval
      literature see PN681.5
    Classical literature in relation to modern
      literature see PN883
    Christian literature see BR66+; BR117
597   Literary movements (General)
599   Idealism
601   Realism. Naturalism
603   Romanticism

Literary history
Special relations, movements, and currents of
literature -- Continued
605.A-Z   Other, A-Z
e. g.
605.C2   Catholic church - Influence on literature
Cf. PN682.C2 Medieval literary history
605.Z9   Curiosa. Eccentric literary history
By period
610   Ancient and medieval
Ancient
For special topics see PN56.A+
611   Origins
Comprehensive works
620   Early through 1800
1801-
620.5   Polyglot
621   American and English
622   Dutch
623   French
624   German
625   Italian
626   Scandinavian
627   Slavic
628   Spanish and Portuguese
629.A-Z   Other, A-Z
630   Addresses, essays, lectures
Alexandrian and early Christian
For Greek and Latin, see subclass PA
640   Early through 1800
1801-
640.5   Polyglot
641   American and English
642   Dutch
643   French
644   German
645   Italian
646   Scandinavian
647   Slavic
648   Spanish and Portuguese
649.A-Z   Other, A-Z
Oriental see PJ306+; PJ806+
Medieval (to 1500)
661   Periodicals and societies
663   Congresses
Collections of medieval literature
665   General works

	Literary history
	By period
	Medieval (to 1500)
	Collections of medieval literature --
	Continued
667	Selections
669	Dictionaries
	General works
670	Early through 1800
	1801-
670.5	Polyglot
671	American and English
672	Dutch
673	French
674	German
675	Italian
676	Scandinavian
677	Slavic
678	Spanish and Portuguese
679.A-Z	Other, A-Z
681	Addresses, essays, lectures
681.5	Classical literature in relation to medieval
	literature
682.A-Z	Special topics, A-Z
682.A5	Allegory
682.A57	Animals
682.A67	Arab influences
682.A7	Art
682.A88	Authors
682.B56	Blood
682.B63	Body and soul
682.B65	Books and reading
682.C2	Catholic church and literature
682.C3	Castles
682.C5	Characters and characteristics
682.C53	Chivalry
682.C54	Cities and towns
682.C58	Confession
682.C6	Courtly love
682.C82	Cuckolds
682.D4	Death
682.D48	Devil
682.D72	Dragons
682.E88	Exoticism
682.F27	Fairies
682.F3	Fall of man
682.F34	Family violence

Literary history
　By period
　　Medieval (to 1500)
　　　Special topics, A-Z -- Continued

682.F6	Forests
682.F64	Four elements (Philosophy)
682.F7	Franciscans
682.F74	Friendship
682.G4	Geis (tabu)
682.G6	Glory
682.G64	Go-betweens
682.G65	Goddesses
682.G74	Grief
682.H47	Hermits
682.H65	Homosexuality
682.H8	Hunting
682.I47	Incest
682.I5	Individuality
682.K54	Knights and knighthood
682.L38	Law
682.L68	Love
682.M34	Magic
682.M37	Marriage
682.M38	Marvelous, The, in literature
682.M42	Mediterranean Region
682.M44	Mental illness
682.M53	Microcosm and macrocosm
682.M57	Military religious orders
682.M65	Monsters
682.N3	Nature
682.N54	Nightingales
682.N65	Nonverbal communication
682.N84	Nudity
682.N86	Numbers
682.N87	Nuns
682.O43	Old age
682.O7	Ordeal
682.O75	Orient
682.O87	Outlaws
682.P27	Paradise
682.P28	Parent and child
682.P3	Patrons
682.P35	Peasantry
682.P5	Pilgrims and pilgrimages
682.Q44	Queens
682.R37	Reality
682.R4	Religion

Literary history
By period
Medieval (to 1500)
Special topics, A-Z -- Continued

682.S32	Seduction
682.S34	Self
682.S38	Sexual deviation
682.S7	Social life
682.S75	Strangers
682.S94	Swine
682.T55	Time
	Towns see PN682.C54
682.T68	The tragic
682.T7	Travel
682.T76	Troubadours
682.U4	Ugliness
682.U5	Unicorns
682.U75	Utopias
682.V4	Venality
682.V55	Violence
682.V56	Virginity
682.V57	Visions
682.V59	Visual perception
682.W35	War
682.W37	Water
682.W6	Women
	Special forms of medieval literature
	Prefer PA-PT
	Legends
683	General works
	Juvenile literature
	see subclass PZ
684	Hero legends (Heldensage)
	Arthurian legends
685	General works
686.A-Z	Special, A-Z
686.A7	Arthur
686.B3	Balin and Balan
686.B65	Bran, son of Llyr
686.B68	Brocêliande. Paimpont Forest
686.G3	Gawain
686.G7	Grail
686.K3	Kay
686.L3	Lancelot
686.M33	Magic
686.M4	Merlin
	Paimpont Forest see PN686.B68

Literary history
　By period
　　Medieval (to 1500)
　　　Special forms of medieval literature
　　　　Legends
　　　　　Arthurian legends
　　　　　　Special, A-Z

686.P4	Perceval (Parsifal, etc.)
686.T7	Tristan
686.W37	Water
686.W65	Women
686.Y8	Ywain
687.A-Z	Other special subjects, A-Z
687.A3	Adalbert, Saint, Bp. of Prague, 950-977
687.A5	Alexander, the Great
	Amantes de Teruel see PN687.L68
687.A73	Argonauts (Greek mythology)
687.B6	Body and soul
687.C5	Charlemagne
687.C55	El Cid Campeador
	Crucifix, Feast of the see PN687.F4
687.D3	Dathi, King
687.D33	David, King of Israel
687.D4	Death
687.D47	Devil
687.D7	Dracula
687.E4	Eginhard and Emma
	Emma and Eginhard see PN687.E4
	Faust
	see PN57.F3, and subclass PT
687.F4	Feast of the Crucifix
687.F45	The fifteen tokens before the last judgment
687.F5	Flights
687.F55	Fortuna (Roman deity)
687.F6	The four daughters of God
687.G4	Geneviève of Brabant
687.G84	Guy of Warwick
687.H34	Hagen
687.H37	Heaven
687.H38	Heinrich der Löwe
687.H4	Herbortsage
687.J4	Jewish boy
687.J62	Job, the patriarch
687.J8	Judas Iscariot
687.K3	Kaisersage
687.L68	Lovers of Teruel

	Literary history
	By period
	Medieval (to 1500)
	Special forms of medieval literature
	Legends
	Other special subjects, A-Z -- Continued
687.M37	Mary, Blessed Virgin, Saint
687.M42	Medea (Greek mythology)
687.M44	Melusine
687.M54	Milon d'Angers
687.M58	Monk and the bird's song
	Nibelungenlied see PT1575+
687.N5	Nicodemus
687.O7	Orpheus
	Orson see PN687.V3
687.P27	Paris (Greek mythology)
687.P3	Saint Patrick's purgatory
687.R4	Reinoldlegende
	Robin Hood see PR2125+; PZ8.1
687.R6	Rodrick
687.S3	Seth (Biblical character)
687.S37	Seven against Thebes (Greek mythology)
687.S43	Seven Sages
687.S5	Seven sleepers
687.S56	Sibille, Queen
687.S6	Sindbad, the philosopher
687.S8	Swan-knight
	Cf. PT509.S8 German literature
687.T5	Theophilus
687.V3	Valentine and Orson
687.W2	Wade
687.W26	Walthari, of Aquitane
687.W3	Wandering Jew
	Poetry
688	General works
	Special topics see PN682.A+
	Epic poetry
689	General works
690.A-Z	Special topics, A-Z
690.A6	Animal epics
690.C7	Crusades
690.D73	Dreams
690.F56	Floire et Blancheflor (Romance)
690.R5	Reynard the Fox
	For special texts, see subclasses PQ - PT
690.T7	Tristan

Literary history
By period
Medieval (to 1500)
Special forms of medieval literature
Poetry -- Continued
691   Lyric poetry
Prose. Prose fiction
692   General works
693.A-Z   Special tales, A-Z
694.A-Z   Other special forms, A-Z
694.E6   Epic literature
(694.E9)   Exempla
see BV4224
Fables see PN980+
694.F3   Fabliaux
Modern
Including medieval and modern, and works on
special areas in Europe, e.g. Southern
Europe
For special topics see PN56.A+
695   Collections
Comprehensive works
700   Early through 1800
1801-
700.5   Polyglot
701   American and English
702   Dutch
703   French
704   German
705   Italian
706   Scandinavian
707   Slavic
708   Spanish and Portuguese
709.A-Z   Other, A-Z
710   Addresses, essays, lectures
Renaissance (1500-1700)
715   Collections
Including sources with commentary
General works
720   Early through 1800
1801-
720.5   Polyglot
721   American and English
722   Dutch
723   French
724   German
725   Italian

Literary history
By period
Modern
Renaissance (1500-1700)
General works
1801- -- Continued

726	Scandinavian
727	Slavic
728	Spanish and Portuguese
729.A-Z	Other, A-Z

16th century
Including works specifically on Humanism
and the Revival of Learning

730	Early through 1800
	1801-
730.5	Polyglot
731	American and English
732	Dutch
733	French
734	German
735	Italian
736	Scandinavian
737	Slavic
738	Spanish and Portuguese
739.A-Z	Other, A-Z

17th century

740	Early through 1800
	1801-
740.5	Polyglot
741	American and English
742	Dutch
743	French
744	German
745	Italian
746	Scandinavian
747	Slavic
748	Spanish and Portuguese
749.A-Z	Other, A-Z

18th (and early 19th) century. Romanticism

750	Early through 1800
	1801-
750.5	Polyglot
751	American and English
752	Dutch
753	French
754	German
755	Italian

Literary history
  By period
    Modern
      18th (and early 19th) century. Romanticism
        1801- -- Continued

756	Scandinavian
757	Slavic
758	Spanish and Portuguese
759.A-Z	Other, A-Z

      19th century
        For early 19th century and Romanticism see
          PN750+

760.5	Polyglot
761	American and English
762	Dutch
763	French
764	German
765	Italian
766	Scandinavian
767	Slavic
768	Spanish and Portuguese
769.A-Z	Other, A-Z

      20th century

770.5	Polyglot
771	American and English
772	Dutch
773	French
774	German
775	Italian
776	Scandinavian
777	Slavic
778	Spanish and Portuguese
779.A-Z	Other, A-Z

      21st century

780.5	Polyglot
781	American and English
782	Dutch
783	French
784	German
785	Italian
786	Scandinavian
787	Slavic
788	Spanish and Portuguese
789.A-Z	Other, A-Z

  Romance literatures
    For combinations of language and literature,
      see subclass PC

Literary history
  Romance literatures -- Continued
    Literary history and criticism

801	Periodicals and societies
802	Congresses
	Collections of monographs, studies, etc.
803	Two or more authors
804	Individual authors
806	Study and teaching
808	History and general works. Criticism, etc.
810.A-Z	Special topics, A-Z
810.A7	Architecture
810.B3	Basques
810.F3	Fate and fatalism
810.G86	Gypsies. Romanies
810.L52	Liberty
810.L65	Love
810.N37	Navarre (Spain)
810.O35	Ocean travel
	Romanies see PN810.G86
810.S44	Senses and sensation
810.W6	Women
	Special periods
811	Medieval
812	Modern, to 1800
813	19th-20th centuries
	Special forms
	Prefer period for medieval literature
814	Poetry
815	Drama
816	Prose (General and fiction)
817	Miscellaneous
	Collections of texts
818	General works
819	Minor collections
820	Translations
	Germanic literatures
	For combinations of language and literature, see subclass PD
	Literary history and criticism
821	Periodicals and societies
822	Congresses
	Collections of monographs, studies, etc.
823	Two or more authors
824	Individual authors
826	Study and teaching
828	History and general works. Criticism, etc.

	Literary history
	Germanic literatures
	Literary history and criticism -- Continued
830.A-Z	Special topics, A-Z
	For list of Cutter numbers, see PN810.A+
	Special periods
831	Medieval
832	Modern, to 1800
833	19th-20th centuries
	Special forms
	Prefer period for medieval literature
834	Poetry
835	Drama
836	Prose (General and fiction)
837	Miscellaneous
	Collections of texts
838	General works
839	Minor collections
840	Translations
841	Black literature (General)
842	Jewish literature in various languages
	Literatures. By region or country
	America
843	History and general works. Criticism, etc.
	Special periods
845	Early to 1800
846	19th-20th centuries
849.A-Z	Other regions or countries, A-Z
	For Asia, see PJ+
849.A35-.A352	Africa (Table P-PZ26)
	Cf. PQ3980+ Literature in French
	Cf. PR9340+ Literature in English
	Cf. PR9340+ Literature in English
849.A355-.A3552	Africa, North. Maghreb (Table P-PZ26)
849.A95-.A952	Australia (Table P-PZ26)
849.B3-.B32	Balkan Peninsula (Table P-PZ26)
	Belgium see PQ3810+
849.C28-.C282	Canada (Table P-PZ26)
	For English and French combined see PR9180+
849.C3-.C32	Caribbean Area. West Indies (Table P-PZ26)
849.C5-.C52	Commonwealth of Nations (Table P-PZ26)
849.C6-.C62	Communist countries (Table P-PZ26)
	Developing countries see PN849.U43+
849.E38-.E382	Egypt (Table P-PZ26)
849.E9-.E92	Europe, Eastern (Table P-PZ26)
849.G74-.G742	Great Britain (Table P-PZ26)
849.I8-.I82	Israel (Table P-PZ26)

Literary history
   Literatures. By region or country
      Other regions or countries, A-Z -- Continued

849.L88-.L882	Luxembourg (Table P-PZ26)
	Maghreb see PN849.A355+
849.M38-.M382	Mauritius (Table P-PZ26)
849.M42-.M422	Mediterranean Region (Table P-PZ26)
849.O26-.O262	Oceania (Table P-PZ26)
849.R9-.R92	Russia. Soviet Union (Table P-PZ26)
849.S25-.S252	Scandinavia (Table P-PZ26)
849.S6-.S62	Spain (Table P-PZ26)
	Soviet Union see PN849.R9+
849.S75-.S752	Suriname (Table P-PZ26)
849.S9-.S92	Switzerland (Table P-PZ26)

         Cf. PQ3870+ Literature in French
         Cf. PQ5961+ Literature in Italian
         Cf. PT3860+ Literature in German

849.U43-.U432	Underdeveloped countries (Table P-PZ26)
849.U5-.U52	United States (Table P-PZ26)
	West Indies see PN849.C3+

Comparative literature
   Prefer PA, PQ-PT for studies of the literary
      relations of special countries and special
      authors
   For works on the literary relations of the
      United States and Great Britain, with
      other countries, see PR
   For special forms of literature, see the
      subject in general literary history
   For special periods see PN611+

851	Periodicals. Serials
855	Societies
858	Congresses
	Collections
861	Series. Monographs by different authors
863	Collected works, essays, papers by different authors
865	Theory. Philosophy. Comparative literature as a discipline
	Study and teaching of comparative literature
867	General works
868.A-Z	By region or country, A-Z
869.A-Z	By school, A-Z
	General works
870	Early through 1800
	1801-
870.5	Polyglot

	Literary history
	Comparative literature
	General works
	1801- -- Continued
871	American and English
872	Dutch
873	French
874	German
875	Italian
876	Scandinavian
877	Slavic
878	Spanish and Portuguese
879.A-Z	Other, A-Z
<881.A-Z>	Special forms or kinds (Genres), A-Z
	Picaresque romances see PN3428+
	Robinsonades see PN3432
883	Classical antiquity and literature in relation to modern literature
	Including general works on "Querelle des anciens et modernes"
	Cf. PQ251.A2+ "Querelle des anciens et modernes" (French literature)
<884.A-Z>	By region or country, A-Z
	Under each country:
	(1) *General works*
	(2) *Special authors*
	Translations
	The art of translating see PN241+
886	General works
	Special
	Prefer subclasses PQ - PT
<888>	English
<889>	German
<890>	Dutch
<891>	Scandinavian
<893>	French
<894>	Italian
<895>	Spanish and Portuguese
<896>	Other Romance
<898>	Slavic
<899>	Other
	Folk literature
	For general works on folk literature, see subclass GR
	For folk literature of special countries, see subclasses PQ - PT
(905)	Periodicals

	Literary history
	Folk literature -- Continued
(907)	Societies
(909)	Congresses
(911)	Collections
(916)	Dictionaries
(921)	Theory, relations, etc.
	Treatises
(930)	Early through 1800
	1801-
(930.5)	Polyglot
(931)	American and English
(932)	Dutch
(933)	French
(934)	German
(935)	Italian
(936)	Scandinavian
(937)	Slavic
(938)	Spanish and Portuguese
(939.A-Z)	Other, A-Z
(945)	Addresses, essays, lectures
(951)	Origins
	Medieval
(953)	Comprehensive
(955)	Early to 1400
(957)	1400-1600
	Modern
(959)	Comprehensive
(961)	1600-1800
(963)	19th-20th centuries
	By class
	Chapbooks and chapbook literature
970	General works
	English see PR972+
	French see PQ783
	German see PT903+
	Folk poetry see PN1341+
	Fables
	For juvenile fables, see PZ8.2; PZ14.2; etc.
980	History. Origins. Theory
	Fables. By language
	For individual authors, see the author
	For Greek and Latin, see subclass PA
980.5	Polyglot
	American and English
	Early through 1800

Literary history
Folk literature
By class
Fables
Fables. By language
American and English
Early through 1800 -- Continued

981.A2	History
981.A3-Z	Collections
	1801-
982.A2	History
982.A3-Z	Collections
	Dutch
983.A2	History
983.A3-Z	Collections
	French
984.A2	History
984.A3-Z	Collections
	German
985.A2	History
985.A3-Z	Collections
	Italian
986.A2	History
986.A3-Z	Collections
	Scandinavian
987.A2	History
987.A3-Z	Collections
	Spanish
988.A2	History
988.A3-Z	Collections
989.A-Z	Other languages (or countries), A-Z
	e. g.
989.I5	India
989.I5B4-.I5B6	Bidpai
989.I5B4	English translations
989.I5B5	Spanish translations
993	Plant fables
994.A-Z	Other special topics, A-Z
	Beast fables see PN980+
994.F3	The family in fables
995.A-Z	Individual fables, A-Z
995.B44	Belly and the members
995.F68	Fox and the stork
	Special authors
	see subclasses PQ, PR, etc.

	Literary history
	Folk literature
	By class -- Continued
999	Prose romances, etc.
	Cf. PQ, PR, etc., Special languages, e.g.
	Anglo-Norman PR2115
	Cf. PN670 Medieval literature
	Cf. PN3451+ History of prose fiction
(1001)	Folk tales and legends
	see subclass GR
	Proverbs see PN6400+
	Folk riddles see PN6366+
1008.A-Z	Other, A-Z
	Exempla see BV4224+
	Juvenile literature
	For special genres see PN1010+
1008.2	Periodicals
1008.3	Congresses
1008.4	Directories
1008.5	Dictionaries
1008.8	Study and teaching
	Authorship see PN147.5
1009.A1	General works. History
	English and American literature
	see subclasses PR, PS
(1009.A5-.Z5)	Juvenile literature in other languages, A-Z
	see PA - PT
1009.5.A-Z	Special topics, A-Z
1009.5.A34	Aesthetics
1009.5.A47	Africans
1009.5.A94	Authority
1009.5.C43	Characters and characteristics
1009.5.C44	Children with disabilities
1009.5.C45	Christianity
1009.5.C65	Communism
1009.5.D43	Death
1009.5.D48	Developing countries
1009.5.E84	Ethnic attitudes
1009.5.F35	Family
1009.5.F66	Food
1009.5.F68	Foreign countries
1009.5.G37	Gardens
1009.5.G73	Grandmothers
1009.5.H47	Heroes
1009.5.H57	History
1009.5.L53	Life
1009.5.L56	Little Red Riding Hood (Tale)

Literary history
  Juvenile literature
    Special topics, A-Z -- Continued

1009.5.M37	Masculinity
1009.5.M54	Middle Ages
1009.5.M64	Money
1009.5.M67	Moral and ethical aspects
1009.5.N34	Names, Personal
1009.5.N36	National socialism
1009.5.O43	Old age
1009.5.P64	Political aspects
1009.5.P78	Psychological aspects
1009.5.R32	Racism
1009.5.S48	Sexism. Sex role
1009.5.S62	Social classes
1009.5.S625	Socialization
1009.5.S67	Sports
1009.5.T43	Technology
1009.5.T55	Time
1009.5.T7	Tragic, The
1009.5.T75	Translating. Translations
(1009.5.U53)	Underdeveloped areas
	see PN1009.5.D48
1009.5.U85	Utopias
1009.5.V54	Violence
1009.5.W35	War

  Poetry

1010	Periodicals. Serials
1012	Societies
1014	Congresses
1016	Collections of monographs
1021	Dictionaries
	Indexes
1022	General
1023	Children's poetry
1024	Poetry by women
1025	Black poetry

    Theory, philosophy, relations, etc.
      For rhythm see BF475

1031	General works
1035	History of the theory of poetry
	Poetics
1039	Polyglot
1040	Greek and Latin

        Including Aristotle, Scaliger, etc.
        For Greek texts of Aristotle's Poetica,
         see subclass PA

Poetry
Theory, philosophy, relations, etc.
Poetics -- Continued
English
1041   Early through 1800
1042   1801-
1043   French
1044   German
1045   Italian
1046   Scandinavian
1047   Slavic
1048   Spanish and Portuguese
1049.A-Z   Other languages, A-Z
1055   Miscellaneous essays, etc.
                    Technique of blank verse
                        see P311, subclass PA, PE515, etc.
1059.A-Z   Special topics, A-Z
1059.A9   Authorship
1059.C6   Computer poetry
(1059.C64)   Conrete poetry
                        see PN1455
1059.C9   Cycles
1059.D45   Dhvani
1059.E35   Editing
1059.E47   Enjambement
1059.E5   Enumeration
1059.E7   Euphonic poetry
1059.E94   Experimental poetry
1059.F7   Free verse
1059.H8   Hypnotism
1059.I17   Iambic
1059.M3   Marketing
1059.M4   Metaphor
1059.M8   Multilingualism
1059.M92   Mysticism
1059.P47   Personification
1059.P7   Poetic license
                    Poetry readings see PN4151
1059.P76   Prose poems
1059.R37   Rasas
1059.R4   Readership
1059.R5   Rhyme
1059.R53   Rhythm
1059.S7   Song-writing
1059.S83   Stanza
1059.S88   Surrealism
1059.S94   Symbolism

	Poetry
	Special topics, A-Z -- Continued
1059.S96	Syntax
1059.T5	Titles
1059.T7	Translating
1064	Poets on poetry. Anthologies in praise of poetry, etc.
	Relations to, and treatment of, special subjects
1065	Nature, landscape, etc.
	Relation to music see ML3849
1069	Relation to art
1072	Relation to other forms of literature
1075	Relation to life
1076	Relation to love
1077	Relation to philosophy, ethics, religion, myth, etc. Religion and theology of the poets
1080	Relation to history and patriotism
1081	Relation to politics, social progress, etc.
	Prefer HN
1082	Relation to economics
1083.A-Z	Other special, A-Z
1083.A48	America
1083.A5	Animals
1083.A72	Architecture
1083.B5	Birds
1083.B55	Blacks
1083.C64	Columbus, Christopher
1083.F35	Fame
1083.M3	Mathematical linguistics
1083.M4	Memory
1083.M64	Mothers
	Negroes see PN1083.B55
1083.P74	Psychoanalysis
1083.R47	Revolutionary poetry
1083.R63	Roca, Julio Argentino
1083.S43	Science
1083.S63	Spanish Civil War
1083.T42	Technology
1083.W37	War
1085	Poetry and children
1091	Women and poetry. Feminine influence
	Cf. HQ1386 Women in literature
	Cf. PN471+ Women authors
1097	Uneducated poets
1101	Study and teaching
	For prosody, metrics, rhythmics, see subclasses P - PM

	Poetry -- Continued
1103	Characters: Heroes, heroines, etc.
	History and criticism
	General works
1110	Early through 1800
	1801-
1110.5	Polyglot
1111	American and English
1112	Dutch
1113	French
1114	German
1115	Italian
1116	Scandinavian
1117	Slavic
1118	Spanish and Portuguese
1119.A-Z	Other, A-Z
1126	General special
	Including origins
1136	Essays
	By period
1140-1149	Ancient (Table PN5)
	Oriental see PJ1+
	Chinese see PL2306+
1160-1169	Medieval and modern (Table PN5)
	For medieval see PN688+
1180-1189	Renaissance (Table PN5)
1200-1209	16th century (Table PN5)
1220-1229	17th century (Table PN5)
1240-1249	18th century (Table PN5)
1260-1269	19th century (Table PN5)
1270-1279	20th century (Table PN5)
1280-1289	21st century (Table PN5)
	Special kinds
	Epic poetry
	Comprehensive treatises
1301	Early
1303	Recent
1305	Minor
	By period
1307	Ancient
	Medieval see PN689+
1317	Modern (since 1500)
	Special topics
1323	National heroic epics
1326	Romantic epics. Romances of chivalry
	Cf. PN683+ Legends
1329	Allegorical epics

	Poetry
	Special kinds
	Epic poetry
	Special topics -- Continued
1332	Descriptive epics
1333.A-Z	Other, A-Z
	e. g.
1333.A6	Animal epics
	For animal epics in medieval literature see PN690.A6
	Folk poetry
1341	General works
1345	General collections
1347	Primitive
	Including collections
	Lyric poetry
	Comprehensive treatises
1351	Early
1356	Recent
1361	Minor
1365	Study and teaching
1371	Odes
1376	Ballads
	Songs
1381	General
1386	Hymns and sacred poems
1389	Elegies. Laments
1401	Didactic poetry
1411	Descriptive poetry
1412	Erotic poetry
1415	Heroids
1421	Pastoral and bucolic poetry
1431	Christmas poetry. Carols
1435	Satire
1441	The poetic epigram. Epitaphs, etc.
1443	Occasional verse
1451	Vers de société
1455	Visual poetry. Concrete poetry
	Minor forms of poetry
1470	General works
1471	Ballads
1475	Cantos, pasticcios, etc.
	Including specimens
1479	Chant royal
1481	Epithalamia
	Haiku see PL729+
1485	Kyrielle

	Poetry
	Minor forms of poetry -- Continued
1489	Macaronic verse (History and collections)
1489.Z7	Individual authors, A-Z
1493	Madrigal
1496	Palinode
1497	Pantoum
1499	Quatrain
1501	Rondeau
1504	Rondel
1507	Roundelay
1511	Sestina
1514	Sonnet
1517	Triolot
1521	Villanelle
1523	Virelai
1525	Other
	Including anagrams, echo verse, nonsense rhymes, etc.
1530	The monologue
1551	The dialogue
	Cf. P95.455 Dialogue as an aspect of communication

The Performing arts. Show business
    Cf. M, Music
    Cf. BP190.5.P4 Islam and the performing arts
    Cf. GV1580+ Dance
    Cf. PN1600+ Drama
    Periodicals. Serials

1560	Early through 1800
	1801-
1560.5	Polyglot
1561	American and English
1562	Dutch
1563	French
1564	German
1565	Italian
1566	Scandinavian
1567	Slavic
1568	Spanish and Portuguese
1569.A-Z	Other, A-Z
	Societies
1570	International
1572	United States
1573.A-Z	Other regions or countries, A-Z
1574	Congresses, conferences, etc.
1575	Expositions
	Study and teaching. Research
1576	General works
1576.5	Audiovisual aids
	By region or country
1577	United States
1578.A-Z	Other regions or countries, A-Z
1579	Dictionaries. Terminology
1580	Performing arts as a profession
1581	History
	By region or country see PN2219.3+
	Biography
1583	Collective (more than one country)
	Collective and individual of specific countries see PN2219.3+
1584	General works
	Centers for the performing arts
1585	General works
	By region or country
	United States
1586	General works
1587.A-Z	By state, region, etc., A-Z
1588.A-Z	By city, A-Z
1589.A-Z	Other regions or countries, A-Z

1590.A-Z	Special topics, A-Z
1590.A54	Animals
1590.A58	Anthropology
1590.A9	Audiences
1590.B5	Blacklisting of entertainers
1590.B53	Blacks
1590.C45	Children and performing arts
1590.C6	Collecting of theatrical paraphernalia
1590.C65	Corrupt practices
1590.D37	Data processing
	Direction see PN1590.P74
	Disabilities, People with see PN1590.H36
1590.D63	Dogs
1590.F47	Festivals
1590.F55	Finance
1590.G73	Graphic arts
1590.H36	Handicapped. People with disabilities
1590.J48	Jews
1590.M27	Marketing
1590.M3	Masters of ceremonies
1590.M87	Museums and the performing arts
	Negroes see PN1590.B53
1590.O7	Oriental influences
	People with disabilities see PN1590.H36
1590.P64	Political aspects
1590.P7	Press agents
1590.P74	Production and direction
1590.P75	Programs
1590.P76	Psychological aspects
1590.S26	Semiotics
1590.S3	Sex
1590.S6	Social aspects
1590.S7	Sponsorship
1590.T43	Technique
	Television and the performing arts see PN1992.66
1590.T53	Tickets
1590.W64	Women
	Including feminism and feminist theater

Drama
    Periodicals. Serials
1600   Early through 1800
                1801-
1600.5   Polyglot
1601   American and English
1602   Dutch
1603   French
1604   German
1605   Italian
1606   Scandinavian
1607   Slavic
1608   Spanish and Portuguese
1609.A-Z   Other, A-Z
1610   Yearbooks. By date
            Societies
1611   American and English
1612   Dutch
1613   French
1614   German
1615   Italian
1616   Scandinavian
1617   Slavic
1618   Spanish and Portuguese
1619.A-Z   Other, A-Z
            Museums, libraries, etc.
                For books alone see Z5781+
1620.A1   General works
1620.A3-Z   Special institutions, A-Z
            Collections
1621   Various authors
1623   Collected essays of individual authors
1625   Dictionaries
1627   Indexes to children's plays
            Philosophy, aesthetics, scope, relations, etc.
1631   General works
1633.A-Z   Special topics, A-Z
1633.C6   Communism
1633.F45   Feminism
1633.I3   Idealism
1633.N16   National socialism
1633.N2   Naturalism
1633.R65   Romanticism
1633.S45   Semiotics
1633.S9   Symbolism
            Relation to, and treatment of, special subjects
1635   Relation to other forms of literature

Philosophy, aesthetics, scope, relations, etc.
Relation to, and treatment of, special subjects
-- Continued

1637	Relation to pictorial art
	Relation to music see ML3849
1641	Relation to life
1643	Relation to sociology, economics, political science, etc.
1647	Relation to philosophy, ethics, and religion
1649	Relation to the church
1650.A-Z	Other special, A-Z
1650.A42	Alchemy
1650.B53	Bible
1650.C48	Christian symbolism
1650.C57	Cities and towns
1650.C59	Clowns
1650.C78	Cruelty
1650.D4	Death
1650.D47	Desire
1650.D65	Don Juan
1650.F44	Femmes fatales
1650.F5	Filicide
1650.F66	Fools and jesters
1650.F88	Future
1650.G56	Ghosts
1650.G7	Grotesque
1650.H64	Holocaust, Jewish (1939-1945)
	Imprisonment see PN1650.P74
1650.J48	Jews
1650.K55	Kings and rulers
1650.L34	Language and languages
1650.M43	Medea
1650.M44	Men
1650.M45	Mental illness
1650.M65	Money
1650.P45	Phaedra
1650.P74	Prisons. Prisoners
1650.P76	Prometheus
1650.R63	Robots
1650.S34	Science
1650.S48	Sex role
1650.S52	Shamanism
1650.T47	Terrorism
1650.T5	Theater rehearsals
1650.T56	Time
1650.T84	Twins
1650.V34	Vampires

	Philosophy, aesthetics, scope, relations, etc.
	Relation to, and treatment of, special subjects
	Other special, A-Z -- Continued
1650.V53	Vietnamese Conflict
1650.V55	Violence
1650.W3	War
1650.W65	Women
	General works on the drama and the stage
1654	Early works through 1800
1655	1801-
	Technique of dramatic composition
	General works
1660	Early through 1800
	1801-
1660.5	Polyglot
1661	American and English
1662	Dutch
1663	French
1664	German
1665	Italian
1666	Scandinavian
1667	Slavic
1668	Spanish and Portuguese
1669.A-Z	Other, A-Z
1670	Pamphlets, etc.
	The unities
1672	General works
1672.9	Place. Setting
1675	Tragic effect. Tragic fault, poetic justice, etc.
	Cf. PN1892+ Tragedy
1676	Deus ex machina
	Comedy effect see PN1922+
1680	Irony
1681	Subtext
1683	Plot
	Exposition. Development of the action
1685	General works
1687	Suspense
1689	Character treatment
1690	Treatment of masses (Crowds, etc.)
	Construction of the play (Acts, scenes, etc.)
1691	General works
1692	Play within a play
1693	Rhythm
	Study and teaching
1701	General works

	Study and teaching -- Continued
1701.5	Audiovisual aids
1707	Criticism
	Including criticism of dramatic presentation
	Biography of critics
1707.9	Collective
1708.A-Z	Individual, A-Z
	Subarrange each by Table P-PZ50
1711	Characters, heroes, heroines
	For individual characters see PN57.A+
	History
	Comprehensive
1720	Early through 1800
	1801-
1720.5	Polyglot
1721	American and English
1722	Dutch
1723	French
1724	German
1725	Italian
1726	Scandinavian
1727	Slavic
1728	Spanish and Portuguese
1729.A-Z	Other, A-Z
1731	Compends, outlines, etc.
1737	Origins of the drama
	By period
1741	Ancient
	Medieval
1751	General works
1761	Miracle plays. Mysteries. Passion plays
1771	Moralities
	By country
	England see PR641+
	France
	see PQ513, PQ1217, PQ1343+
	Other
	see subclasses PQ - PT
	Renaissance
1785	General works
1791	Special
	By period
1800	Early to 1550
1801	1550-1650
	Modern
	Including medieval, renaissance, and modern
1811	General works

	History
	By period
	Modern -- Continued
1821	Special
	By period
1831	17th century
1841	18th century
1851	19th century
1861	20th century
1861.2	21st century
	Special types
	Opera, comic opera, etc. see ML1699+
1865	One-act plays
	Historical plays
1872	General works
1879.A-Z	Special topics, A-Z
1879.H65	Holocaust, Jewish (1939-1945)
1879.M37	Mary Stuart, Queen of Scots, 1542-1587
1879.M67	More, Thomas, Sir, Saint, 1478-1535
1880	Religious plays
	Cf. PN1647 Drama and religion
	Cf. PN1761 Miracle plays
	Cf. PN3235+ Oberammergau
1883	Pastoral drama
	Tragedy
1892	General works
1899.A-Z	Special topics, A-Z
1899.C48	Christianity
1899.C6	Comic episodes in tragedies (Drama)
1899.F27	Family
1899.G74	Greek influences
1899.M68	Mourning customs
	Tragicomedy
1902	General works
1909.A-Z	Special topics, A-Z
	Melodrama
1912	General works
1919.A-Z	Special topics, A-Z
	Comedy
	Cf. PN1969.C65 Vaudeville
1922	General works
1929.A-Z	Special topics, A-Z
	Acting see PN2071.C57
1929.B6	Boastfulness
1929.C4	Characters and characteristics
1929.C5	Closure (Rhetoric)
1929.I7	Irony

Special types
Comedy
Special topics, A-Z -- Continued
1929.S45   Semiotics
1929.S6   Social problems
1929.W35   War
1934   Interludes, masques, etc.
1936   Monodrama
Farces. Burlesques. Mimes
For burlesque as a literary form see PN6149.B8
1942   General works
1949.A-Z   Special topics, A-Z
1949.S7   Striptease
1950   Science fiction plays
1955   Clowns
For circus clowns see GV1828
Vaudeville. Varieties
1962   General works
1968.A-Z   By region or country, A-Z
1969.A-Z   Special topics, A-Z
1969.C3   Cabarets
1969.C34   Café chantants
1969.C65   Comedy acts. Stand-up comedy
1969.H85   Human body
1969.M5   Minstrels
Stand-up comedy see PN1969.C65
Puppet theater
Cf. BV1535.9.P8 Puppet plays in religious
education
Cf. TT174.7 Puppet making
1972   General works
1978.A-Z   By region or country, A-Z
1979.A-Z   Special topics, A-Z
1979.B57   Black box theaters
1979.E4   Educational puppetry
1979.F48   Festivals
1979.G84   Guignol
1979.K3   Kamishibai. Kamishibai plays
Including those for educational purposes
1979.K34   Kasper
1979.M87   Museums
1979.P9   Punch and Judy, Punchinello, Polichinelle,
etc.
1979.S5   Shadow plays, Wayang, etc.
1979.T6   Toy theaters
Wayang see PN1979.S5
Plays (Texts). Collections and separate plays

	Special types
	Puppet theater
	Plays (Texts). Collections and separate plays
	-- Continued
1980	English
1981	Other
	Biography
1982.A2	Collective
1982.A3-Z	Individual, A-Z
	Subarrange each by Table P-PZ50
	Pantomimes
1985	General works
	Plays (Texts) see PN6120.P3+; PN6120.P3
	Biography
1986.A2	Collective
1986.A3-Z	Individual, A-Z
	Subarrange each by Table P-PZ50
1987.A-Z	By region or country, A-Z
1988.A-Z	Special topics, A-Z
	Amateur entertainments see PN4305.T3
1988.C57	Christmas entertainments
1988.H3	Harlequin
	Ballet see GV1580+
	Broadcasting
	Cf. HE8689+ Radio and television industry
	Cf. TK6540+ Radio engineering
	Cf. TK6630+ Television engineering
1990	Periodicals. Societies. Serials
1990.1	Yearbooks
1990.2	Congresses
1990.3	Collections. Collected essays
1990.36	Archives
1990.4	Dictionaries
1990.5	History
1990.55	Vocational guidance
1990.6.A-Z	By region or country, A-Z
	Biography
1990.7	Collective
1990.72.A-Z	Individual, A-Z
	Subarrange each by Table P-PZ50
1990.8	General works
1990.83	General special
1990.85	Juvenile works
1990.87	Anecdotes, facetiae, etc.
1990.9.A-Z	Special topics, A-Z
	For relation to special subjects, see the
	subjects in classes B - Z

	Broadcasting
	Special topics, A-Z -- Continued
1990.9.A54	Announcing
1990.9.A88	Authorship. Technique of script writing
1990.9.C45	Children's programs
1990.9.C73	Criticism
	Direction see PN1990.9.P76
	Gays see PN1990.9.H64
1990.9.H64	Homosexuality. Gays
1990.9.L3	Language
1990.9.M56	Minorities
1990.9.P76	Production and direction
1990.9.P82	Public service programs
	Script writing technique see PN1990.9.A88
1990.9.T34	Talk shows
1990.9.W64	Women
	Radio broadcasts
	For relation to special subjects, see the subject in classes B - Z, e.g., BV656, Radio in religion; PN4784.R2, Radio journalism
	Cf. GV742.3 Sports broadcasting
	Cf. HE8690+ Radio and television broadcasting industry
	Cf. LB1044.8 Educational radio broadcasting
	Cf. QC877.5 Weather broadcasting
1991	Periodicals. Societies. Serials
1991.1	Yearbooks
1991.15	Collections
1991.2	History
1991.3.A-Z	By region or country, A-Z
	Biography
1991.4.A2	Collective
1991.4.A3-Z	Individual, A-Z
	Subarrange each by Table P-PZ50
1991.5	General works
1991.55	General special
1991.57	Juvenile works
1991.58	Anecdotes, facetiae, etc.
	Special topics
1991.6	Influence. Moral and religious aspects
1991.65	The drama in radio
	Cf. PN1991.73 The writing of radio plays
	Format radio broadcasting
1991.66	General works
1991.67.A-Z	Special format stations, A-Z
	Cf. ML68 Radio and music

PN
1560-3307

Broadcasting
   Radio broadcasts
      Special topics
         Format radio broadcasting
            Special format stations, A-Z -- Continued

1991.67.C64	College radio stations
	Contemporary music stations see PN1991.67.P67
1991.67.M86	Music radio stations
1991.67.P67	Popular music stations
	Top forty stations see PN1991.67.P67
	Authorship. Technique of script writing
1991.7	General works
1991.73	Radio plays
1991.75	Production and direction
	Programs. Scripts
	Prefer the subject in classes B - Z
1991.77.A1	Collections
	For collections of radio plays see PN6120.R2
1991.77.A2-Z	Individual, A-Z
	Subarrange each by Table P-PZ50
	For radio plays by individual authors, see subclasses PR, PS, etc.
1991.8.A-Z	Other special topics, A-Z
1991.8.A32	Acting
1991.8.A35	African Americans. Blacks
1991.8.A6	Announcing
	Blacks see PN1991.8.A35
1991.8.B66	Book review programs
	Children and radio see HQ784.R3
1991.8.C45	Children's programs
1991.8.C65	Comedy programs
1991.8.D47	Detective and mystery programs
1991.8.D63	Documentary programs
1991.8.E84	Ethnic broadcasting and programs
1991.8.E94	Experimental radio programs
1991.8.I53	Indians
1991.8.I57	Interviewing
1991.8.L3	Language
1991.8.L5	Literature
1991.8.M5	Microphone technique
	Music see ML68
	Mystery programs see PN1991.8.D47
1991.8.P6	Poetry and radio
1991.8.P83	Public service programs
1991.8.Q58	Quiz programs

	Broadcasting
	Radio broadcasts
	Special topics
	Other special topics, A-Z -- Continued
1991.8.S34	Science fiction programs
1991.8.S4	Serials
1991.8.S44	Sex
1991.8.S69	Sound effects
1991.8.T35	Talk shows
1991.8.W47	Westerns
1991.8.W65	Women
1991.9	Miscellaneous works
	Including catalogs
	Television broadcasts
	Cf. GV742.3 Sports broadcasting
	Cf. LB1044.8 Educational television
	broadcasting
	Cf. PN1992.95 Nonbroadcast video programs and
	programming
	Cf. QC877.5 Weather broadcasting
1992	Periodicals. Societies. Serials
1992.1	Yearbooks
1992.13	Congresses
1992.15	Collections
1992.16	Archives
1992.18	Dictionaries
1992.2	History
1992.3.A-Z	By region or country, A-Z
	Biography
1992.4.A2	Collective
1992.4.A3-Z	Individual, A-Z
	Subarrange each by Table P-PZ50
	For individual actors and actresses, see
	PN2287, PN2308, etc.
1992.45	Study and teaching
1992.5	General works
1992.55	General special
1992.56	Relation to history
1992.57	Juvenile works
1992.58	Anecdotes. Humor. Quotations, maxims, etc.
	Special topics
1992.6	Influence. Political, moral and religious
	aspects
1992.63	Motion pictures and television
	Cf. PN1992.8.F5 Films in programming
	Cf. TR898 Cinematography

PN
1560-3307

Broadcasting
Television broadcasts
Special topics -- Continued
1992.65   Drama in television
                                          Cf. PN1992.7 Writing of television plays
1992.655   Literature and television
1992.66   Performing arts and television
1992.7   Authorship. Technique of script writing.
                                             Selling the script
1992.75   Production and direction
                                       Programs. Scripts
                                          Prefer the subject in classes B - Z
1992.77.A1   Collections
                                             For collections of television plays see
                                                PN6120.T4
1992.77.A2-Z   Individual, A-Z
                                             For television plays by individual
                                                authors, see subclasses PR, PS, etc.
                                       Locations
1992.78   General works
1992.783.A-Z   By place, A-Z
1992.8.A-Z   Other special topics, A-Z
1992.8.A3   Acting
                                             Including auditions
1992.8.A317   Adventure programs
1992.8.A32   Advertising of television programs
                                             Cf. HF6146.T42 Business advertising
                                                methods
1992.8.A34   African Americans. Blacks
1992.8.A37   Aging
                                             Cf. HQ1063.4 Television and older people
1992.8.A58   Animals
                                             Including individual animals
1992.8.A59   Animated programs
1992.8.A6   Announcing. Voice-overs
1992.8.A7   Arabs
1992.8.A75   Art
1992.8.A76   Art direction
1992.8.A78   Asian Americans
                                       Blacks see PN1992.8.A34
1992.8.B64   Body, Human
1992.8.B87   Businessmen
                                       Cable TV see HE8700.7+
1992.8.C36   Casting
                                       Children and television see HQ784.T4
1992.8.C46   Children's programs
1992.8.C64   Collectibles

Broadcasting
  Television broadcasts
    Special topics
      Other special topics, A-Z -- Continued

1992.8.C66	Comedy programs
1992.8.C7	Criticism
1992.8.D3	Dance parties
1992.8.D4	Death
1992.8.D48	Detective and mystery programs
	Disabilities, People with see PN1992.8.H36
1992.8.D6	Documentary programs
1992.8.D74	Drinking of alcoholic beverages
1992.8.E84	Ethnic broadcasting and programs
1992.8.F33	Family and family life
	Cf. HQ520 Television and family
1992.8.F35	Fantastic programs
1992.8.F5	Films in programming
1992.8.F67	Foreign programs
	Game shows see PN1992.8.Q5
1992.8.G47	Germany
1992.8.G7	Graphics
1992.8.H36	Handicapped. People with disabilities
1992.8.H54	Hispanic Americans
1992.8.H56	Historical programs
1992.8.H63	Holocaust, Jewish (1939-1945)
1992.8.H64	Homosexuality
	Human body see PN1992.8.B64
1992.8.I68	Interviewing
1992.8.J48	Jews
1992.8.J87	Justice. Law
1992.8.L35	Language
	Law see PN1992.8.J87
1992.8.L5	Lighting
1992.8.L54	Lincoln, Abraham
1992.8.M33	Magazine format
1992.8.M36	Makeup
1992.8.M43	Medicine
1992.8.M54	Minorities
1992.8.M58	Mothers
1992.8.M6	Motion-picture cartoons
1992.8.M87	Music
	Including music videos, rock videos, etc.
	Mystery programs see PN1992.8.D48
	News see PN4784.T4
1992.8.N65	Nonverbal communication
1992.8.N87	Nurses
1992.8.O27	Occupations (as a theme)

Broadcasting
Television broadcasts
Special topics
Other special topics, A-Z -- Continued

1992.8.O72	Organizational behavior
	People with disabilities see PN1992.8.H36
1992.8.P4	Personal appearance
	Including clothing, makeup, movement, etc.
1992.8.P54	Pilot programs
	Private detective programs see PN1992.8.D48
1992.8.P8	Public service programs
1992.8.P83	Public speaking
1992.8.P86	Puppets. Puppet plays
1992.8.Q5	Quiz programs
1992.8.R26	Rape
1992.8.R3	Rating
1992.8.R4	Realism
1992.8.R43	Reality programs
	Rock videos see PN1992.8.M87
1992.8.S35	Science fiction
1992.8.S36	Scooby-Doo television programs
1992.8.S37	Sensationalism
1992.8.S4	Serials
1992.8.S44	Sex role
1992.8.S62	Spacebridges
1992.8.S64	Special programs. Specials
1992.8.S67	Spy television programs
1992.8.S7	Stage-setting
1992.8.S74	Star Trek television programs
	For individual television programs see
	PN1992.77.A2+
1992.8.S76	Superhero films
1992.8.S78	Student television
	Subscription television. Pay TV. Cable TV
	see HE8700.7+
1992.8.T3	Talk shows
1992.8.T75	Travel
1992.8.T78	True crime programs
1992.8.V3	Variety shows
	Video art see N6494.V53
1992.8.V55	Violence
	Voice-overs see PN1992.8.A6
1992.8.W36	Weddings
1992.8.W4	Westerns
1992.8.W65	Women
1992.8.Y68	Youth
1992.9	Miscellaneous works

Broadcasting
Television broadcasts -- Continued
1992.92.A-Z   Individual corporations, A-Z
Online dramas
1992.924   General works
1992.925.A-Z   Individual. By title, A-Z
Nonbroadcast video recordings
       Including videotapes, videocassettes, and
          videodiscs
       For relation to special subjects, see the
          subject in classes B - Z
1992.93   Periodicals. Societies. Serials
1992.934.A-Z   By region or country, A-Z
1992.935   General works
Special topics
1992.94   Production and direction
1992.945   Other special
1992.95   Catalogs
          Class here general catalogs of dramatic videos
          For catalogs of nonfiction videos not limited
             to a particular topic see ZA4550
Motion pictures
       Cf. BV1643 Motion pictures in the Church
       Cf. NC1765+ Animated cartoons
       Cf. TR845+ Photography
1993   Periodicals. Societies. Serials
1993.3   Yearbooks
1993.4   Museums, archives, exhibitions, festivals, etc.
1993.45   Dictionaries
History
       Including finance
1993.5.A1   General works
1993.5.A3-Z   By region or country, A-Z
           United States
1993.5.U6   General
1993.5.U65   Hollywood, Calif.
1993.5.U7-.U8   Other local. By state
1993.7-.8   Study and teaching
       Cf. TR852 Photography of moving objects
1993.7   General works
1993.75   Audiovisual aids about motion pictures
1993.8.A-Z   By region or country, A-Z
          Under each country:
           .x   *General works*
           .x2A-.x2Z   *Individual schools, A-Z*
1993.85   Examinations, questions, etc.
Competitions, prizes, etc.

PN
1560-3307

Motion pictures
Competitions, prizes, etc. -- Continued
1993.9   General and international
1993.92   United States
1993.93.A-Z   Other regions or countries, A-Z
                  Laws, regulations, etc.
                      see class K
1994.A52-Z   General works
1994.5   Juvenile literature
1994.9   Anecdotes, facetiae, satire
1995   General special
                      Including criticism, aesthetics, etc.
                      For film music, see class M
1995.2   Relation to history
1995.25   Relation to the arts
1995.3   Relation to literature
1995.4   Relation to language
1995.5   Relation to ethics, etc.
                  Motion pictures and television see PN1992.63
                  Censorship
1995.6   General works
                  United States
1995.62   General works
1995.63.A-.W   By state, A-W
1995.64.A-Z   By city, A-Z
1995.65.A-Z   Other regions or countries, A-Z
                  Locations
1995.67.A1   General works
1995.67.A3-Z   By place, A-Z
1995.7   Pictures and sound. Talking pictures
1995.75   Silent films
1995.8   Amateur motion pictures
1995.9.A-Z   Other special topics, A-Z
                      Aboriginal Australians see PN1995.9.A835
1995.9.A26   Acting. Auditions
1995.9.A3   Adventure films
                      Aeronautics see PN1995.9.F58
1995.9.A43   Africa
1995.9.A435   AIDS (Disease)
1995.9.A44   Alamo (San Antonio, Tex.)
1995.9.A45   Alcoholism
1995.9.A457   Alien films
1995.9.A46   Alien labor
1995.9.A47   Alienation (Social psychology). Rebels
1995.9.A48   Aliens
                      American Civil War see E656
1995.9.A487   Anarchism

	Motion pictures
	Other special topics, A-Z -- Continued
1995.9.A49	Angélique films
	Angels see PN1995.9.S8
1995.9.A5	Animals
	Including individual animals
1995.9.A55	Antisemitism
	Appalachians (People) see PN1995.9.M67
	Arab-Jewish relations see PN1995.9.J45
1995.9.A68	Arabs
1995.9.A69	Archaeology
1995.9.A695	Architects
1995.9.A7	Argentina
1995.9.A72	Armed Forces
1995.9.A73	Art and the arts
1995.9.A74	Art direction
1995.9.A75	Arthur and Arthurian romances
1995.9.A77	Asian Americans
1995.9.A78	Asians
1995.9.A8	Audiences
	Auditions see PN1995.9.A26
1995.9.A835	Australians, Aboriginal
1995.9.A837	Auteur theory
1995.9.A84	Authors
1995.9.A85	Automobiles. Motor vehicles
1995.9.B28	Baseball films
1995.9.B29	Basques
1995.9.B3	Baths
1995.9.B42	Beauty, Personal
1995.9.B47	Berlin (Germany)
1995.9.B53	Bible films
	Biker films see PN1995.9.M66
1995.9.B55	Biographical films
1995.9.B57	Bisexuality
	Blacks see PN1995.9.N4
1995.9.B62	Body, Human
1995.9.B63	Bogotá (Colombia)
1995.9.B64	Bondage (Sexual behavior)
1995.9.B68	Bowery Boys films
1995.9.B72	Brazil
1995.9.B76	Brooklyn
1995.9.B8	Bullfights
1995.9.B85	Bureaucracy
1995.9.B87	Business
1995.9.C32	Calabria (Italy)
1995.9.C33	Canada
1995.9.C332	Cannibalism

Motion pictures
Other special topics, A-Z -- Continued

1995.9.C333	Captivity
1995.9.C335	Carry on films
1995.9.C34	Casting
1995.9.C35	Catholic Church. Catholics
	Catholics see PN1995.9.C35
	Ceremonies see PN1995.9.R56
1995.9.C36	Characters and characteristics
1995.9.C37	Charlie Chan films
	Chicanos see PN1995.9.M49
1995.9.C39	Child sexual abuse
1995.9.C4	Childhood
1995.9.C45	Children and adolescents
1995.9.C47	China
1995.9.C5113	Christmas
1995.9.C512	Circus
1995.9.C5125	Cisco Kid
1995.9.C513	City and town life
	Civil War, American see E656
	Civil War, Spanish see DP269.8.M6
1995.9.C52	Clergy
1995.9.C53	Collectibles. Memorabilia
1995.9.C54	Collecting of motion pictures
1995.9.C543	College life films
1995.9.C55	Comedy
	Communism and motion pictures see HX550.M65
1995.9.C553	Composers
1995.9.C56	Costume
1995.9.C58	Country life
1995.9.C65	Credit titles
	Cf. TR886.9 Cinematography
	Credits for individual producers, directors,
	actors, etc.
	see PN1998.3; PN2287; PN2308; etc.
1995.9.C7	Cruelty
1995.9.C85	Culture conflict
1995.9.C9	Cyborgs
	Dead End kids see PN1995.9.B68
1995.9.D35	Deaf
1995.9.D37	Death
1995.9.D4	Detective and mystery films
1995.9.D44	Developing countries
1995.9.D46	Devil
1995.9.D49	Dialogue
1995.9.D52	Dinners and dining
1995.9.D53	Dinosaurs

	Motion pictures
	Other special topics, A-Z
	Direction see PN1995.9.P7
	Disabilities, People with see PN1995.9.H34
1995.9.D55	Disasters
1995.9.D58	Doctor Mabuse films
1995.9.D6	Documentary films
	Including catalogs
	Cf. TR895.4 Cinematography
1995.9.D62	Documentary-style films
1995.9.D63	Don Juan films
1995.9.D64	Dracula
1995.9.D67	Dreams
1995.9.D68	Drifters
1995.9.D78	Drugs
	Eastside Kids films see PN1995.9.B68
1995.9.E44	Emigration and immigration
1995.9.E77	Entertainers
1995.9.E79	Epic films
	Erotic films see PN1995.9.S45
	Espionage films see PN1995.9.S68
1995.9.E83	Eskimos
1995.9.E9	Evaluation
1995.9.E93	Evil
1995.9.E95	Exoticism
1995.9.E96	Experimental films
	Exploitation films see PN1995.9.S284
1995.9.E97	Extras (Actors)
1995.9.F27	Face
1995.9.F34	Fairy tales
1995.9.F35	Family
1995.9.F36	Fantastic films
	Feminism see PN1995.9.W6
	Feminist films see PN1995.9.W6
1995.9.F44	Femmes fatales
1995.9.F54	Films noirs
1995.9.F56	Flashbacks
1995.9.F58	Flight. Aeronautics
1995.9.F65	Food
1995.9.F67	Foreign films
1995.9.F78	France
1995.9.F79	Francis, of Assisi, Saint, 1182-1226
1995.9.F8	Frankenstein
1995.9.F85	Futurism in motion pictures
1995.9.G26	Gambling
1995.9.G3	Gangster films
	Gender see PN1995.9.S47

PN
1560-3307

Motion pictures
Other special topics, A-Z
1995.9.G39	Geopolitics
1995.9.G43	German reunification question (1949-1990)
1995.9.G45	Germans
	Ghosts see PN1995.9.S8
1995.9.G57	Girls
1995.9.G6	Godfather films
1995.9.G63	Godzilla
	Gypsies see PN1995.9.R67
1995.9.H3	Hand-to-hand fighting, Oriental. Martial arts films
1995.9.H34	Handicapped. People with disabilities
1995.9.H38	Hawaii
1995.9.H4	Heimatfilme
1995.9.H43	Helsinki (Finland)
1995.9.H47	Hispanic Americans
1995.9.H5	Historical films
1995.9.H514	Hitler, Adolf, 1889-1945
1995.9.H52	Hô Chí Minh, 1890-1969
1995.9.H53	Holocaust, Jewish (1939-1945)
1995.9.H54	Home
1995.9.H55	Homosexuality
1995.9.H56	Hopalong Cassidy films
1995.9.H6	Horror films
	Human body see PN1995.9.B62
1995.9.H84	Hunting
1995.9.H95	Hypnotism
1995.9.I43	Impersonators
1995.9.I45	Impressionism
1995.9.I48	Indians
1995.9.I49	Indigenous peoples
1995.9.I55	Intercultural communication
1995.9.I57	International relations
1995.9.I67	Irish Americans
1995.9.I68	Irish question
1995.9.I7	Islands of the Pacific
1995.9.I72	Israel
1995.9.I73	Italian Americans
1995.9.J3	James Bond films
1995.9.J34	Japan
1995.9.J37	Jazz
1995.9.J4	Jesus Christ
1995.9.J45	Jewish-Arab relations
1995.9.J46	Jews
	Cf. PN1995.9.A55 Antisemitism
1995.9.J57	Joan, of Arc, Saint, 1412=1431

Motion pictures
    Other special topics, A-Z -- Continued

1995.9.J6	Journalists
1995.9.J8	Justice. Law
1995.9.J87	Juvenile delinquency
1995.9.K35	Kanagawa-ken (Japan)
1995.9.K57	Kissing
1995.9.K95	Kyūshū Region (Japan)
1995.9.L28	Labor. Working class
1995.9.L37	Latin America. Latin Americans
1995.9.L38	Latin lovers
	Law see PN1995.9.J8
1995.9.L46	Lenin, Vladimir Il'ich, 1870-1924
1995.9.L48	Lesbianism
1995.9.L49	Libraries
1995.9.L53	Lincoln, Abraham, 1809-1865
1995.9.L55	Lisbon (Portugal)
1995.9.L57	London (England)
1995.9.L6	Love
1995.9.M23	Mafia
1995.9.M25	Makeup
1995.9.M27	Man-woman relationships
1995.9.M29	Marketing
1995.9.M3	Marriage. Weddings
	Martial arts films see PN1995.9.H3
1995.9.M38	Masochism
	Medical personnel see PN1995.9.P44
1995.9.M43	Medici, House of
1995.9.M45	Melodrama
	Memorabilia see PN1995.9.C53
1995.9.M46	Men
1995.9.M462	Mental health personnel
	Including psychiatrists, psychotherapists, etc.
1995.9.M463	Mental illness
1995.9.M472	Metaphor
1995.9.M48	Mexican-American Border region
1995.9.M49	Mexican-Americans
1995.9.M5	Mexico
1995.9.M52	Middle Ages
1995.9.M54	Miners
1995.9.M56	Minorities
1995.9.M6	Monsters
1995.9.M63	Mothers
1995.9.M65	Motion picture industry in motion pictures
	Motion pictures as a profession see PN1995.9.P75
	Motor vehicles see PN1995.9.A85

Motion pictures
Other special topics, A-Z
1995.9.M66	Motorcycles. Biker films
1995.9.M67	Mountain whites (Southern States).
	Appalachians (People)
1995.9.M68	Mountains
1995.9.M83	Mummies
	Music
	see class M
1995.9.M86	Musical films. Rock musical films
1995.9.M96	Myth
1995.9.M97	Mythology
1995.9.N3	Naples (Italy)
1995.9.N32	Napoleon I, Emperor of the French, 1769-1821
1995.9.N33	National characteristics
1995.9.N34	National characteristics, American
1995.9.N35	National characteristics, Australian
1995.9.N352	National characteristics, British
1995.9.N354	National characteristics, German
1995.9.N36	National socialism
1995.9.N38	Nature films
1995.9.N4	Negroes. Blacks
1995.9.N47	New Deal, 1933-1939
1995.9.N49	New York
1995.9.N53	Nightmare on Elm Street films
1995.9.N55	Nihilism (Philosophy)
1995.9.N57	Niskavuori films
1995.9.N59	Nixon, Richard M. (Richard Milhous), 1913-
1995.9.N67	Nostalgia
1995.9.N92	Nudity
1995.9.O28	Occultism
1995.9.O64	Opera
1995.9.O75	Organizational behavior
1995.9.O8	Our Gang films
1995.9.O84	Outlaws
1995.9.P3	Paris
1995.9.P34	Passion plays
1995.9.P36	Peasants
	People with disabilities see PN1995.9.H34
1995.9.P38	Peronism
1995.9.P42	Philosophy
1995.9.P44	Physicians. Medical personnel
1995.9.P48	Picasso, Pablo, 1881-1973
1995.9.P49	Pirates
1995.9.P495	Planet of the Apes films

	Motion pictures
	Other special topics, A-Z -- Continued
1995.9.P5	Playbills. Posters
	For posters by individual artists see
	NC1850.A+
1995.9.P57	Police films
1995.9.P6	Politics
1995.9.P64	Populist films
	Posters see PN1995.9.P5
1995.9.P67	Prehistoric animals
1995.9.P68	Prison films
1995.9.P7	Production and direction
1995.9.P75	Profession, Motion pictures as
	Props see PN1995.9.S69
1995.9.P76	Prostitutes
1995.9.P77	Prussia
	Psychiatrists see PN1995.9.M462
1995.9.P78	Psychiatry
1995.9.P783	Psychoanalysis
1995.9.P785	Psychopaths
	Psychotherapists see PN1995.9.M462
1995.9.P79	Public relations
1995.9.P793	Puerto Rico
1995.9.P8	Puppet films
1995.9.Q36	Queensland
1995.9.R25	Railroads
1995.9.R27	Rape
1995.9.R3	Realism
1995.9.R34	Refugees
1995.9.R35	Regeneration
1995.9.R4	Religion
1995.9.R45	Remakes
1995.9.R56	Rites and ceremonies
	Rock musical films see PN1995.9.M86
1995.9.R63	Road films
1995.9.R65	Robin Hood
1995.9.R67	Romanies
1995.9.R68	Rome
1995.9.S23	Sadism
1995.9.S237	Sami (European people)
1995.9.S24	Samurai films
1995.9.S253	Schools
1995.9.S26	Science fiction films
1995.9.S265	Science films
1995.9.S27	Scotland
1995.9.S28	Sea
1995.9.S284	Sensationalism. Exploitation films

Motion pictures
Other special topics, A-Z -- Continued

1995.9.S29	Sequels
1995.9.S297	Serial murderers
1995.9.S3	Serials
1995.9.S4	Setting and scenery
1995.9.S45	Sex. Erotic films
1995.9.S47	Sex role
1995.9.S48	Shamanism
1995.9.S5	Sherlock Holmes films
1995.9.S54	Sicily (Italy)
1995.9.S55	Sisters
1995.9.S554	Slasher films
1995.9.S557	Slavery
1995.9.S56	Slovakia
1995.9.S58	Smoking
1995.9.S6	Social aspects
1995.9.S62	Social problems
1995.9.S63	Socialist realism
1995.9.S655	South Africa
1995.9.S66	Southern States
1995.9.S665	Soviet Union
	Spanish Civil War see DP269.8.M6
1995.9.S67	Sports
1995.9.S68	Spy films
1995.9.S69	Stage props
1995.9.S694	Star Trek films
1995.9.S695	Star Wars films
1995.9.S696	Stills
1995.9.S697	Strong men
1995.9.S7	Stunt men
1995.9.S74	Suburbs
1995.9.S75	Subways
1995.9.S76	Superhero films
1995.9.S77	Superman films
1995.9.S8	Supernatural. Angels. Ghosts
1995.9.S85	Surrealism
1995.9.S87	Suspense
1995.9.T3	Tarzan
1995.9.T4	Teachers
1995.9.T45	Telephone
1995.9.T47	Texas
1995.9.T5	Three Stooges films
1995.9.T55	Time
1995.9.T57	Titles
	Cf. PN1995.9.C65 Credit titles
	Cf. TR886.9 Cinematography

	Motion pictures
	Other special topics, A-Z -- Continued
1995.9.T64	Tokyo
	Town and city life see PN1995.9.C513
1995.9.T685	Trailers
1995.9.T72	Trapalhões films
1995.9.T75	Trials
1995.9.T87	Turks
1995.9.U45	Ukrainians
1995.9.U6	Underground movements
1995.9.U62	Unidentified flying objects
1995.9.U64	United States
1995.9.V3	Vampire films
1995.9.V4	Veneto (Italy)
1995.9.V44	Veterans
	Vietnamese Conflict see DS557.73
1995.9.V47	Villains
1995.9.V5	Violence
1995.9.V63	Voice-overs
1995.9.V66	Voodooism
1995.9.W3	War

> For motion pictures about a particular war, see the war

	Weddings see PN1995.9.M3
1995.9.W38	Werewolves
1995.9.W4	Western films
1995.9.W45	Whites
1995.9.W6	Women

> Including feminism and feminist films

1995.9.W65	Women murderers
	Working class see PN1995.9.L28
	World War I see D522.23
	World War II see D743.23
1995.9.Y54	Yiddish films
1995.9.Y6	Youth
1995.9.Z63	Zombie films
1995.9.Z67	Zorro films
1996	Authorship, scenario writing, etc.
	Plays, scenarios, etc.
1997.A1	Collections

> Class collections by an individual literary author in the author's literary author number

Individual motion pictures

> For non-fiction documentary films, see the subject in classes B - Z

	Motion pictures
	Plays, scenarios, etc.
	Individual motion pictures -- Continued
1997.A2-.Z8	Motion pictures produced through 2000. By title of motion picture, A-Z

Under each:

.x		*Text. By date*
		Including translations
.xA-.xZ		*Criticism*

1997.Z9	Uncatalogued
1997.2.A-Z	Motion pictures produced 2001- . By title of motion picture, A-Z

Under each:

.x		*Text. By date*
		Including translations
.xA-Z		*Criticism*

1997.3	Plays, scenarios, etc. of unproduced films. By author, A-Z
1997.5	Cartoon plays, scenarios, etc.
	For individual motion pictures see PN1997.A2+
1997.8	Plots, themes, etc.
1997.85	Film and video adaptations
	Miscellaneous
1998.A1	Directories
1998.A5-Z	Other miscellaneous works
	Including catalogs of dramatic motion pictures
	For catalogs of non-fiction motion pictures not limited to a particular topic see ZA4550
	Biography
1998.2	Collective
1998.3.A-Z	Individual, A-Z
	Subarrange each by Table P-PZ50
	For individual screen writers, see subclasses PA - PT
	For individual actors and actresses, see PN2287, PN2308, etc.
1999.A-Z	Special corporations, A-Z
	Dramatic representation. The theater
	Cf. HV2508 Theater for the deaf. Sign language theater
	Cf. MT955 Production of operas, musical comedies, etc.
	Periodicals
2000.A1	Polyglot
	American

	Dramatic representation. The theater
	Periodicals
	American -- Continued
2000.A2	Early to 1821
2000.A3-Z	1821-
2001	English
2002	Dutch
2003	French
2004	German
2005	Italian
2006	Scandinavian
2007	Slavic
2008	Spanish and Portuguese
2009	Other
2012	Yearbooks
	Class here general yearbooks only
	For local see PN2300+
	Societies
2015	International
	By region or country
2016	United States
2017.A-Z	Other regions or countries, A-Z
2018	Congresses
2019	Expositions. By date
	Collections
2020	Various authors
2021	Individual authors
2035	Dictionaries. Terminology
	General works on the theater
	Cf. PN1654+ Drama and theater
	Cf. PN2085+ The stage
2036	Early through 1800
2037	1801-
2038	Addresses, essays, lectures
	Philosophy, aesthetics, relation to other arts, etc.
	Cf. NX180.A78 Artists and the theater
2039	General works
2041.A-Z	Special topics, A-Z
2041.A57	Anthropology
2041.S45	Semiotics
	Relation to the state. Regulation and control. Censorship. Government patronage
2042	General works
2044.A-Z	By region or country, A-Z
2045.A-Z	Special topics, A-Z

PN
1560-3307

Dramatic representation. The theater
Philosophy, aesthetics, relation to other arts,
  etc. -- Continued
  Influence of the drama
      Including relation to the church, etc.,
        moral, religious, social, psychological
        and political aspects of the theater, etc.
    English
2047   Early through 1800
2049   1801-
2051   Other
2052 Directories. Guidebooks, etc. (International)
      For local, see the country
2053 Management, administration, production, and
        direction
      Cf. PN2085+ Stage management
2053.5 Public relations
2054 Guides to the selection of plays
  Acting
2055   Acting as a profession
2056   Professional ethics for actors
2058   Psychology of the actor
    Art of acting
        For television acting see PN1992.8.A3
        For motion picture acting see PN1995
        Cf. PN4001+ Oratory, elocution
2061   Treatises
2062   Method acting
          Including Stanislavsky, Strasberg, et. al.
      Special topics
2067   Theatrical costume and costume design
2068   Makeup
2071.A-Z   Other, A-Z
2071.A92   Auditioning
2071.B58   Blackface
2071.B74   Breathing
2071.C57   Comedy
2071.C58   Computer network resources
2071.F4   Fencing
2071.F5   Fighting
2071.F6   Foreign and regional dialect imitation
2071.G4   Gestures. Miming
              Cf. PN4165 Oratory
2071.I47   Impersonation
2071.I5   Improvisation
2071.M37   Masks
              Miming see PN2071.G4

	Dramatic representation. The theater
	Acting
	Art of acting
	Special topics
	Other, A-Z -- Continued
2071.M6	Movement
2071.M87	Music
2071.P78	Psychological aspects
2071.R45	Rehearsals
2071.S63	Social aspects
2071.S65	Speech
	Including Stage English, Transatlantic, etc.
	Cf. PN2071.F6 Foreign and regional dialect imitation
	Stage English see PN2071.S65
	Transatlantic see PN2071.S65
2073	Contracts, blanks, forms, diaries, etc.
2074	Theater as a profession
	Cf. PN2055+ Acting as a profession
	Study and teaching
2075	General works
2078.A-Z	By region or country, A-Z

Under each country:

.x	General works
.x2	Dramatic schools, research institutes, etc. By place, A-Z

2080	Selections for practice
	Criticism see PN1707
2081.A-Z	Special methods of presentation, A-Z
2081.A7	Arena stage
2081.E58	Environmental theater
2081.O6	Open stage (open on three sides)
2081.R4	Readers' theater
	Sign language theater see HV2508
	The stage and accessories
	For the architecture of buildings see NA6820+
2085	Treatises
2086	General special
2087.A-Z	By region or country, A-Z
2091.A-Z	Special topics, A-Z
2091.C65	Corrugated paperboard
2091.C85	Curtains
2091.E4	Electric devices. Stage lighting
	Cf. TK4399.T6 Electric lighting companies
	Electronic sound control see TK7881.9

Dramatic representation. The theater
The stage and accessories
Special topics, A-Z -- Continued

2091.F54	Fireworks
2091.F58	Flying
2091.M3	Machinery. Stage rigging
2091.M48	Metals in stage setting
2091.M6	Models of stage and theater
2091.P3	Panics
2091.S6	Sound effects
	Stage lighting see PN2091.E4
	Stage rigging see PN2091.M3
2091.S8	Stage settings, scenery, etc.
	Cf. ND2885+ Scene painting
2093	Miscellaneous
2095	Satire, humor, etc.
	Biography of stage designers
2096.A1	Collective
2096.A2-Z	Individual, A-Z
	Subarrange each by Table P-PZ50
	Theatrical posters
2098	General works
2099.A-Z	By region or country, A-Z
	History
	Comprehensive works
2100	Early through 1800
	1801-
2100.5	Polyglot
2101	American and English
2102	Dutch
2103	French
2104	German
2105	Italian
2106	Scandinavian
2107	Slavic
2108	Spanish and Portuguese
2109.A-Z	Other, A-Z
2111	Pictorial works
2115	Addresses, essays, lectures
2122	General special
	e.g. First performance
2125	Primitive
	Prefer classification by region or country
	By period
	Ancient
	Cf. PA, Classical literature
2131	General works

Dramatic representation. The theater
  History
    By period
      Ancient -- Continued

2132	General special
2135.A-Z	Special topics, A-Z
	By region or country
	Greece see PA3201+
	Rome see PA6073+
2145	Other
	Medieval
2152	General works
2154	Early to 1400
2156	Fifteenth century
2159.A-Z	Special topics, A-Z
2160	Byzantine Empire
	Renaissance
2171	General works
2173	Sixteenth century
2174	Seventeenth century
2179.A-Z	Special topics, A-Z
	Modern
2181	General works
2183	Eighteenth century
2185	Nineteenth century
2189	Twentieth century
2193.A-Z	Special topics, A-Z
2193.A8	Audiences
	Avant-garde theater see PN2193.E86
2193.C57	Circus
2193.E86	Experimental theater. Avant-garde theater
2193.E87	Expressionism
	Biography
	Special see PN2285+; PN2307+
2205	Collections
2208	Dictionaries
2215	Homes and haunts of actors
2217	Anecdotes. Wit. Humor, etc.
2219.A-Z	Special topics, A-Z
	Cabarets see PN1969.C3
	Café chantants see PN1969.C34
	Deaf, Theater for see HV2508
2219.O8	Outdoor theater
	Prison theater see HV8861
	Sign language theater see HV2508
	Vaudeville see PN1962+
	Women see PN1590.W64

PN
1560-3307

	Dramatic representation. The theater -- Continued
	Special regions or countries
2219.3	America
	North America
2219.5	General works
	United States
	Periodicals see PN2000.A+
	Societies see PN2015+
2220	Collections
	History
2221	Comprehensive
2226	General special
2232	Addresses, essays, lectures
	By period
	Early to 1800
2237	General works
2239	Contemporary works
	Nineteenth century
2245	Comprehensive
	1800-1859
2248	General works
2251	Contemporary works
	1860-1900
2256	General works
2259	Contemporary works
	Twentieth century
2266	Comprehensive
2266.3	1900-1959
2266.5	1960-
2267	Little theater movement. Community theater. Folk theater
2268	Municipal theaters
2269	Summer theater, barn theater, open-air theater, etc.
2270.A-Z	Other special topics, A-Z
2270.A35	African American theater
2270.A54	Animals
	Including individual animals
2270.A89	Audiences
2270.A93	Awards, prizes, etc. Tony awards
2270.D56	Dinner theater
2270.F43	Federal Theatre Project (United States)
2270.F45	Feminist theater
2270.G39	Gay theater
2270.H57	Hispanic American theater
2270.I53	Indian theater

PN
1560-3307

Dramatic representation. The theater
Special regions or countries
America
North America
United States
History
By period
Twentieth century
Other special topics, A-Z -- Continued
2270.I73	Italian-American theater
2270.L38	Latvian American theater
2270.L47	Lesbian theater
2270.M48	Mexican American theater
2270.P58	Plays-in-progress
2270.P64	Polish American theater

Local
2273.A-Z	Regions, A-Z
	Including East, South, etc.
2275.A-.W	States, A-W
2277.A-Z	Cities, A-Z
	Subarrange each by Table PN8a

Biography
Collective
Including portrait albums, etc.
2285	General
2286	African Americans
2286.2	Asian Americans
2286.5	Gays
2286.8	Women
2287.A-Z	Individual, A-Z
	Subarrange each by Table P-PZ50
	Including actors (Stage names),
	producers, directors, etc.
	For producers, directors, etc. of
	motion pictures see PN1998.3.A+
2289	Directories
	Class here general works only
	For local see PN2275.A+
2291	Management, organization, administration,
	etc.
	Including syndicates, circuits,
	troupes, etc.
2293.A-Z	Special topics, A-Z
2293.C38	Casting
2293.E35	Economics. Finance
	Finance see PN2293.E35
2293.I4	Independent theaters

Dramatic representation. The theater
Special regions or countries
America
North America
United States
Management, organization, administration, etc.
Special topics, A-Z -- Continued

2293.N67	Nonprofit theater
2293.P53	Planning
2293.S4	Showboats
2293.T8	Theatrical trusts
2295.A-Z	Corporations and institutions, A-Z
	Theatrical troupes
2297.A2	General works
2297.A3-Z	Individual, A-Z
	Subarrange each by Table P-PZ50
	e. g.
2297.L5	Living Theater
2297.M3	Marx Brothers
2297.P7	Provincetown Players
2298	Special plays, spectacles, etc. By name
	Canada
2300	Collections
	History
2301	General works
2302	Early to 1800
2303	19th century
2304	20th century
2304.2	21st century
2305.A-Z	Provinces, A-Z
2306.A-Z	Cities, A-Z
	Subarrange each by Table PN8a
	Biography
2307	Collective
2308.A-Z	Individual, A-Z
	Subarrange each by Table P-PZ50
2308.5	Directories. Guidebooks, etc.
	For local see PN2305.A+
2309	Latin America
2310-2318	Mexico (Table PN6)
	Central America
2320	General works
	Belize
2325	Collections
	History
2326	General works

	Dramatic representation. The theater
	Special regions or countries
	America
	North America
	Central America
	Belize
	History -- Continued
2327.A-Z	Local, A-Z
	Subarrange each by Table PN8a
	Biography
2328	Collective
2329.A-Z	Individual, A-Z
	Subarrange each by Table P-PZ50
	Costa Rica
2330	Collections
	History
2331	General works
2332.A-Z	Local, A-Z
	Subarrange each by Table PN8a
	Biography
2333	Collective
2334.A-Z	Individual, A-Z
	Subarrange each by Table P-PZ50
2340-2344	Guatemala (Table PN7)
2350-2354	Honduras (Table PN7)
2360-2364	Nicaragua (Table PN7)
2370-2374	Panama (Table PN7)
2380-2384	Salvador (Table PN7)
2389	Caribbean Area
	West Indies
2390	General works
2395-2399	Bahamas (Table PN7)
2400-2404	Cuba (Table PN7)
2410-2414	Dominican Republic (Table PN7)
2415-2419	Haiti (Table PN7)
2420-2424	Jamaica (Table PN7)
2430-2434	Puerto Rico (Table PN7)
2440.A-Z	Others, A-Z
	South America
2445	General works
2450-2454	Argentina (Table PN7)
2460-2464	Bolivia (Table PN7)
2470-2474	Brazil (Table PN7)
2480-2484	Guyana (Table PN7)
2490-2494	Chile (Table PN7)
2500-2504	Colombia (Table PN7)
2510-2514	Suriname (Table PN7)

PN
1560-3307

Dramatic representation. The theater
　　Special regions or countries
　　　America
　　　　South America -- Continued

2515-2519	Ecuador (Table PN7)
2520-2524	French Guiana (Table PN7)
2525-2529	Paraguay (Table PN7)
2530-2534	Peru (Table PN7)
2540-2544	Uruguay (Table PN7)
2550-2554	Venezuela (Table PN7)

　　　Europe
2570	General works

　　　　Great Britain. England
2575.A-Z	Theatrical clubs, A-Z
	e. g.
2575.G2	Garrick Club, Cambridge
2575.G3	Garrick Club, London
2580	Collections
	History
2581	General works
2582.A-Z	Special topics, A-Z
2582.B4	Benefit performances
	Censorship see PN2042+
2582.K55	Kings and rulers
	Including command performances
2582.N3	National theater
2582.P54	Playbills
2582.S64	Special effects
2582.T5	Ticket prices
2582.W65	Women
2583	Addresses, essays, lectures
	By period
2585	Early to 1800
2586	Origins
	Medieval
2587	General works
2588.A-Z	Special topics, A-Z
	Renaissance
2589	General works
2590.A-Z	Special topics, A-Z
2590.B6	Boy actors
2590.C45	Children of Paul's
2590.C66	Court theater
2590.L67	Lord Chamberlain's Servants
2590.R35	Religious aspects
2590.T7	Traveling theater
	Modern

Dramatic representation. The theater
  Special regions or countries
    Europe
      Great Britain. England
        History
          By period
            Modern -- Continued

2592	17th century (17th-18th centuries)
2593	18th century
2594	19th century
	20th century
2595	General works
2595.13.A-Z	Special topics, A-Z
2595.13.E97	Experimental theater
2595.13.W65	Women's theater. Feminist theater
2595.132	21st century
2595.15	Awards, prizes, etc.
2595.3	Little theater. Repertory theater
2595.5	Special counties, regions, etc.
2596.A-Z	Special English cities, A-Z
	e. g.
	London
2596.L6	General works
2596.L7.A-Z	Special theaters, A-Z
	Biography
2597	Collective
2598.A-Z	Individual, A-Z
	Subarrange each by Table P-PZ50
2598.5	Directories. Guidebooks, etc.
	For local see PN2595.5; PN2600+
	Management, etc.
2599	General works
2599.5.A-Z	Special topics, A-Z
	Companies, Theatrical see PN2599.5.T54
2599.5.E25	Economics. Finance
	Finance see PN2599.5.E25
2599.5.T54	Theatrical troupes and companies
2599.5.T73	Traveling theater
	Ireland
2600	Collections
2601	History, biography, etc.
2602.A-Z	Local, A-Z
	Subarrange each by Table PN8a
	Scotland
2603	Collections
2604	History, biography, etc.

PN
1560-3307

Dramatic representation. The theater
Special regions or countries
Europe
Great Britain. England
Scotland -- Continued
2605.A-Z   Local, A-Z
Subarrange each by Table PN8a
Wales
2606   Collections
2607   History, biography, etc.
2608.A-Z   Local, A-Z
Subarrange each by Table PN8a
2609.A-Z   Other local, A-Z
Austria. Austria-Hungary
For Hungary see PN2859.H8+
2610   Periodicals. Serials
History
2611   General works
2611.5   General special
2612   Early to 1800
2613   19th century
2614   20th century
2614.2   21st century
2615.A-Z   Special states, provinces, etc., A-Z
Czechoslovakia see PN2859.C9+
2616.A-Z   Special cities, A-Z
Subarrange each by Table PN8a
Biography
2617   Collective
2618.A-Z   Individual, A-Z
Subarrange each by Table P-PZ50
France
2620   Collections
History
2621   General works
2622.A-Z   Special topics, A-Z
2622.A8   Audiences
2622.C37   Caricatures and cartoons
2622.P53   Playbills
Posters see PN2098+
2622.W65   Women
2623   Addresses, essays, lectures
By period
2625   Early to 1800
2626   Origins
Medieval
2627   General works

Dramatic representation. The theater
Special regions or countries
Europe
France
History
By period
Medieval -- Continued

2628.A-Z	Special topics, A-Z
	Renaissance
2629	General works
2630.A-Z	Special topics, A-Z
	Modern
2631	General works
2632	17th century (17th-18th centuries)
2633	18th century
2634	19th century
2635	20th century
2635.2	21st century
2636.A-Z	Local, A-Z
	Subarrange each by Table PN8a
	Biography
2637	Collective
2638.A-Z	Individual, A-Z
	Subarrange each by Table P-PZ50
2638.5	Directories. Guidebooks, etc.
	For local see PN2636.A+
	Management, etc.
2639	General works
2639.5.A-Z	Special topics, A-Z
	Companies, Theatrical see PN2639.5.T54
2639.5.E35	Economics. Finance
	Finance see PN2639.5.E35
2639.5.T54	Theatrical troupes and companies
2639.5.T73	Traveling theater
	Germany
2640	Collections
	History
2641	General works
2642.A-Z	Special topics, A-Z
2642.A84	Audiences
2642.H4	Heralds
2642.O6	Open-air theater
2642.P5	Playbills
	Posters see PN2098+
2642.W65	Women
2643	Addresses, essays, lectures
	By period

Dramatic representation. The theater
Special regions or countries
Europe
Germany
History
By period -- Continued
2645 Early to 1800
2646 Origins
Medieval
2647 General works
2648.A-Z Special topics, A-Z
2648.M55 Minstrels
Renaissance
2649 General works
2650.A-Z Special topics, A-Z
Modern
2652 17th-18th centuries
2653 19th century
2654 20th century
2654.2 21st century
2655.A-Z States, provinces, etc., A-Z
2656.A-Z Cities, A-Z
Subarrange each by Table PN8a
Biography
2657 Collective
2658.A-Z Individual, A-Z
Subarrange each by Table P-PZ50
Management, etc.
2659 General works
2659.5.A-Z Special topics, A-Z
2659.5.E35 Economics. Finance
Finance see PN2659.5.E35
2659.5.T47 Theatrical troupes and companies
2660-2668 Greece (Modern) (Table PN6a)
Italy
2670 Collections
History
2671 General works
2672.A-Z Special topics, A-Z
For list of Cutter numbers, see
PN2642.A+
2673 Addresses, essays, lectures
By period
2675 Early to 1800
2676 Origins
Medieval
2677 General works

Dramatic representation. The theater
Special regions or countries
Europe
Italy
History
By period
Medieval -- Continued

2678.A-Z	Special topics, A-Z
	For list of Cutter numbers, see PN2648.A+
	Renaissance
2679	General works
2680.A-Z	Special topics, A-Z
	Modern
2682	17th-18th centuries
2683	19th century
2684	20th century
2684.2	21st century
2685.A-Z	States, provinces, etc., A-Z
2686.A-Z	Cities, A-Z
	Subarrange each by Table PN8a
	Biography
2687	Collective
2688.A-Z	Individual, A-Z
	Subarrange each by Table P-PZ50
	Management, etc.
2689	General works
2689.5.A-Z	Special topics, A-Z
	For list of Cutter numbers, see PN2659.5.A+
	Low countries
	General
2690	Periodicals. Serials
	History
2691	General works
2691.5	General special
2692	Early to 1800
2693	19th century
2694	20th century
2694.2	21st century
2700-2708	Belgium (Table PN6a)
2710-2718	Netherlands (Table PN6a)
2719	Luxembourg
2720-2728	Russia. Soviet Union. Russia (Federation) (Table PN6a)
	Scandinavia
2730-2738	General (Table PN6a)

PN
1560-3307

Dramatic representation. The theater
Special regions or countries
Europe
Scandinavia -- Continued

2740-2748	Denmark (Table PN6a)
2750-2758	Iceland (Table PN6a)
2760-2768	Norway (Table PN6a)
2770-2778	Sweden (Table PN6a)
2780-2788	Spain (Table PN6a)
2790-2798	Portugal (Table PN6a)
2800-2808	Switzerland (Table PN6a)
	Balkan States
2818.5	General works
	Albania
2819	General works
2819.2.A-.Z	Local, A-Z
	Each city subarranged by author
	Biography
2819.3	Collective
2819.4.A-Z	Individual, A-Z
	Subarrange each by Table P-PZ50
	Bosnia and Hercegovina see PN2859.B67+
2820-2828	Bulgaria (Table PN6a)
	Croatia see PN2859.C7+
	Macedonia (Republic) see PN2859.M275+
	Montenegro see PN2850+
2840-2848	Romania (Table PN6a)
	Slovenia see PN2859.S57+
	Turkey see PN2959+
2850-2858	Yugoslavia (Table PN6a)
2859.A-Z	Other European regions or countries, A-Z
	Belarus
2859.B44	General works
2859.B443A-.B443Z	Local, A-Z
	Each city subarranged by author
	Biography
2859.B445	Collective
2859.B446A-.B446Z	Individual, A-Z
	Bosnia and Hercegovina
2859.B67	General works
2859.B673A-.B673Z	Local, A-Z
	Each city subarranged by author
	Biography
2859.B675	Collective
2859.B676A-.B676Z	Individual, A-Z
	Croatia
2859.C7	General works

Dramatic representation. The theater
Special regions or countries
Europe
Other European regions or countries, A-Z
Croatia -- Continued

2859.C73A-.C73Z	Local, A-Z
	Each city subarranged by author
	Biography
2859.C75	Collective
2859.C76A-.C76Z	Individual, A-Z
	Czech Republic
2859.C9	General works
2859.C93A-.C93Z	Local, A-Z
	Each city subarranged by author
	Biography
2859.C95	Collective
2859.C96A-.C96Z	Individual, A-Z
2859.E17	Eastern Europe
	Estonia
2859.E7	General works
2859.E73A-.E73Z	Local, A-Z
	Each city subarranged by author
	Biography
2859.E75	Collective
2859.E76A-.E76Z	Individual, A-Z
	Finland
2859.F5	General works
2859.F53A-.F53Z	Local, A-Z
	Each city subarranged by author
	Biography
2859.F55	Collective
2859.F56A-2859Z	Individual, A-Z
	Hungary
2859.H8	General works
2859.H83A-.H83Z	Local, A-Z
	Each city subarranged by author
	Biography
2859.H85	Collective
2859.H86A-.H86Z	Individual, A-Z
	Latvia
2859.L3	General works
2859.L33A-.L33Z	Local, A-Z
	Each city subarranged by author
	Biography
2859.L35	Collective
2859.L36A-.L36Z	Individual, A-Z
	Lithuania

Dramatic representation. The theater
Special regions or countries
Europe
Other European regions or countries, A-Z
Lithuania -- Continued

2859.L5	General works
2859.L53A-.L53Z	Local, A-Z
	Each city subarranged by author
	Biography
2859.L55	Collective
2859.L56A-.L56Z	Individual, A-Z

Macedonia (Republic)

2859.M275	General works
2859.M2753A- .M2753Z	Local, A-Z
	Each city subarranged by author
	Biography
2859.M2755	Collective
2859.M2756A- .M2756Z	Individual, A-Z

Malta

2859.M3	General works
2859.M33A-.M33Z	Local, A-Z
	Each city subarranged by author
	Biography
2859.M35	Collective
2859.M36A-.M36Z	Individual, A-Z

Moldova

2859.M64	General works
2859.M643A-.M643Z	Local, A-Z
	Each city subarranged by author
	Biography
2859.M645	Collective
2859.M646A-.M646Z	Individual, A-Z

Poland

2859.P6	General works
2859.P63A-.P63Z	Local, A-Z
	Each city subarranged by author
	Biography
2859.P65	Collective
2859.P66A-.P66Z	Individual, A-Z

San Marino

2859.S27	General works
2859.S273A-.S273Z	Local, A-Z
	Each city subarranged by author
	Biography
2859.S275	Collective
2859.S276A-.S276Z	Individual, A-Z

	Dramatic representation. The theater
	Special regions or countries
	Europe
	Other European regions or countries, A-Z --
	Continued
	Slovakia
2859.S56	General works
2859.S563A-.S563Z	Local, A-Z
	Each city subarranged by author
	Biography
2859.S565	Collective
2859.S566A-.S566Z	Individual, A-Z
	Slovenia
2859.S57	General works
2859.S573A-.S573Z	Local, A-Z
	Each city subarranged by author
	Biography
2859.S575	Collective
2859.S576A-.S576Z	Individual, A-Z
	Ukraine
2859.U47	General works
2859.U473A-.U473Z	Local, A-Z
	Each city subarranged by author
	Biography
2859.U475	Collective
2859.U476A-.U476Z	Individual, A-Z
	Asia
2860	General works
2870-2878	China (Table PN6a modified)
2874.5.A-Z	Special types of theater, A-Z
2874.5.H75	Hsiang sheng. Xiang sheng
2874.5.K83	Kuai shu
2874.5.P56	Ping ju (Folk dramas)
2874.5.P58	Ping shu
	Xiang sheng see PN2874.5.H75
2879	Taiwan
2880-2888	India (Table PN6a modified)
2884.5.A-Z	Special types of theater, A-Z
2884.5.K36	Kathakali (Dance drama)
2884.5.N38	Nautanki
2884.5.P36	Pandava
2884.5.T45	Thumri (Dance drama)
2884.5.Y35	Yaksagana (Dance drama)
2889	Indochina
	Burma
2889.2	Periodicals. Serials
	History

Dramatic representation. The theater
Special regions or countries
Asia
Burma
History -- Continued
2889.22   General works
2889.23   Early to 1800
2889.24   19th century
2889.25   20th century
2889.252   21st century
2889.255.A-Z   Special types of theater, A-Z
2889.26.A-Z   Special states, provinces, A-Z
2889.27.A-Z   Special cities, A-Z
Biography
2889.28   Collective
2889.29.A-Z   Individual, A-Z
Subarrange each by Table P-PZ50
Cambodia
2889.3   Periodicals. Serials
History
2889.32   General works
2889.33   Early to 1800
2889.34   19th century
2889.35   20th century
2889.352   21st century
2889.355.A-Z   Special types of theater, A-Z
2889.36.A-Z   Special states, provinces, etc., A-Z
2889.37.A-Z   Special cities, A-Z
Biography
2889.38   Collective
2889.39.A-Z   Individual, A-Z
Subarrange each by Table P-PZ50
Laos
2889.4   Periodicals. Serials
History
2889.42   General works
2889.43   Early to 1800
2889.44   19th century
2889.45   20th century
2889.452   21st century
2889.455.A-Z   Special types of theater, A-Z
2889.46.A-Z   Special states, provinces, etc., A-Z
2889.47.A-Z   Special cities, A-Z
Biography
2889.48   Collective
2889.49.A-Z   Individual, A-Z
Subarrange each by Table P-PZ50

Dramatic representation. The theater
Special regions or countries
Asia -- Continued
Thailand

2889.7	Periodicals. Serials
	History
2889.72	General works
2889.73	Early to 1800
2889.74	19th century
2889.75	20th century
2889.752	21st century
2889.755.A-Z	Special types of theater, A-Z
2889.76.A-Z	Special states, provinces, etc., A-Z
2889.77.A-Z	Special cities, A-Z
	Biography
2889.78	Collective
2889.79.A-Z	Individual, A-Z
	Subarrange each by Table P-PZ50

Vietnam

2889.8	Periodicals. Serials
	History
2889.82	General works
2889.83	Early to 1800
2889.84	19th century
2889.85	20th century
2889.852	21st century
2889.855.A-Z	Special types of theater, A-Z
2889.86.A-Z	Special states, provinces, etc., A-Z
2889.87.A-Z	Special cities, A-Z
	Biography
2889.88	Collective
2889.89.A-Z	Individual, A-Z
	Subarrange each by Table P-PZ50
(2890-2898)	Indochina, Thailand, Vietnam, etc.
	see PN2889+

Indonesia, Malay Archipelago
Malaysia

2899	Periodicals. Serials
	History
2899.1	General works
2899.2	Early to 1800
2899.3	19th century
2899.4	20th century
2899.42	21st century
2899.45	Special types of theater, A-Z
2899.5.A-Z	Special states, provinces, etc., A-Z
2899.6.A-Z	Special cities, A-Z

PN
1560-3307

Dramatic representation. The theater
Special regions or countries
Asia
Indonesia, Malay Archipelago
Malaysia -- Continued
Biography

2899.7	Collective
2899.8.A-Z	Individual, A-Z
	Subarrange each by Table P-PZ50
2900-2908	Indonesia (Table PN6a modified)
2904.5.A-Z	Special types of theater, A-Z
2904.5.K43	Kecak
2904.5.L45	Lenong
2904.5.L83	Ludruk
2904.5.R35	Randai
2904.5.W38	Wayang wong (Dance drama)
2910-2918	Philippines (Table PN6a)
2919-2919.8	Israel. Palestine (Table PN8)
	Cf. PN3035 Jewish theater

Japan

2920	Collections
	History
2921	General works
	By period
2922	Early to 1868
2923	1868-1900
2924	20th century
2924.2	21st century
2924.5.A-Z	Special types of theater, A-Z
2924.5.D45	Dengaku
2924.5.G54	Gigaku
2924.5.K3	Kabuki
2924.5.K6	Kowaka
2924.5.K9	Kyogen
2924.5.M36	Manzai
	Cf. GV1796.M32 Manzai (Dance)
2924.5.N36	Naniwabushi
2924.5.N6	Nō
2924.5.N65	Nōmai
2924.5.R34	Rakugo
2924.5.S3	Sarugaku
2925.A-Z	Special provinces, A-Z
2926.A-Z	Special cities, A-Z
	Subarrange each by Table PN8a
	Biography
2927	Collective

Dramatic representation. The theater

Special regions or countries

Asia

Japan

Biography -- Continued

2928.A-Z	Individual, A-Z
	Subarrange each by Table P-PZ50
2930-2938	Korea (Table PN6a)
	Including South Korea
2939-2939.8	North Korea (Table PN8)
2940-2948	Pakistan (Table PN6a)
2950-2958	Iran (Table PN6a)
2959-2959.8	Turkey (Table PN8)
2960.A-Z	Other Asian regions or countries, A-Z
	Each country subarranged by author
	e. g.
2960.A67	Arab countries
2960.A7	Armenia

Africa

2969	General works

Egypt

2970	Periodicals. Serials

History

2971	General works
2971.5	General special
2972	Early to 1800
2973	19th century
2974	20th century
2974.2	21st century
2975.A-Z	Special states, provinces, etc., A-Z
2976.A-Z	Special cities, A-Z
	Subarrange each by Table PN8a

Biography

2977	Collective
2978.A-Z	Individual, A-Z
	Subarrange each by Table P-PZ50

Sub-Saharan Africa

2979	General works

South Africa

2980	Periodicals. Serials

History

2981	General works
2981.5	General special
2982	Early to 1800
2983	19th century
2984	20th century
2984.2	21st century

Dramatic representation. The theater
Special regions or countries
Africa
Sub-Saharan Africa
South Africa -- Continued

2985.A-Z	Special states, provinces, etc., A-Z
2986.A-Z	Special cities, A-Z
	Subarrange each by Table PN8a
	Biography
2987	Collective
2988.A-Z	Individual, A-Z
	Subarrange each by Table P-PZ50
2989-2989.8	Cameroon (Table PN8)
2990-2990.8	Ghana (Table PN8)
2991-2991.8	Kenya (Table PN8)
2992-2992.8	Liberia (Table PN8)
2993-2993.8	Nigeria (Table PN8)
2994-2994.8	Somalia (Table PN8)
2995-2995.8	Tanzania (Table PN8)
2996-2996.8	Uganda (Table PN8)
2997-2997.8	Zambia (Table PN8)
2998-2998.8	Zimbabwe (Table PN8)
3000.A-Z	Other African regions or countries, A-Z
	Each country subarranged by author
	Australia and New Zealand
3010	Periodicals. Serials
	History
3011	General works
3011.5	General special
3012	Early to 1800
3013	19th century
3014	20th century
3014.2	21st century
3015.A-Z	Special states, provinces, etc., A-Z
3016.A-Z	Special cities, A-Z
	Subarrange each by Table PN8a
	Biography
3017	Collective
3018.A-Z	Individual, A-Z
	Subarrange each by Table P-PZ50
3030.A-Z	Pacific islands, A-Z
3035	The Jewish theater
	Cf. PN2919+ Theater in Israel

Dramatic representation. The theater -- Continued
   Amateur theater
      For pageants (Processionals, dances, and
         songs interwoven with dramatic episodes or
         miniature plays) see PN3203+
      For plays see PN6119.9
      General works

3151	Treatises
3155	Popular works
3156	General special
	Children's theater
	Including children as actors or audience,
	and presentation, etc., of plays
3157	General works
3159.A-Z	By region or country, A-Z
3160.A-Z	Other special topics, A-Z
3160.A34	Aged. Older people
3160.C34	Camping
	Older people see PN3160.A34
3160.W64	Women
	By region or country
	United States
3161	General works
3166.A-Z	Local. By place, A-Z
	e. g.
3166.S3	San Francisco. Bohemian Club of San Francisco
3169.A-Z	Other regions or countries, A-Z
	Under each country:
	.x *General works*
	.x2 *Local. By place, A-Z*
3171	The drama as a method of teaching
	For drama as a method in religious education
	see BV1534.4
	College and school theatricals
3175	General works
3178.A-Z	Special topics, A-Z
3178.C6	Competitions
3178.C64	Convent theater
3178.J46	Jesuit theater
3178.P52	Piarist theater
3178.P7	Production and direction
3178.S8	Stage setting and scenery
3178.T68	Theater management
	By region or country
	United States
3182	General works

Dramatic representation. The theater
College and school theatricals
By region or country
United States -- Continued

3185.A-Z	By institution, A-Z
3191.A-Z	Other regions or countries, A-Z

Under each country:

.x	*General works*
.x2	*By institution, A-Z*

3195   Minstrel shows, etc.
For collections and separate plays see
PN4305.N5; PN6120.N4

Tableaux, pageants, "Happenings," etc.
Class here works on pageants with tableaux,
songs, dances, dramatic episodes, etc.
For all pageants of local historical
interest, see classes D-F
Cf. GT3925+ Festivals and holidays (Manners
and customs)
Cf. GV1743 National dances, folk dances
Cf. LB3525+ School exercises (Special days,
etc.)
Cf. PN6120.T3 Tableaux

3203   Treatises. Production of (Amateur) pageants,
masques, plays, etc.
e.g. Bates, Pageants and pageantry; Chubb,
Festivals and plays

3205   Collections of texts, scenarios, etc.
3206   Special pageants, etc. By author or title
By region or country
United States
3209   General works
3211.A-Z   Local, A-Z
3215.A-Z   Other America. By region or country, A-Z
Europe
3220   General works
Austria
3221   General works
3222.A-Z   Local, A-Z
France
3225   General works
3226.A-Z   Local, A-Z
Germany
3233   General works
Special
Oberammergau
3235   General works

PN
1560-3307

Dramatic representation. The theater
Tableaux, pageants, "Happenings," etc.
By region or country
Europe
Germany
Special
Oberammergau -- Continued
3238   Minor works
3241   Texts of the play
3244.A-Z   Other local, A-Z
Great Britain
3251   General works
3252.A-Z   Local, A-Z
Kenilworth pageant, 1575 see DA690.K4
Greece
3255   General works
3256.A-Z   Local, A-Z
Italy
3261   General works
3262.A-Z   Local, A-Z
Netherlands
3265   General works
3266.A-Z   Local, A-Z
Spain
3271   General works
3272.A-Z   Local, A-Z
Portugal
3275   General works
3276.A-Z   Local, A-Z
Switzerland
3281   General works
3282.A-Z   Local, A-Z
3299.A-Z   Other regions or countries, A-Z
Workers' theaters. Agitprop. Popular theater
for community development
3305   General works
3306   Collections of texts
3307.A-Z   By region or country, A-Z
Lyceum courses, etc. see LC6501+

Prose
Prose. Prose fiction
3311   Periodicals. Societies. Serials
3315   Yearbooks
3318   Statistics
3319   Congresses
                Collections
3321   Various authors
3324   Collected essays by individual authors
                Dictionaries see PN41+
3326   Digests, synopses, etc.
            Philosophy, theory, etc.
                General
3329   Early
3331   Recent
3335   Aesthetics. Criticism, etc.
              Relation to and treatment of special subjects
3338   General works
3340   Realism and romanticism in prose fiction
3341   Relation to life
3342   Relation to art
3343   Relation to history
3344   Relation to sociology
3347   Relation to philosophy, ethics, etc.
3351   Relation to religion, mythology, etc.
3352.A-Z   Other special, A-Z
3352.A34   Absurdity
3352.A38   Adultery
3352.A55   Animals
3352.A77   Artists
3352.A84   Asia
3352.B53   Bible
3352.C37   Carnival
3352.C5   Cities and towns
3352.C6   The comic
                Con artists see PN3352.S94
3352.C74   Crime
3352.E2   Economics
3352.E38   Education
3352.E56   Emotions
3352.G76   Grotesque
3352.G85   Guilt
3352.H65   Homosexuality
3352.I53   Illegitimacy
3352.I56   Interpersonal relations
3352.J9   Judicial error
3352.K56   Knowledge

	Prose. Prose fiction
	Philosophy, theory, etc.
	Relation to and treatment of special subjects
	Other special, A-Z -- Continued
3352.L33	Labor. Working class
3352.M3	Management
3352.M34	Marginality, Social
3352.M87	Murder
3352.N83	Nuclear warfare
3352.P3	Paris
3352.P67	Probability. Verisimilitude
3352.P7	Psychology
	Cf. PN3448.P8 Psychological novel
3352.Q37	Quests
3352.R34	Railroads
3352.R43	Regionalism
3352.S3	School
3352.S34	Science
3352.S44	Self
3352.S48	Sex
3352.S5	Sickness
3352.S74	Storytelling
3352.S94	Swindlers and swindling
3352.T35	Terrorism
3352.T45	Theater
3352.T5	Time
	Verisimilitude see PN3352.P67
3352.W34	Walking
	Working class see PN3352.L33
3353	General works
3354	Addresses, essays, lectures
	Technique. Authorship
	Including marketing
3355	General works (Fiction in general)
	Special forms, subjects, etc.
3365	The novel
3373	The short story
3377	Juvenile stories
3377.5.A-Z	Other, A-Z
3377.5.A37	Adventure stories
3377.5.C47	Christian fiction
3377.5.C57	Computer-produced fiction
3377.5.C6	Confession stories
3377.5.C75	Crime writing
3377.5.D4	Detective and mystery stories
3377.5.E76	Erotic stories
3377.5.F34	Fantastic fiction

Prose. Prose fiction
 Technique. Authorship
  Special forms, subjects, etc.
   Other, A-Z -- Continued

3377.5.H57	Historical fiction
3377.5.H67	Horror tales
3377.5.L68	Love stories
3377.5.O9	Outdoor life
3377.5.R45	Reportage literature
3377.5.R48	Revolutionary literature
3377.5.S3	Science fiction
3377.5.S77	Stream of consciousness fiction
3377.5.W37	War stories
3377.5.W47	Western stories

   Special aspects of technique

3378	Plots
3383.A-Z	Other, A-Z
3383.C4	Characterization
3383.C55	Closure
3383.D53	Dialogue

     Cf. PN1551 The dialogue (General)

3383.E96	Exposition
3383.F74	Free indirect speech
3383.I5	Indirect discourse
3383.M48	Metaphor
3383.N35	Narration
3383.P37	Parody
3383.P64	Point of view
3383.R46	Repetition
3383.S42	Setting
3383.S67	Space
3383.S79	Style

  Study and teaching

3385	General works

   Story telling. Reading of stories to children,
    etc. see LB1042; LB1179
  Special topics

3401	Women writers. Feminism in fiction
3403	Men writers. Masculinity in fiction
3411	Characters: Heroes and heroines, etc.

   Special races, classes, types, etc., in fiction

3418	Jews
3423	Blacks
3426.A-Z	Other, A-Z
3426.A75	Armenians
3426.A77	Artists
3426.C5	Children

Prose. Prose fiction
  Special topics
    Special races, classes, types, etc., in fiction
      Other, A-Z -- Continued

3426.K65	Knights and knighthood
3426.L3	Labor. Working class
3426.L37	Lawyers
3426.N85	Nuns
3426.P4	Peasants
3426.P46	People with mental disabilities
3426.P75	Prostitutes
3426.S24	Saints
3426.W65	Women
	Working class see PN3426.L3

    Special kinds of fiction. Fiction genres

3427	General works
	Picaresque novels. Romances of roguery
3428	General
	By region or country
	Spain see PQ6147.P5
	Other regions or countries, A-Z
	see the national literature
3432	Robinsonades, "Avanturiers," etc.
	Science fiction
3433	Periodicals. Societies. Serials
3433.2	Congresses
3433.3	Exhibitions, museums, etc.
3433.4	Encyclopedias. Dictionaries
3433.5	General works
3433.6	Special topics (not A-Z)
3433.7	Study and teaching
	Authorship. Technique see PN3377.5.S3
3433.8	History
3435	Tales of wonder, terror, etc. Fantastic fiction
3437	Fairy tales
	Cf. GR550+ Fairy tales (Folk literature)
3441	The historical novel
3443	Juvenile and young adult fiction
3448.A-Z	Other, A-Z
3448.A3	Adventure stories
3448.A8	Autobiographical fiction
3448.B54	Bildungsroman
3448.C48	Christian fiction
3448.D4	Detective and mystery stories
3448.E6	Epistolary novel
3448.E76	Erotic stories
3448.H4	Heroic romance

PN
3311-4500

	Prose. Prose fiction
	Special kinds of fiction. Fiction genres
	Other, A-Z -- Continued
3448.K85	Künstlerroman
3448.L4	Legal novels
3448.L67	Love stories
3448.P38	Pastoral fiction
3448.P6	Political novel
3448.P8	Psychological novel
3448.S46	Sentimental novel
3448.S47	Sequels
3448.S6	Sociological novel
3448.S66	Spy stories
3448.U7	Utopian literature
3448.W3	War stories
3448.W4	Western stories
	History
	Comprehensive works
3451	American and English
3452	Dutch
3453	French
3454	German
3455	Italian
3456	Scandinavian
3457	Slavic
3458	Spanish and Portuguese
3459.A-Z	Other, A-Z
3463	Addresses, essays, lectures
	By period
3466	Ancient
	Medieval see PN692+
3481	Renaissance
	Modern
3491	General works
3493	17th century
3495	18th century
3499	19th century
3500	Early 19th century. Romanticism
3503	20th century
3504	21st century

Oratory
   Oratory. Elocution, etc.
     Cf. PN4199+ Recitations
    Periodicals. Serials

4001	English
4003	Other
4005	Yearbooks
4007	Directories
4009	Societies
4012	Collections (of monographs, etc., on the art, history, etc., of oratory)
	Collections of speeches see PN6121+
4016	Dictionaries
	History
4021	Comprehensive
4023	General special
	By period
	Antiquity
	see subclass PA
4031	Middle Ages
	Modern
4036	Comprehensive
	By period
4039	16th century
4042	17th century
4045	18th century
4048	19th century
4051	20th century
4051.2	21st century
4055.A-Z	By region or country, A-Z

        Under each country:

	.x	*General works*
	.x2	*By place, A-Z*
	.x3	*Special topics, A-Z*

    Biography of orators, lecturers, etc.

4057	Collected
	Individual
	Orators
	see D-F, PQ, PR, PS, etc.
4058	Lecturers
	Prefer PQ, PR, etc.
	Cf. LC6501+ Lyceums
4059	Elocutionists
4061	Philosophy. Theory. Relations

	Oratory. Elocution, etc. -- Continued
4066	Satire. Humor
	Cf. PN4250+ Humorous recitations
	Cf. PN6146.2+ Wit and humor
	Cf. PN6231.S2 Collections (Satire)
	Study and teaching
4071	Periodicals. Serials
4073	Societies
4075	Congresses
4076	Competitions. Oratorical contests
4086	General works. History
4088	Audiovisual aids
4089	Examinations, questions, etc.
	By region or country
	United States
4091	General works
4092.A-Z	By place, A-Z
4093.A-Z	Schools. By city, A-Z
	Biography
4093.8	Collective
4094.A-Z	Individual, A-Z
	Subarrange each by Table P-PZ50
4095.A-Z	Other regions or countries, A-Z
4096	Criticism
4098	Vocational guidance
	Treatises. Compends. Textbooks
	Early to 1800
4103	Latin
4105	Other
	19th century
4111	American and English
4112	Dutch
4113	French
4114	German
4115	Italian
4116	Scandinavian
4117	Slavic
4118	Spanish and Portuguese
4119.A-Z	Other, A-Z
	20th century
4121	American and English
4122	Dutch
4123	French
4124	German
4125	Italian
4126	Scandinavian
4127	Slavic

       Oratory. Elocution, etc.
        Treatises. Compends. Textbooks
         20th century -- Continued
4128   Spanish and Portuguese
4129.A-Z   Other, A-Z
         21st century
4129.15   American and English
4129.2   Dutch
4129.3   French
4129.4   German
4129.5   Italian
4129.6   Scandinavian
4129.7   Slavic
4129.8   Spanish and Portuguese
4129.9.A-Z   Other, A-Z
4130   Addresses, essays, lectures, etc.
        Special
4135   Audiences
4140   Subjects
4142   Composition, style, etc.
         Reading, emphasis, etc. Oral interpretation
4145   General works
4148   Chamber theater
          Choral speaking see PN4193.C5
4151   Poetry. Poetry readings
          Readers' theater see PN2081.R4
         Expression
          For general works on voice and gesture see
           PN4103+
         Theory. Philosophy
4155   General works
4157   Delsarte system
         The voice
          Cf. MT820 Musical instruction
          Cf. PN2071.S65 Speech and voice culture
           for actors
          Cf. QP306 Physiology
4162   General works
4163.A-Z   Special topics, A-Z
4163.C5   Children's voices
4163.S8   Stimulants, Effect of
4165   Gestures
          Cf. PN2071.G4 Art of acting
4168   Extemporaneous speaking
          For conversation see BJ2120+
4171   Forensic oratory

PN
3311-4500

Oratory. Elocution, etc.
 Special -- Continued
4173 Pulpit oratory and elocution
  Cf. BV4200+ Preaching
 Debating
  For outlines with arguments in extenso, see
   the subject
  For outlines and references on public
   questions see Z7161+
  Cf. PE1431 Modern English rhetoric
4177 Periodicals. Societies. Serials
4181 Treatises
  Including topics for debate
4183.A-Z Special topics, A-Z
4183.C74 Cross-examination
4183.J83 Judging
 Local
  United States
4185 Associations, leagues, etc.
4187 General works
4189.A-Z Special colleges, schools, etc., A-Z
4191.A-Z Other regions or countries, A-Z
4192.A-Z Special classes of persons, A-Z
4192.A72 Architects
4192.B87 Businesspeople
4192.C45 Church leaders
4192.C63 Coaches
 Educators see PN4192.T43
4192.E53 Engineers
4192.M43 Medical personnel
4192.S35 School administrators
4192.S39 Scientists
4192.S94 Supervisors
4192.T43 Teachers. Educators
4192.U54 Union representatives
4192.W65 Women
4193.A-Z Other special, A-Z
4193.B6 Biographical speeches
4193.B8 Business speeches
4193.C5 Choral speaking
  Cf. PN4305.C4 Choral recitations
 Discussion see LC6519
4193.I5 Illustrative incidents, stories, etc.
4193.L4 Lectures and lecturing
4193.M5 Military service
4193.O4 Occasional speeches
  Including after-dinner speeches, etc.

	Oratory. Elocution, etc.
	Special
	Other special, A-Z -- Continued
4193.O7	Open-air meeting
4193.P5	Poetry recitation
	Cf. PN4151 Poetry readings
4193.P6	Political oratory
4193.P73	Press conferences
	Cf. PN4784.P69 Journalism
4193.R63	Roasts
	Storytelling see PN4193.R63
(4193.S8)	Supervisor's speech
	see PN4192.S94
(4193.T4)	Teacher's speech
	see PN4192.T43
	Theater speech see PN2071.S65
(4193.W7)	Women speakers
	see PN4192.W65
	Exercises
4197	Drill books. Voice culture
	Cf. QP306 Physiology
	Recitations (in English)
	Collections of recitations (Poetry and prose)
4199	Serials
	General works
4200	Early through 1830
4201	1831-
	Indexes see PN4321
	Regional, sectional, etc.
4215	New England
4217	South
4219	West
4221	Pacific
4225.A-.W	By state, A-W
4228.A-Z	Foreign. By nationality, A-Z
	e.g. Canadian, Scotch, etc.
	Special
	Religious
	Cf. PE1123+ Readers for religious students
4230	Early through 1830
4231	1831-
	Patriotic
	Cf. PE1127.H4+ "Patriotic" readers
4240	Early through 1830
4241	1831-
	Humorous
4250	Early through 1830

PN
3311-4500

	Oratory. Elocution, etc.
	Recitations (in English)
	Special
	Humorous -- Continued
4251	1831-
	Juvenile
4270	Early through 1830
4271	1831-
	Dialogues
	Class here general and miscellaneous works
	For special, see the subject in PN4230+,
	PN4305; for plays, see PN6111+,
	PN1241+; etc.
4290	Early to 1830
4291	1831-
4305.A-Z	Other special. By subject, A-Z
	Blacks see PN4305.N5
4305.C3	Catholic
4305.C4	Choral recitations
	Cf. PN4193.C5 Choral speaking
4305.C5	Christmas
4305.C6	Club and lodge-room
4305.C7	College, commencement parts, etc
4305.D6	Dialect
4305.E2	Easter
4305.H7	Holidays
	Cf. PN4305.C4 Christmas
	Cf. PN4305.T5 Thanksgiving
4305.I5	Impersonations
4305.I6	Indians
4305.I7	Introduction of speakers
4305.J48	Jewish
4305.M3	Martial, heroic, etc.
4305.M6	Monologues
4305.M8	Musical recitations
4305.N3	Nature
4305.N5	Negroes. Blacks
4305.O4	Occasional addresses. After-dinner speeches
4305.P3	Pathetic, etc.
4305.R3	Radio talks, etc.
4305.S3	St. Valentine's day
4305.S4	School exercises
4305.T3	Tableaux, drills, etc., with recitations
4305.T5	Thanksgiving
	Toasts see PN6340+
	Valentine's Day see PN4305.S3
4305.W44	Weddings

Oratory. Elocution, etc.
Recitations (in English) -- Continued
Selections from particular authors
see the author's works in PR, PS, etc.

4309	Addresses, essays, lectures
4321	Indexes
	Recitations in foreign languages
4331-4333	Dutch (Table PN10)
4336-4338	French (Table PN10)
4341-4343	German (Table PN10)
4346-4348	Italian (Table PN10)
4351-4353	Spanish (Table PN10)
4355.A-Z	Other, A-Z
	e. g.
4355.D2	Danish
4355.N8	Norwegian
4355.S8	Swedish
4390	Diaries
	Cf. CT25 Autobiography
4395	Notebooks. Commonplace books
4397	Anthologies
4400	Letters (Literary history)
	For letter writing (in English) see PE1481+
4500	Essays
	Including history, criticism, technique
	Wit and humor see PN6146.2+

Journalism
Journalism. The periodical press, etc.
Periodicals
4699	International. Polyglot
4700	American
4701	English
4702	French
4703	German
4705	Other
4709	Yearbooks

Directories see Z6941
Societies
For local societies and associations see
PN4841.A+
4712	General works
4714	News agencies

For local agencies see PN4841.A+; PN4901+
4714.A1	General works, manuals, directories, etc.
4715	Press councils

For local councils see PN4846; PN4901+
Museums
4716	General works
4716.2.A-Z	Special institutions, A-Z
4717	Congresses. Conferences

For local congresses and conferences see
PN4848
4720.A-Z	Exhibitions. By place, A-Z

Collections
4722	Series: Monographs, etc.
4724	Collected works of two or more authors
4725	Collected works, essays, papers, etc., by individual authors
4726	Specimens of journalistic writings
4728	Encyclopedias. Dictionaries

Communication in journalism
4729	General works
4729.2	Information services
4729.3	Computer network resources

Including the Internet
4731	General works. Theory, scope, influence, etc.

For influence on children see HQ784.N4
4733	Addresses, essays, lectures

Periodical and newspaper publishing
Cf. Z286.N48 Publishing of newspapers
Cf. Z286.P4 Publishing of periodicals
4734	General works
4734.5.A-Z	Individual international firms and groups, A-Z

	Journalism. The periodical press, etc. --
	Continued
	Special relations
	Relation to the state. Government and the press. Liberty of the press
	For press law, see class K
	Cf. Z657+ Censorship, freedom of the press
4735	General works
4736	International press
4737	Government press services
	Prefer special countries
	By region or country
	United States
4738	General works
4739.A-Z	Local, A-Z
	Special topics
4741	Newspaper libel
	Cf. K, Law
4745	Other special
4748.A-Z	Other regions or countries, A-Z
4749	Relation to social questions
4751	Relation to politics
4756	Relation to ethics, religion, etc.
4759	Relation to literature
4762	Relation to art
4765	Relation to the stage, etc.
4771	Other
	Technique. Practical journalism
	For practices in individual countries see PN4840+
4775	General works
4776	Juvenile works
	Special
4778	The editor. Editing
	For editorial writing see PN4784.E28
4781	Reporting, correspondence, etc.
4783	Newspaper style
4784.A-Z	Other, A-Z
	For press coverage of specific events, see the event in classes B-Z
4784.A18	Abortion
4784.A26	Aeronautical journalism
4784.A3	Agricultural journalism
4784.A5	Anniversary editions
4784.A94	Automotive journalism
4784.B75	Broadcast journalism
4784.C3	Catholic press

PN
4699-5650

Journalism. The periodical press, etc.
  Technique. Practical journalism
    Special
      Other, A-Z -- Continued

4784.C6	Circulation. Marketing
4784.C62	City editor
4784.C63	The coach
4784.C64	Colombia
4784.C65	Column writing
	Comics see PN6700+
4784.C7	Commercial journalism
	Including economic and financial
	journalism
	For House organs see PN4784.H6
4784.C72	Communist press
4784.C73	Community newspapers
4784.C75	Copyreading
4784.C77	Country newspapers. Rural journalism
4784.C88	Crime and journalism
4784.C9	Cub reporters
4784.D4	Dental journalism
4784.D57	Disaster reporting
	Economic journalism see PN4784.C7
4784.E28	Editorial writing. Editorials
4784.E3	Educational journalism
4784.E5	Electronic data processing
4784.E53	Electronic news gathering
4784.E6	Employees' magazines
4784.E7	Equipment and supplies
4784.F3	Family in the press
4784.F33	Fashion
4784.F37	Feature writing
4784.F4	Feuilletons
4784.F5	Finance
	Financial journalism see PN4784.C7
4784.F55	Food
4784.F6	Foreign news
	For transmission see HE7700
4784.F74	Free circulation newspapers and periodicals
4784.F76	Freelance journalism
4784.G5	Ghost writing
4784.H4	Headlines
4784.H6	House organs
4784.I6	Interviewing
	Islamic press see PN4784.R35
4784.I82	Italy
4784.L3	Labor press

Journalism. The periodical press, etc.
Technique. Practical journalism
Special
Other, A-Z -- Continued

4784.L44	Legal journalism
4784.L6	Local editions
4784.M34	Management
4784.M36	Maps
	Marketing see PN4784.C6
4784.M37	Mathematics
4784.M4	Medical journalism
4784.M5	Military journalism
4784.M54	Mining journalism
4784.M6	Motion picture journalism
	Cf. TR895 Newsreel cinematography
4784.N4	New literates
4784.N48	News audiences
4784.N5	Newsletters
4784.N6	Notetaking
4784.O24	Objectivity
4784.O6	Ombudsmen
4784.O62	Online journalism
4784.O64	Open letters
4784.O9	Outdoor journalism
4784.P2	Paragraphers
4784.P4	Personnel management
4784.P5	Pictorial journalism
	For photojournalism see TR820
4784.P69	Press conferences
	Cf. PN4193.P73 Public speaking
4784.P7	Prison journalism
4784.P8	Publicity
4784.Q6	Quotation
4784.R2	Radio journalism
4784.R27	Readership surveys
4784.R29	Regional journalism
4784.R3	Religious press
4784.R35	Islam
4784.R38	Research
4784.R4	Reviews. Critical writing
	Rural journalism see PN4784.C77
	Scientific journalism see PN4784.T3
4784.S4	Sensationalism
4784.S5	Small town journalism
4784.S55	Socialist journalism
4784.S58	Specialization

PN
4699-5650

	Journalism. The periodical press, etc.
	Technique. Practical journalism
	Special
	Other, A-Z -- Continued
4784.S6	Sports journalism
	Cf. GV742.4+ Sports writers (Biography)
4784.S7	Stories
4784.S73	Stringers (Journalists)
4784.S75	Subjects for articles
4784.S8	Syndicating
4784.T23	Tabloid newspapers
4784.T3	Technical journalism
4784.T4	Television
4784.T45	Terrorism
4784.U53	Underground press
4784.W37	War in the press
4784.W7	Women in journalism
	Study and teaching
4785	General works
4786	Audiovisual aids
	By region or country
	United States
4788	General works
4789.A-Z	By region or state, A-Z
4791.A-Z	By school, A-Z
4793.A-Z	Other regions or countries, A-Z
	Under each country:
	.x *General works*
	.x2 *By school, A-Z*
4797	Journalism as a profession
4798	Competitions, prizes, etc.
	History
4801	Comprehensive
	By period
4805	Origins
4808	18th century
4811	19th century
4815	20th century
4815.2	21st century
	Special regions or countries see PN4840+
	Biography
4820	General works
	Special regions or countries see PN4871+
4823	War correspondents
	For individual correspondents, see under country

Journalism. The periodical press, etc. --
　　　Continued
　　　Amateur journalism
　　　　　Cf. LB3620+ School journalism
　　　　　Cf. PN147 Popular authorship
　　　　　Cf. PN157 Amateur authors
　　　　　Cf. Z6944.A6 Bibliography

4825	General works. History
	By region or country
	United States
4826	Associations, societies, etc.
4827	General works
4828	By state
4829	By city
4830.A-Z	Other regions or countries, A-Z

　　　　　　　Under each country:
　　　　　　　　.x　　　　　　　　　　*General works*
　　　　　　　　.x2　　　　　　　　　　*Local*

Magazines and other periodicals
　　　For magazine writing see PN147

4832	History and other general
	Special
4833	Electronic journals
4834	Illustrated magazines
4835	Juvenile periodicals
4835.5	Women's periodicals
4836	Other special

Foreign language press
　　　For foreign language newspapers and
　　　　　periodicals in the United States see
　　　　　PN4884+

4837.A2	General works
4837.A3-Z	By language, A-Z
4838	Miscellaneous. Anecdotes, stories, etc.
4839	Curiosities, oddities, etc. of newspapers

　　　　　Including Clay, The agony column of the
　　　　　　"Times," and miniature newspapers

	By region or country
4840	America. North America
	United States
	Periodicals see PN4700
	Societies
	Amateur press associations see PN4826+
	National
4841.A1	General works
4841.A2-Z	Individual, A-Z

　　　　　　　Subarrange each by Table P-PZ50

PN
4699-5650

Journalism. The periodical press, etc.
By region or country
America. North America
United States
Societies -- Continued

4844.A-.W	State societies. By state, A-W
	Local see PN4899.A+
4846	Press councils
4848	Conferences. Conventions
4853	Collections
	For collections of a university see PN4722+
	General works. History, etc.
4855	Comprehensive
4857	Addresses, essays, lectures
	By period
4858	Early
4861	18th century
4864	19th century
4867	20th century
4867.2	21st century
	Biography of editors, journalists, etc.
	For historical characters, see classes E-F
4871	Collective
4872	Women
4874.A-Z	Individual, A-Z
	Subarrange each by Table P-PZ50
	Directories see Z6951+
	Special topics
	Periodicals. Magazines
4877	General
4878	Juvenile periodicals
4878.1	Electronic journals
4878.3	Little magazines
4878.5	Pulp magazines
4878.7	Regional periodicals
4879	Women's magazines
4880	Humorous magazines
4881	University magazines
	Ethnic press. Minority press
4882	General works
4882.5	African American press
4883	American Indian press
4883.5	Irish-American press
	Foreign language press
4884	General works
4885.A-Z	Special, A-Z

Journalism. The periodical press, etc.
By region or country
America. North America
United States
Special topics
Ethnic press. Minority press
Foreign language press
Special, A-Z -- Continued

4885.A4	Albanian (Table PN4)
4885.A73	Arabic (Table PN4)
4885.A75	Armenian (Table PN4)
4885.C5	Chinese (Table PN4)
4885.D35	Danish (Table PN4)
4885.E87	Estonian (Table PN4)
4885.F55	Finnish (Table PN4)
4885.F72	French (Table PN4)
4885.G3	German (Table PN4)
4885.I8	Italian (Table PN4)
4885.J35	Japanese (Table PN4)
4885.L37	Latvian (Table PN4)
4885.L54	Lithuanian (Table PN4)
4885.N6	Norwegian (Table PN4)
4885.P7	Polish (Table PN4)
	Ruthenian see PN4885.U4
4885.S2	Scandinavian (Table PN4)
4885.S45	Slavic (Table PN4)
4885.S47	Slovak (Table PN4)
4885.S5	Slovenian (Table PN4)
4885.S75	Spanish (Table PN4)
4885.S8	Swedish (Table PN4)
4885.U4	Ukrainian. Ruthenian (Table PN4)
4885.V53	Vietnamese (Table PN4)
4885.W44	Welsh (Table PN4)
4885.Y5	Yiddish (Table PN4)
4888.A-Z	Other special topics, A-Z
	For press coverage of specific events
	or organizations, see the event or
	organization in classes B-Z
4888.A2	Abortion
4888.A4	Aeronautical journalism
	African American journalism. Black
	journalism see PN4882.5
4888.A43	Agricultural journalism
	Air Force newspapers see PN4888.M54
	Amateur journalism see PN4826+
4888.A67	Arabs in the press

PN
4699-5650

Journalism. The periodical press, etc.
  By region or country
    America. North America
      United States
        Special topics
          Other special topics, A-Z -- Continued

(4888.A7)	Armed Forces newspapers
	see PN4888.M54
	Army newspapers see PN4888.M54
4888.A87	Awards
4888.B57	Birth control
4888.B74	Broadcast journalism
	Cf. PN4888.T4 Television journalism
	Business journalism see PN4888.C59
4888.C4	Cable dispatches
	Camp (Army) newspapers see PN4888.M54
4888.C47	Caribbean Area
4888.C5	Catholic press
4888.C54	China
4888.C56	Circulation. Marketing
4888.C57	Collectors and collecting
4888.C59	Commercial journalism
4888.C593	Communist press
4888.C594	Community newspapers
4888.C598	Conservatism in the press
4888.C6	Corruption of the press
	Cf. HV6631 Libel
	Cf. Z657+ Liberty of the press
4888.C7	Country newspapers
4888.C8	Crime and the press
4888.D57	Disaster reporting
4888.E3	Educational journalism
4888.E58	Employees
4888.E6	Employees' magazines
4888.E65	Environmental protection
4888.E8	Ethics of journalism
4888.E94	Evolution
4888.E97	Explorers
4888.F5	Fiction
4888.F6	Finance
4888.F67	Food contamination in the press
4888.F69	Foreign news
4888.G6	German literature in American magazines
4888.G63	Germany
4888.H57	Hispanic Americans
	Including Mexican Americans, Puerto
	Ricans, etc.

Journalism. The periodical press, etc.
By region or country
America. North America
United States
Special topics
Other special topics, A-Z -- Continued

4888.H65	Homophobia
4888.I52	Indians
4888.I53	Influence
4888.I56	Investigative reporting
4888.J48	Jewish-Arab relations
4888.L27	Labor, Portrayal of. Working class
4888.L3	Labor press
4888.L47	Letters to the editor. Readers' opinions, etc.
	Literary reviews
	see subclasses PQ - PT
4888.M37	Maps
	Marketing see PN4888.C56
4888.M43	Medical journalism
	Mexican Americans see PN4888.H57
4888.M54	Military journalism. Armed Forces newspapers
4888.M56	Minorities in the press
4888.M6	Motion picture journalism
	Navy newspapers see PN4888.M54
4888.N48	Newsletters
4888.N53	Nicaragua
4888.O25	Objectivity
4888.O73	Op-ed pages
4888.O85	Ownership
4888.P45	Personnel management
4888.P6	Political aspects
4888.P75	Prison journalism
4888.P82	Public opinion
	Puerto Ricans see PN4888.H57
4888.R3	Racism
4888.R33	Radio journalism
	Readers' opinions see PN4888.L47
4888.R37	Readership surveys
4888.R44	Religious journalism
4888.R45	Research
4888.S43	Securities fraud in the press
4888.S46	Sensationalism
4888.S49	Sex crimes in the press
4888.S6	Social aspects
4888.S67	Standards

Journalism. The periodical press, etc.
  By region or country
    America. North America
      United States
        Special topics
          Other special topics, A-Z -- Continued

4888.S77	Supernatural
4888.S8	Supplements
	For Christmas supplements see AY21+
4888.S9	Syndicates
4888.T3	Tabloid newspapers
4888.T4	Television journalism
4888.T55	Time management
4888.U5	Underground press
4888.W34	Wages
4888.W65	Women, Portrayal of
	Working class see PN4888.L27
4889	Newspaper and periodical distributors
	Local. By region
4891	New England
4892	Middle States
4893	South
4894	West
4895	Pacific
4897.A-.W	Local. By state, A-W

           Under each:

.x	*Manuals*
	Associations see PN4844
.x3	*General works. History*
.x4	*Special topics*

4899.A-Z	Local. By place, A-Z

           Under each:

.x	*Manuals*
.x2	*Associations*
.x3	*General works. History*
.x4	*Special topics*
.x5A-.x5Z	*Special papers, etc., A-Z*
	For foreign language
	newspapers, see PN4885

4900.A-Z	Particular magazines and other periodicals.
	By name, A-Z
	For newspapers see PN4899.A+
4901-4920	Canada (Table PN1)
	Latin America
4930	General works
	Caribbean Area. West Indies
4930.5	General works

Journalism. The periodical press, etc.
  By region or country
    Latin America
      Caribbean Area. West Indies -- Continued

4931-4940	Cuba (Table PN2)
4941-4950	Puerto Rico (Table PN2)
4959.A-Z	Other West Indies, A-Z
	Subarrange each by Table PN4
4961-4980	Mexico (Table PN1)

      Central America

4988	General works
4989.A-Z	By region or country, A-Z
	Subarrange each by Table PN4

      South America

5000	General works
5001-5010	Argentina (Table PN2)
5011-5015	Bolivia (Table PN3)
5021-5030	Brazil (Table PN2)
5031-5035	Guyana. British Guiana (Table PN3)
5041-5050	Chile (Table PN2)
5051-5055	Colombia (Table PN3)
5061-5065	Suriname (Table PN3)
5066-5070	Ecuador (Table PN3)
5071-5075	French Guiana (Table PN3)
5076-5080	Paraguay (Table PN3)
5081-5085	Peru (Table PN3)
5091-5095	Uruguay (Table PN3)
5101-5105	Venezuela (Table PN3)
5106.A-Z	Other South American regions or countries, A-Z
	Subarrange each by Table PN4

    Europe

5110	General works
5111-5130	Great Britain. England (Table PN1)
5131-5140	Scotland (Table PN2)
5141-5150	Ireland (Table PN2)
5151-5160	Wales (Table PN2)
5161-5170	Austria (Table PN2)
5171-5190	France (Table PN1)
5201-5220	Germany (Table PN1)
5231-5240	Greece (Table PN2)
5241-5250	Italy (Table PN2)

      Low countries

5251-5260	Netherlands (Table PN2)
5261-5270	Belgium (Table PN2)
5271-5280	Russia (Table PN2)

      Scandinavia

	Journalism. The periodical press, etc.
	By region or country
	Europe
	Scandinavia -- Continued
5280.5	General works
5281-5290	Denmark (Table PN2)
5290.1-.5	Iceland (Table PN3)
5291-5300	Norway (Table PN2)
5301-5310	Sweden (Table PN2)
5311-5320	Spain (Table PN2)
5321-5330	Portugal (Table PN2)
5331-5340	Switzerland (Table PN2)
5355.A-Z	Other European regions or countries, A-Z
5355.M43	Malta (Table PN4)
5355.S53	Slavic (General) (Table PN4)
5359	Near East. Arab countries
	Asia. Far East
5360	General works
5361-5370	China (Table PN2)
5370.1-.5	Taiwan (Table PN3)
5371-5380	India (Table PN2)
5401-5410	Japan (Table PN2)
5411-5420	Korea (Table PN2)
	Including South Korea
5420.1-.5	North Korea (Table PN3)
5421-5430	Philippines (Table PN2)
5449.A-Z	Other Asian regions or countries, A-Z
	Subarrange each by Table PN4
	Africa
5450	General works
5450.5.A-Z	By region, A-Z
	e. g.
5450.5.W34	West Africa (Table PN4)
	By country
5461-5465	Egypt (Table PN3)
5471-5480	Republic of South Africa (Table PN2)
5499.A-Z	Other African countries, A-Z
	Subarrange each by Table PN4
	Australia
	Periodicals
	see PN4699+
5511	Societies, conferences, collections
	History and other general works
5512	Comprehensive
5513	Early
5514	Recent

Journalism. The periodical press, etc.
By region or country
Australia -- Continued
Biography of editors, journalists, etc.
For historical characters, see classes D-F

5516.A1-.A5	Collective
5516.A6-Z	Individual, A-Z
	Subarrange each by Table P-PZ50
5517.A-Z	Special topics, A-Z
	For list of Cutter numbers, see Table PN1 14
	For press coverage of specific events, see the event in Classes B-Z
	Local
	Class individual biography with Australia (General)
5521-5530	New South Wales (Table PN2)
5531-5540	North Australia (Table PN2)
5541-5550	Queensland (Table PN2)
5551-5560	South Australia (Table PN2)
5561-5570	Tasmania (Table PN2)
5571-5580	Victoria (Table PN2)
5581-5590	West Australia (Table PN2)
5591-5600	New Zealand (Table PN2)
	Pacific islands
5620	General works
5621-5630	Hawaii (Table PN2)
5639.A-Z	Other islands, A-Z
	Subarrange each by Table PN4
	Arctic regions
5645	Greenland
5648	Developing countries
5650	The Jewish press

PN
4699-5650

	Collections of general literature
	General collections
6010	Polyglot
	English
6010.5	Periodicals
	Early to 1800
6011	Comprehensive
6012	Selections, anthologies, etc.
	Recent
6013	Comprehensive. "Libraries of world's best literature"
6013.5	Condensed books
6014	Selections, anthologies, etc.
	Annuals, keepsakes, etc. see AY10+
	Translations of foreign classics
6019.A-Z	By several translators. By editor or title, A-Z
6020.A-Z	By individual translators, A-Z
	French
	Early to 1800
6021	Comprehensive
6022	Selections, anthologies, etc.
	Recent
6023	Comprehensive. "Libraries of world's best literature"
6023.5	Condensed books
6024	Selections, anthologies, etc.
	German
	Early to 1800
6031	Comprehensive
6032	Selections, anthologies, etc.
	Recent
6033	Comprehensive. "Libraries of world's best literature"
6033.5	Condensed books
6034	Selections, anthologies, etc.
	Italian
	Early to 1800
6041	Comprehensive
6042	Selections, anthologies, etc.
	Recent
6043	Comprehensive. "Libraries of world's best literature"
6043.5	Condensed books
6044	Selections, anthologies, etc.
	Spanish
	Early to 1800

	General collections
	Spanish
	Early to 1800 -- Continued
6051	Comprehensive
6052	Selections, anthologies, etc.
	Recent
6053	Comprehensive. "Libraries of world's best literature"
6053.5	Condensed books
6054	Selections, anthologies, etc.
6065.A-Z	Other. By language, A-Z
	Special classes of authors
6066	Child authors
6067	Jewish authors
	Including contributions of Jews to world literature
6068	Black authors
	Cf. PS508.N3 American literature
6069.A-Z	Other special groups, A-Z
6069.E94	Exiles
6069.I53	Indians, American
6069.N63	Nobel Prize winners
6069.P7	Prisoners
6069.W65	Women
6071.A-Z	Collections, extracts, etc. By subject, A-Z
6071.A3	Adolescence
6071.A35	Adultery
6071.A36	Adulthood
6071.A38	Adventure stories
6071.A4	Aeronautics
6071.A45	Africa
6071.A48	Aging
6071.A56	Air
6071.A57	Airships
6071.A6	Alienation (Social psychology)
6071.A65	Angels
6071.A7	Animals
6071.A75	Anti-clericalism
6071.A775	Apartheid
6071.A78	Apocalyptic literature
6071.A79	Apostles
6071.A8	Archers and archery
6071.A83	Art
6071.A84	Arthurian romances. King Arthur
6071.A85	Artisans
6071.A87	Atheism
6071.A9	Authors

Collections, extracts, etc. By subject, A-Z --
Continued

6071.A94	Automata
6071.A95	Automobiles
6071.A97	Autumn
6071.B23	Babel, Tower of
6071.B3	Barrel organs
6071.B34	Beans
6071.B36	Beauty
6071.B38	Beds
6071.B42	Berlin (Germany)
6071.B43	Beverages
6071.B5	Bibles
	Bicycles see PN6071.C95
6071.B55	Birds
6071.B57	Blacks
6071.B65	Boats and boating
6071.B7	Books
6071.B72	Borges, Jorge Luis, 1899-
6071.B73	Boxing
6071.B75	Brancusi, Constantin, 1876-1957
6071.B76	Brigands and robbers
6071.B78	Brothers
6071.B8	Bruges (Belgium)
6071.B84	Bullfights
6071.B86	Business
6071.B88	Butterflies
6071.C27	Caribbean Area
6071.C3	Cats
6071.C37	Central America
6071.C43	Chairs
6071.C437	Champagne (Wine)
6071.C44	Character sketches
6071.C45	Chess
6071.C5	Children
6071.C54	China
	For Hong Kong see PN6071.H725
6071.C6	Christmas
6071.C62	Cid, ca. 1043-1099
6071.C63	Circus
6071.C66	Codfish
6071.C7	Contentment
6071.C76	Cosmogony
6071.C8	Country life
6071.C815	Courage
6071.C82	Cows
6071.C85	Creative ability (Literary, artistic, etc.)

Collections, extracts, etc. By subject, A-Z --
    Continued

6071.C87	Crowds
6071.C95	Cycling. Bicycles
6071.D26	Dance
6071.D28	Dandies
6071.D3	Daughters
6071.D33	Deadly sins
6071.D35	Deafness
6071.D4	Death
6071.D45	Detective and mystery stories
6071.D46	Developing countries
6071.D47	Devil
6071.D5	Didactic literature
6071.D53	Dimitrov, Georgi
6071.D56	Disasters
6071.D58	Diseases
6071.D6	Dogs
6071.D64	Dolphins
6071.D67	Dreams
6071.D7	Drinking customs
6071.D77	Drugs
6071.E2	Easter
6071.E4	Elephants
6071.E44	Embarrassment
6071.E46	Emigration and immigration
6071.E5	End of the world
6071.E56	Entertaining
6071.E6	Epic literature

        For prose adaptations of epic poetry see
          PN6110.E6

6071.E7	Erotic literature
6071.E78	Europe
6071.E8	European War, 1914-1918
6071.E87	Exiles
6071.E9	Existentialism
6071.F15	Fairy tales. Fairies

        Cf. GR549+ Fairies and fairy tales (Folklore)

6071.F17	Faith
	Fall see PN6071.A97
6071.F2	Family
6071.F25	Fantastic literature
6071.F27	Fashion
6071.F28	Fate and fatalism
6071.F3	Fathers
6071.F33	Faust
6071.F37	Festivals

Collections, extracts, etc. By subject, A-Z --
Continued

6071.F47	Fishing
6071.F48	Flight
6071.F49	Florence (Italy)
6071.F5	Flowers
6071.F6	Food
6071.F64	Fools and jesters
6071.F65	Forgiveness
6071.F66	Fortune
6071.F68	France
6071.F7	Friendship
6071.F74	Frogs and toads
6071.F76	Fruit
6071.F86	Future life
6071.G23	Galicia (Poland and Ukraine)
6071.G24	Gambling
6071.G27	Gardens
6071.G3	Gastronomy
6071.G42	Generosity
6071.G45	Ghost stories
6071.G5	Gipsies. Romanies
6071.G53	Girls
6071.G55	Gluttony
6071.G57	God
6071.G6	Golem
6071.G64	Gothic revival (Literature)
6071.G7	Grandparents
	Gypsies see PN6071.G5
6071.H18	Hallucinations and illusions
6071.H2	Happiness
6071.H26	Havana (Cuba)
6071.H37	Heaven
6071.H4	Heroes
6071.H5	History
6071.H7	Holidays
6071.H713	Holocaust, Jewish
6071.H72	Home
6071.H724	Homosexuality
6071.H725	Hong Kong
6071.H727	Horror tales
6071.H73	Horses
6071.H78	Human ecology
6071.H784	Human rights
6071.H79	Humanism
6071.H795	Humorous stories
6071.H8	Hunting

Collections, extracts, etc. By subject, A-Z --
Continued
Illusions see PN6071.H18

6071.I5	Incest
6071.I52	Infants
6071.I58	Insomnia
6071.I6	Inspiration
6071.I64	Interplanetary voyages
6071.I67	Inventions
6071.I7	Iron
6071.I75	Islands
6071.I8	Italy
6071.J28	Jazz music. Jazz musicians
6071.J38	Jerusalem
6071.J4	Jesus Christ
6071.J5	Jewish legends and tales
	Cf. BM530+ Jewish myths and legends
6071.J6	Jews
6071.J84	Judas Iscariot
6071.K4	Kenya
6071.K44	King Kong (Fictitious character)
6071.K45	Kissing
6071.K5	Knight, Death and the Devil (Painting)
6071.L3	Labor. Working class
6071.L33	Law
6071.L35	Lazarus
6071.L37	Laziness
6071.L47	Lesbians
6071.L48	Letter writing
6071.L5	Liberty
6071.L554	Libraries. Librarians
6071.L6	Life
6071.L64	Lists
6071.L66	Lodginghouses
6071.L68	Loneliness
6071.L69	Loss (Psychology)
6071.L7	Love
6071.L86	Lust
6071.M12	Macau
6071.M14	Mafia
6071.M15	Magi
6071.M155	Magic
6071.M167	Man
6071.M17	Man, Primitive
6071.M2	Marriage
6071.M25	The marvelous
6071.M27	Mary, Blessed Virgin

PN
6010-6790

Collections, extracts, etc. By subject, A-Z --
Continued

6071.M28	Matches
6071.M3	Mathematics
6071.M35	May Day (Labor holiday)
6071.M38	Medicine
6071.M387	Men
6071.M39	Menstruation
6071.M4	Mental illness
6071.M45	Merchants
6071.M46	Merlin
6071.M49	Mexico
6071.M54	Miracles
6071.M55	Money
6071.M6	Moon
6071.M7	Mothers
6071.M73	Motion pictures
6071.M738	Mountaineering
6071.M77	Mummies
6071.M8	Music
6071.N28	National characteristics
6071.N3	Nature
	Negroes see PN6071.B57
6071.N5	Night
6071.N53	Nihilism
6071.N57	Nomads
6071.N6	Noses
6071.N87	Nursing
6071.O22	Occult sciences
6071.O49	Odysseus (Greek mythology)
6071.O5	Old age
6071.O7	Optimistic thought
6071.O72	Organ (Musical instrument)
6071.O74	Orpheus
6071.O87	Outdoor life
6071.P27	Parables
6071.P28	Parent and child
6071.P29	Paris (France)
6071.P3	Patriotism
6071.P34	Peace
6071.P42	Photographers
6071.P45	Physicians
6071.P5	Picaresque novels
	Pigs see PN6071.S94
6071.P57	Political science
6071.P575	Pool (Game)
6071.P58	Pottery

Collections, extracts, etc. By subject, A-Z --
Continued

6071.P6	Poverty
6071.P617	Prague (Czech Republic)
6071.P62	Pregnancy
6071.P63	Prejudice
6071.P65	The press
6071.P68	Prisons
6071.P695	Prometheus
6071.P7	Proposals of marriage
6071.P75	Prostitution
6071.P77	Prussia, East
6071.P8	Psychology
6071.P9	Puppet plays
6071.P95	Pygmalion (Greek mythology)
6071.Q47	Quests
6071.R2	Rabbits
6071.R23	Race discrimination
6071.R25	Radicalism
6071.R27	Radio stories
6071.R3	Railroads
6071.R35	Rain forests
6071.R37	Ravenna (Italy)
6071.R39	Reincarnation
6071.R4	Religion
	Cf. PN6071.B5 Bibles
6071.R42	Revenge
6071.R43	Revolutionary literature
6071.R5	Rivers
6071.R55	Rogues and vagabonds
	Romanies see PN6071.G5
6071.R57	Rome
6071.R58	Roses
6071.R6	Rotterdam
6071.R8	Russia
6071.R83	Russian Revolution, 1917-1921
6071.S16	Saint Petersburg (Russia)
6071.S19	Santa Claus
6071.S2	Satanism
6071.S23	Scapegoat
6071.S27	School prose
6071.S3	Science
6071.S33	Science fiction
6071.S4	Sea. Sea stories
6071.S4114	Seasons
6071.S412	Self-realization
6071.S414	Servants

Collections, extracts, etc. By subject, A-Z --
Continued

6071.S416	Sex
6071.S418	Sheep
6071.S42	Siebengebirge
6071.S425	Sisters
6071.S43	Sky
6071.S45	Sleep
6071.S47	Slovak Uprising, 1944
6071.S49	Snakes
6071.S5	Snow
6071.S52	Socialism
6071.S53	Sociology
6071.S55	Soldiers
6071.S56	Solitude
6071.S57	Sons
	Soviet Union see PN6071.R8
6071.S58	Space flight to the moon
6071.S6	Spanish Civil War
6071.S615	Spiritual life
6071.S62	Sports
6071.S63	Spring
6071.S64	Spy stories. Spies
6071.S67	Stars
6071.S68	Statisticians
6071.S7	Street scenes
6071.S75	Students
6071.S78	Substance abuse
6071.S79	Subversive activities
6071.S8	Success
6071.S85	Sufi tales
6071.S87	Suicide
6071.S88	Sun
6071.S9	Supernatural
6071.S92	Suspense
6071.S93	Swearing
6071.S94	Swine
6071.S96	Symbolism
6071.T25	Tangier (Morocco)
6071.T3	Teachers
6071.T35	Textile industry. Textile fabrics
6071.T4	Theater
6071.T5	Time
6071.T55	Titanic (Steamship)
	Toads see PN6071.F74
	Tower of Babel see PN6071.B23
6071.T7	Travel

	Collections, extracts, etc. By subject, A-Z --
	Continued
6071.T74	Trees
6071.T746	Tricksters
6071.T75	Tristan
6071.T82	Tuberculosis
6071.U85	Utopias
6071.V3	Vampires
6071.V4	Venice
6071.V46	Vietnamese Conflict, 1961-
6071.V5	Violence
	Voyages and travel see PN6071.T7
6071.W3	Walking
6071.W32	Walthari, of Aquitaine
6071.W35	War
6071.W37	Water
6071.W4	Weddings
6071.W47	Werewolves
6071.W56	Windows
6071.W57	Wine
6071.W6	Winter
6071.W7	Women
6071.W72	Women travelers
6071.W74	Work
	Working class see PN6071.L3
	World War I see PN6071.E8
6071.W75	World War II
6071.Z8	Zurich
	Selections for daily reading
6075	English
	Cf. PN6084.B5 Birthdays
	Cf. PN6084.S7 The South
6076	French
6077	German
6078.A-Z	Other languages, A-Z
	Selections from special authors
	see their works
	Quotations
6080	Polyglot
	Including classical (Latin and Greek)
6080.5	Latin
	For Latin with English translations see PN6080
	English
6081	General works
6081.3	Black authors
6081.4	Indian authors
6081.5	Women authors

PN
6010-6790

	Quotations
	English -- Continued
6082	Poetry
6083	Prose
6084.A-Z	Special topics, A-Z
6084.A25	Acting
6084.A3	Adoption
6084.A35	Age
6084.A55	Angels
6084.A57	Animals
6084.A75	Architecture
6084.A8	Art
	Including painting
6084.A83	Arthurian romances
6084.B3	Banquet quotations
6084.B35	Baseball
	Bicycles see PN6084.C95
6084.B48	Birds
6084.B5	Birthdays
6084.B65	Books and reading
6084.B7	Brotherliness
6084.B87	Business
6084.C15	Canada
6084.C17	Cape Cod (Mass.)
6084.C2	Catholic
6084.C23	Cats
6084.C44	Celebrities
6084.C46	Charity
6084.C48	Child rearing
6084.C49	Childhood
6084.C5	Children
6084.C52	Christmas
6084.C524	Cigars
6084.C53	Civil service
6084.C535	Clothing and dress
6084.C54	Coaching (Athletics)
6084.C55	Compliments
6084.C556	Conduct of life
6084.C56	Conservatism
6084.C57	Consolation
6084.C58	Contentment
6084.C6	Courage
6084.C7	Criminals
6084.C95	Cycling. Bicycles
6084.D34	Dance
6084.D37	Daughters
6084.D39	Deadly sins

Quotations
English
Special topics, A-Z -- Continued

6084.D394	Deafness
6084.D4	Death
6084.D46	Design
6084.D64	Dogs
6084.D65	Dogsledding
6084.D74	Drinking customs
6084.E34	Eccentrics and eccentricities
6084.E36	Economics
6084.E38	Education
6084.E53	End of the world
6084.E82	Espionage
6084.E85	Etiquette
6084.E88	Evolution (Biology)
6084.E9	Experience
6084.F23	Family
6084.F25	Farewells
6084.F27	Fashion
6084.F3	Fathers
6084.F47	Fishing
6084.F5	Flowers
6084.F6	Food
6084.F8	Friendship
6084.F83	Fruit
6084.F85	Frustration
6084.F89	Future life
6084.G32	Gambling
6084.G33	Gardens
6084.G35	Gays
6084.G6	Grandparents
6084.G63	Gratitude
6084.G66	Great Britain
6084.G7	Great men
6084.H3	Happiness
6084.H4	Heart
6084.H47	Hispanic Americans
6084.H57	Home
6084.H62	Hope
6084.H66	Horses
6084.H8	Humorous quotations
6084.H84	Hunting
6084.H9	Hygiene
6084.I48	Infants
6084.I5	Interpersonal relations
6084.I6	Ireland. Irish

Quotations
English
Special topics, A-Z -- Continued

6084.I73	Italian Americans
6084.J65	Joy
6084.K5	Kissing
6084.L15	Leadership
(6084.L2)	Legal quotations
	see class K
6084.L45	Lesbians
6084.L5	Liberty
6084.L54	Lighthouses
6084.L56	London (England)
6084.L565	Lord's Supper
6084.L57	Loss (Psychology)
6084.L6	Love
6084.M25	Man-woman relationships
6084.M27	Maps
6084.M3	Marriage
6084.M35	Medicine
6084.M4	Men
6084.M56	Money
6084.M57	Monkeys
6084.M6	Mothers
	Motion pictures see PN1994.9
6084.M75	Multiculturalism
6084.M8	Music
6084.N2	Nature
6084.N38	New York (N.Y.)
6084.N5	Night
6084.N53	Nihilism
6084.O3	Occasions
6084.O35	Ocean
6084.O5	Old age
6084.O63	Openings (Rhetoric)
6084.O93	Owls
	Painting see PN6084.A8
6084.P3	Patience
6084.P4	Patriotism
6084.P45	Peace
6084.P52	Phobias
6084.P55	Places
6084.P6	Political science
6084.P73	Pregnancy
6084.Q3	Quarreling
6084.Q4	Queens
6084.Q54	Quilting

	Quotations
	English
	Special topics, A-Z -- Continued
	Reading see PN6084.B65
6084.R3	Religious quotations
6084.R62	Rock music
6084.S2	Sacred quotations
6084.S26	Sailing
6084.S34	Science fiction
6084.S38	Scotland. Scots
6084.S45	Self-realization
6084.S49	Sex
6084.S493	Sexism
6084.S5	Simile
6084.S56	Sisters
6084.S58	Smiles
6084.S62	Social problems
6084.S65	Solitude
6084.S67	Sons
6084.S7	The South
6084.S72	Sports
6084.S73	Spring
6084.S78	Success
6084.S79	Suffering
6084.S8	Sunshine
6084.S84	Supervisors
6084.T48	Theater
6084.T5	Time
6084.T68	Toys
6084.T7	Travel
6084.T75	Trees
6084.T83	Twenty-first century
6084.U53	United States
6084.V3	Valentines
6084.V35	Vampires
6084.V44	Vegetables
6084.V58	Visual perception
6084.W3	Wales
6084.W32	Walking
6084.W35	War
6084.W39	West (U.S.)
6084.W47	Wilderness areas
6084.W5	Wine
6084.W53	Wishes
6084.W55	Wives
6084.W6	Women
6084.W65	Words

Quotations
  English
    Special topics, A-Z -- Continued

6084.W67	Work
6084.Y6	Youth
	French
6086	General works
6087	Poetry
6088	Prose
6089.A-Z	Special topics, A-Z
6089.A2	Absurdity
6089.D43	Death
6089.E9	Eye
6089.G63	God
6089.H85	Humorous quotations
6089.L6	Love
6089.P6	Political science
6089.S4	Sex
6089.S5	Sins
6089.W3	War
6089.W6	Women
	German
6090	General works
6091	Poetry
6092	Prose
6093.A-Z	Special topics, A-Z
6093.A3	Aesthetics
6093.A5	Animals
6093.A8	Art
6093.A9	Automobiles
6093.B5	Birthdays
6093.B6	Boats and boating
6093.C5	Children
6093.C56	Closings (Rhetoric)
6093.C6	Consolation
6093.E35	Economics
6093.F25	Fashion
6093.F3	Fate and fatalism
6093.F6	Food
6093.F7	Friendship
6093.F8	Future life
6093.G3	Gardens
6093.G6	God
6093.H3	Happiness
6093.H85	Humorous quotations
6093.J6	Joy
6093.K5	Kissing

Quotations
German
Special topics, A-Z -- Continued

6093.L4	Leisure
6093.L6	Love
6093.M27	Man
6093.M3	Marriage
6093.M6	Mothers
6093.N3	Nature
6093.O4	Old age
6093.P3	Patriotism
6093.P43	Peace
6093.R27	Relaxation
6093.R3	Religious quotations
6093.R4	Rest
6093.S4	Sex
6093.S5	Silence
6093.T5	Theater
6093.T7	Travel
6093.W5	Wine
6093.W6	Women
6095.A-Z	Other, A-Z
6095.A35	Afrikaans
6095.A42	Albanian
6095.A7	Arabic
6095.A75	Armenian
6095.A9	Azerbaijani
6095.B3	Bengali
6095.B8	Bulgarian
6095.B86	Burmese
6095.C37	Catalan
6095.C4	Chinese
6095.C93	Czech
6095.D3	Danish
6095.D8	Dutch
6095.E76	Estonian
6095.F56	Finnish
6095.G7	Greek, Modern
6095.H4	Hebrew
6095.H5	Hindi
6095.H8	Hungarian
6095.I32	Icelandic
6095.I45	Indic
6095.I5	Indonesian
6095.I7	Italian
6095.J3	Japanese
6095.J4	Jewish

Quotations
    Other, A-Z -- Continued

6095.K3	Kannada
6095.K6	Korean
6095.L37	Latvian
6095.M3	Malayalam
6095.M35	Marathi
6095.N4	Nepali
6095.N6	Norwegian
6095.O7	Oriental
6095.O74	Oriya
6095.P27	Papiamento
6095.P35	Persian
6095.P4	Philippine
6095.P6	Polish
6095.P7	Portuguese
6095.P8	Pushto
6095.R6	Romanian
6095.R8	Russian
6095.S3	Sanskrit
6095.S4	Serbo-Croatian
6095.S44	Sinhalese
6095.S46	Slovenian
6095.S5	Spanish
6095.S8	Swedish
6095.T3	Tamil
6095.T4	Telugu
6095.T5	Thai
6095.T8	Turkish
6095.U5	Ukrainian
6095.U7	Urdu
6095.V53	Vietnamese

Poetry
    Cf. PN1345 Folk poetry
    Cf. PN6080+ Quotations
  By language

6099	Polyglot
6099.3	Uncataloged poetry in pamphlet collections
	English
6099.6	Periodicals
6100	To 1800
6101	1800-
6102	Dutch
6103	French
6104	German
6105	Italian
6106	Scandinavian

	Poetry
	By language -- Continued
6107	Slavic
6108	Spanish
6109.A-Z	Other languages, A-Z
	Special categories of authors
6109.3	Catholic authors
6109.5	Jewish authors
6109.7	Black authors
6109.8	Male authors
6109.9	Women authors
6109.95.A-Z	Other special groups, A-Z
6109.95.B34	Bahai
6109.95.L54	Linguists
6109.95.M55	Minority authors
6109.95.U55	Unification Church
6109.97	Poetry for children
	Class here general multi-national works only
	For collections by authors of a specific country, see the national literature
	For works by one author, see that author's literary number
	For multi-national collections on special topics see PN6110.A+
6110.A-Z	Special. By subject or form, A-Z
	For collections including both poetry and prose see PN6071.A+
6110.A2	Aeronautics
6110.A4	Album verse
6110.A44	Alphabet rhymes
6110.A5	Altruism
6110.A58	Amvrosil, Metropolitan of Novgorod and St. Petersburg, 1742-1818
6110.A59	Angels
6110.A6	Angling
6110.A7	Animals
6110.A77	Art
6110.A88	Astronautics
6110.B2	Ballads
6110.B25	Barrel organs
	Battlesongs see PN6110.H3
6110.B28	Bees
6110.B3	Bells
6110.B38	Bible
6110.B4	Bicycling
6110.B6	Birds
6110.B65	Birthdays

PN
6010-6790

149

Poetry
    Special. By subject or form, A-Z -- Continued

6110.B66	Boxing
6110.B68	Blind
6110.B75	Body, Human
	Books see Z992.5
6110.B8	Boys
6110.B85	Brotherhood
6110.B88	Bulls. Bullfights
6110.B9	Business
6110.C28	Carols
6110.C3	Cats
6110.C36	Cheerfulness
6110.C4	Children
	Children and parents see PN6110.P25
6110.C5	Christmas
6110.C55	City life
6110.C57	Clocks and watches
6110.C59	Clothing and dress
6110.C7	College verse
6110.C75	Communism
6110.C77	Concrete poetry
	Cf. PN6110.V56 Visual poetry
6110.C78	Cookery
6110.C8	Country life
6110.C85	Courage
6110.C88	Crime. Criminals
6110.C9	Crusades
6110.D33	Dali, Salvador
6110.D35	Day
6110.D4	Death and immortality
	Cf. PN6110.R4 Religion
6110.D43	Debate poetry
6110.D45	Destruction
6110.D53	Didactic poetry
6110.D6	Dogs
6110.D7	Donkeys and mules
6110.D8	Dreams
6110.D85	Drinking
	For literary works of a hortatory nature see HV5070
	For collections in praise of drinking see PN6237
	Cf. PN6231.D7 Wit and humor
6110.E2	Easter
6110.E4	Eccentric poetry
	Cf. PN6110.N6 Nonsense

Poetry
Special. By subject or form, A-Z -- Continued

6110.E47	Eminescu, Mihail
6110.E5	Emotions
6110.E6	Epics
	Epistolary poetry see PN6110.L4
6110.E65	Eroticism
6110.E8	"Evolution" poetry
6110.E9	Eyes
6110.F2	Fables in verse
6110.F3	Fairies
6110.F32	Family
6110.F33	Fantastic poetry
6110.F34	Farm life
6110.F36	Fathers
6110.F4	"Favorite poems"
	Fishing see PN6110.A6
6110.F6	Flowers
	Cf. PN6110.N2 Nature
	Folk poetry see PN1345
6110.F7	Folklore
6110.F73	Food
	Forests see PN6110.T75
6110.F75	Free thought
6110.F8	Friendship
6110.F9	Fugitive verse
6110.F95	Futurism (Literary movement)
6110.G2	Gardens
6110.G3	Gems
6110.G5	Ghosts
6110.G52	Giants
6110.G54	Girls
6110.G58	God
6110.G59	Goddess religion
6110.G6	Good fellowship
6110.G83	Grandparents
6110.H13	Haiku
6110.H14	Happiness. Optimism
6110.H17	Heaven
6110.H2	Heroism
6110.H3	Historical poems
6110.H4	Holidays
	For specific holidays, see PN6110.C5, etc.
6110.H45	Holocaust, Jewish (1939-1945)
6110.H5	Holy Spirit
6110.H6	Home
6110.H65	Homosexuality

Poetry

Special. By subject or form, A-Z -- Continued

6110.H75	Horses
	Human body see PN6110.B75
6110.H8	Humor
6110.H83	Hunters and hunting
6110.I3	Icarus
	Immortality see PN6110.D4
6110.I52	Infants
6110.I55	Insects
6110.I56	Insomnia
6110.I57	Interpersonal relationships
6110.J4	Jesus Christ
	Jewels see PN6110.G3
6110.J45	Jews
6110.J69	Joyce, James, 1882-1941
6110.K55	Kim, Il-song, 1912-
6110.L15	Labor
6110.L2	Law
6110.L37	Lenin, Vladimir Il'ich, 1870-1924
6110.L4	Letters
6110.L43	Liberty
6110.L5	Life
	Cf. PN6110.D4 Death and immortality
	Limericks see PN6231.L5
6110.L6	Love
	Cf. HQ450+ Erotica
	Cf. PN6110.W6 Women
	Cf. PR1184 English literature
	Lullabies see PN6110.C4
	Macaronis see PN1489
6110.M23	Magi
6110.M24	Mandela, Nelson, 1918-
6110.M25	Mandel'shtam, Osip, 1891-1938
6110.M27	Marriage
6110.M28	Mary, Virgin
6110.M29	Mathematics
6110.M3	Medicine
6110.M4	Memorizing, Selections for
6110.M43	Mice
6110.M45	Military life
6110.M6	Moon
6110.M64	Mother
6110.M65	Mountains
6110.M7	Music
6110.M8	Mythology

Poetry
    Special. By subject or form, A-Z -- Continued

6110.N15	Names
	For poems on names of women see PN6110.W6
6110.N17	Narration
6110.N19	National songs
6110.N2	Nature
	For specific aspects of nature, see
	PN6110.A6, PN6110.C8, etc.
6110.N35	Neruda, Pablo, 1904-1973
6110.N46	Night
6110.N6	Nonsense
	Cf. PN6110.E4 Eccentric poetry
6110.O3	Occasions
6110.O4	Old age
	Optimism see PN6110.H14
6110.P2	Pain
6110.P25	Parent and child
6110.P3	Parodies
	Pastorals see PN6110.C8
6110.P4	Peace
	Places
6110.P6	General collections
6110.P7A-.P7Z	By place (country, region, etc.), A-Z
6110.P72	Plants
6110.P728	Political poetry
6110.P73	Potatoes
	Precious stones see PN6110.G3
6110.P8	Prisons and prisoners
6110.P82	Prose poems
6110.P83	Protest poetry
6110.Q3	Quakers
6110.Q33	Quatrains
6110.Q8	Quiet life
6110.R2	Railways
6110.R4	Religion
	Cf. PN6110.D4 Death and immortality
6110.R42	Renga
6110.R48	Revolutionary poetry
6110.R6	Roses
	Rural life see PN6110.C8
	Sacred poems and hymns see PN6110.R4
6110.S22	Sailing
6110.S23	Saints
6110.S25	Salutations
6110.S27	Satire
6110.S3	School days, etc.

Poetry
    Special. By subject or form, A-Z -- Continued

6110.S35	School verse
6110.S37	Science
6110.S4	Sea and sailors
6110.S5	Seasons
6110.S513	Self
6110.S515	Serra, Junípero
6110.S517	Shakespeare, William, 1564-1616
6110.S52	Sick, Poems for the
6110.S525	Sky
6110.S53	Slavery
6110.S55	Sleep
6110.S556	Slums
6110.S56	Social conditions. Social justice
6110.S57	Socialism
6110.S58	Solitude
6110.S6	Sonnets
6110.S65	Sports

        For a specific sport, see PN6110.A6,
           PN6110.B4, etc.

6110.S7	Spring
6110.S75	Stars
6110.S8	Stenography
6110.S85	Summer
6110.S87	Sun
6110.S9	Supernatural
6110.S92	Swans
6110.S93	Swine
6110.T4	Technology
6110.T5	Terror and wonder
6110.T6	Thanksgiving
6110.T63	Theater
	Tobacco see GT3020+
6110.T7	Traveling
6110.T75	Trees and forests
6110.T8	Typography
6110.V3	Vagabond
6110.V35	Valentine verses
6110.V37	Vampires
6110.V4	Vers de société
6110.V53	Vietnamese Conflict, 1961-1975
6110.V54	Virtues
6110.V56	Visual poetry

        Cf. PN6110.C77 Concrete poetry

6110.W28	War
	Watches see PN6110.C57

	Poetry
	Special. By subject or form, A-Z -- Continued
6110.W3	Water
6110.W4	Weddings
6110.W6	Women
	Cf. HQ450+ Erotica
6110.W7	Work
6110.Z45	Zen poetry
	Drama
6110.5	Polyglot
	English
6110.7	Periodicals
6111	Comprehensive collections
6112	Minor collections
6112.5	Digests. Stories of great plays
6113	French
	German
6114	Collections
6114.5	Digests. Stories of great plays
	Italian
6115	Collections
6115.5	Digests. Stories of great plays
6116	Scandinavian
	Spanish
6117	Collections
6117.5	Digests. Stories of great plays
6118	Slavic
6119.A-Z	Other, A-Z
	Special classes of authors
6119.7	Black authors
6119.8	Women authors
6119.9	Amateur drama. Children's plays
	Class here general multi-national works only
	For collections by authors of a specific country, see the national literature
	For works by one author, see the author's literary number
	For multi-national collections on special topics see PN6120.A+
6120.A-Z	Special. By subject or form, A-Z
6120.A3	Alcestis
6120.A6	Amphitryon
6120.A7	Animal plays
6120.A75	Antigone
6120.A77	Architecture
6120.A9	Avarice
6120.B3	Ballets

PN
6010-6790

	Drama
	Special. By subject or form, A-Z -- Continued
	Blacks see PN6120.N4
	Blackouts see PN6120.R5
6120.C3	Camping
	Christmas pantomimes (Drury Lane, etc.) see
	PN6120.P4
6120.C5	Christmas plays
6120.C6	College plays
6120.C65	Conflict of generations
	Detective and mystery plays see PN6120.M9
6120.D6	"District school," etc.
6120.D7	Don Juan
6120.E2	Easter plays
6120.E43	Electra
6120.E9	Everyman
6120.F3	Farces
6120.F33	Faust
6120.F6	Folk drama
6120.G34	Gay men
	Generations, Conflict of see PN6120.C65
6120.G4	Geography
6120.G45	Ghost plays
6120.G5	Girl Scout plays
6120.H3	Halloween
6120.H5	Historical. Patriotic
6120.H7	Holidays
6120.H73	Holocaust, Jewish (1939-1945)
6120.H8	Humorous drama
6120.I6	Indian drama
6120.I7	Iphigenia
6120.J35	Jesus Christ
	Cf. PN6120.C5 Christmas plays
	Cf. PN6120.E2 Easter plays
6120.J4	Jewish plays
6120.J6	Joan, of Arc, Saint
6120.L3	Labor
6120.L5	Library plays
6120.M3	Masques
6120.M4	Medea
6120.M5	Miracle plays
6120.M7	Mock trials
6120.M75	Mother's Day
6120.M8	Mumming plays
6120.M9	Mystery plays (Modern)
6120.N4	Negroes. Blacks
6120.O3	Oedipus

Drama
    Special. By subject or form, A-Z -- Continued

6120.O5	One-act plays
6120.O7	Orestes
	Pantomimes
6120.P3	General
6120.P4	Christmas pantomimes (Drury Lane, etc.)
6120.P5	Peace plays
6120.P64	Political plays
	Puppet plays see PN1980+
6120.R2	Radio plays
6120.R4	Religious drama
	For missionary plays see BV2086
6120.R47	Revolutions
6120.R5	Revues
	Including blackouts
6120.S3	Safety plays
	School plays see PN6119.9
6120.S5	Shadow pantomimes
6120.S7	Song pantomimes
6120.S8	Stunts and skits
6120.T3	Tableaux
	Cf. PN4305.T3 Recitations
6120.T4	Television plays
	Temperance plays see HV5069
6120.T5	Thanksgiving
6120.T8	Twelfth-night
6120.U5	United Nations
6120.V3	Vaudeville
6120.V4	Ventriloquism
6120.V48	Vietnamese Conflict, 1961-1975
6120.W3	Wax works
6120.W5	Wine
6120.W6	Women
6120.Z9	Miscellaneous entertainments
	For amateur circuses see GV1838
	Fiction
6120.15	Polyglot
6120.2	English
6120.3	French
6120.4	German
6120.5	Italian
6120.6	Scandinavian
6120.7	Slavic
6120.8	Spanish
6120.9.A-Z	Other languages, A-Z
6120.92.A-Z	Special classes of authors, A-Z

Fiction
   Special classes of authors, A-Z -- Continued

6120.92.B45	Blacks
6120.92.C38	Catholics
6120.92.H56	Hispanic authors
6120.92.W65	Women authors
6120.95.A-Z	Special. By subject or form, A-Z

       For list of Cutter numbers see PN6071.A+

Orations
   English

6121	Comprehensive collections
6122	Minor collections
6123	French
6124	German
6125	Italian
6126	Scandinavian
6127	Spanish
6128	Slavic
6129.A-Z	Other, A-Z

Letters

6130	Polyglot
6131	English
6132	French
6133	German
6135.A-Z	Other, A-Z

     Classical Latin see PA6139.E7
     Medieval and modern Latin see PA8147

6140.A-Z	Special topics, A-Z
6140.C5	Christmas
6140.F35	Fathers' letters
6140.H38	Hate mail
6140.L3	Last letters before death
6140.L7	Love letters

Essays
   English

6141	Comprehensive collections
6142	Minor collections
6143	French
6144	German
6145.A-Z	Other, A-Z
6146	Meditations

     Class here collections only
     For individual authors, see PQ, PT, etc.
     Cf. BL-BX, Religion
     Cf. BJ1548+ Ethics
     Cf. PN6329+ Thoughts

	Wit and humor
	For humor and religion, see BL+
	Periodicals see AP101+
	Humorous periodicals see AP101+
6146.5	Congresses
	History and criticism
6147	General works
6149.A-Z	Special topics, A-Z
6149.A88	Authorship
6149.B8	Burlesque
	For burlesque as a theatrical form see PN1942+
6149.E83	Ethnic wit and humor
	Geriatric therapy see RC953.8.H85
6149.J4	Jews
6149.L35	Lampoon
6149.L5	Limericks
6149.M55	Mock-heroic literature
6149.P3	Parody
6149.P5	Philosophy. Theory
	Cf. BF575.L3 Laughter (Psychology)
6149.P64	Political satire
	Psychotherapy see RC489.H85
6149.P85	Puns
(6149.R44)	Religious aspects
	see BL-BX
6149.S2	Satire and irony
6149.S37	Sex
6149.S4	Shaggy dog stories
6149.S62	Social aspects
6151	General collections
	Cf. PN6110.H8 Humorous poetry
	Cf. PN6120.H8 Humorous drama
6153	Minor collections
	Ancient (Classical) Greek see PA3469.W5
	Ancient Latin see PA6137.5.W5
	Medieval and modern Latin see PA8148
	Byzantine and modern Greek see PA5197+
	Arabic see PN6222.A6
	By region or country
	Including works of individual authors who have not written in other literary forms
	United States
	History see PS430+
6157	Comprehensive collections
	Minor collections
6158	Early to 1850

PN
6010-6790

Wit and humor
By region or country
United States
Minor collections -- Continued
6161 1850-1950
1951-2000
6162 General works
6163 Juvenile works
2001-
6165 General works
6166 Juvenile works
Great Britain
History see PR931+
6173 Early to 1850
6175 1850-
6178.A-Z Colonial, provincial, etc., A-Z
Including English-speaking former colonies
For local humor of England, see PN6173+
6178.A8 Australian
6178.C3 Canadian
6178.G43 Ghanian
6178.I6 Irish
6178.N4 New Zealand
6178.S4 Scotch
6178.W44 Welsh
France
6183 Early to 1850
6185 1850-
Germany
6193 Early to 1850
6195 1850-
Italy
6203 Early to 1850
6205 1850-
Russia. Soviet Union
6209 Early to 1850
6210 1850-
6211.A-Z Local, A-Z
e. g.
(6211.U4) Ukraine
see PN6222.U4
Spain
6213 Early to 1850
6215 1850-
6222.A-Z Other regions or countries, A-Z
e. g.
6222.A6 Arab countries (General)

	Wit and humor
	By region or country
	Other regions or countries, A-Z -- Continued
6222.U4	Ukraine
6231.A-Z	Collections on special topics, A-Z
6231.A22	Accidents
6231.A24	Accounting
6231.A25	Acronyms
6231.A26	Adolescence. Youth
6231.A28	Adultery
6231.A3	Advertising
6231.A4	Aeronautics
6231.A42	Affirmations
6231.A43	Aging
6231.A44	Agriculture
6231.A445	Air travel
6231.A448	Alcoholics
	Aliens see PN6231.F74
6231.A45	Alphabet
6231.A47	Amateur radio
6231.A5	Animals
6231.A54	Animals, Mythical
6231.A65	Appalachian Region
6231.A68	Arab countries. Arabs
6231.A69	Arizona
6231.A7	Artisans
6231.A72	Assertiveness (Psychology)
6231.A73	Astrology
6231.A76	Australia
6231.A762	Australian football
6231.A764	Austria
6231.A77	Authorship
6231.A8	Automobiles. Automobile travel
6231.B22	Baby boom generation
6231.B24	Baby sitters
6231.B25	Bachelors
6231.B26	Bahamas. Bahamians
	Bahamians see PN6231.B26
6231.B27	Baldness
6231.B28	Balgansang (Legendary character)
6231.B3	Banks and banking
6231.B32	Barbers
6231.B324	Barbie dolls
6231.B33	Bartenders
6231.B35	Baseball
6231.B38	Bathing
6231.B39	Bavaria

Wit and humor
Collections on special topics, A-Z -- Continued

6231.B396	Beads
6231.B4	Beards
6231.B42	Bears
6231.B43	Beer
6231.B45	Bible
	Bicycles see PN6231.C92
6231.B457	Biographies
6231.B46	Birds
	Blacks see PN6231.N5
6231.B5	Blue glass
6231.B6	Boating
6231.B62	Books
6231.B63	Boredom
6231.B65	Bowling
6231.B67	Breasts
6231.B69	Bubble wrap
6231.B7	Building
6231.B78	Bullfights
6231.B8	Bulls and blunders
	For Irish bulls see PN6178.I6
6231.B83	Bundling
6231.B834	Bungee jumping
6231.B84	Burlesques
6231.B85	Business
	For general works on the benefits of humor
	in the workplace see HF5549.5.H85
6231.B87	Buttocks
6231.C14	Cabbage Patch Kids dolls
6231.C16	California
6231.C18	Camps
6231.C19	Canada
6231.C195	Capitalism
6231.C2	Card games
6231.C215	Carter family
6231.C22	Catholics
6231.C23	Cats
6231.C24	Cattle. Cows
6231.C25	Celebrities
6231.C255	Cellular telephones
6231.C265	Censorship
6231.C28	Cheating (Education)
6231.C284	Cheese
	Chess see GV1449
6231.C29	Chickens
6231.C3	Child care

Wit and humor
Collections on special topics, A-Z -- Continued

6231.C315	Child rearing
6231.C32	Children
6231.C33	Chocolate
6231.C35	Christianity
6231.C36	Christmas
6231.C367	Church of England
6231.C37	Church year
	Cigarette habit see PN6231.S56
6231.C45	Circus
6231.C455	City and town life
	Civil service see PN6231.P79
6231.C46	Civilization
6231.C5	Clergy
6231.C53	Clinton, Chelsea
6231.C55	Clothing trade
6231.C554	Clowns
6231.C56	Cockroaches
6231.C563	Codependency
6231.C565	Coffee
6231.C57	Colds
6231.C58	Collectors and collecting
6231.C6	College
6231.C6114	Columbus, Christopher
	Commercial travelers see PN6231.S17
6231.C6117	Committees
	Common colds see PN6231.C57
6231.C612	Communism
6231.C614	Commuting
	Computers see PN6231.E4
6231.C6142	Conduct of life
6231.C6143	Conformity
6231.C6145	Consumer credit
6231.C615	Contract bridge
6231.C617	Contracts
6231.C62	Convalescence
6231.C624	Cookery
6231.C63	Corporation reports
6231.C635	Corpulence
6231.C64	Cost and standard of living
6231.C65	Country life
6231.C66	Courtship
6231.C67	Courtship of animals
	Cows see PN6231.C24
6231.C69	Crazy Bones (Trademark)
6231.C7	Cremation

PN
6010-6790

Wit and humor
Collections on special topics, A-Z -- Continued

6231.C73	Crime. Criminals
6231.C75	Criticism
6231.C78	Croatia
6231.C85	Curiosities and wonders
6231.C92	Cycling. Bicycles
6231.C95	Czechs
6231.D3	Dating
6231.D33	Deaf. Hearing impaired
6231.D35	Death
6231.D37	Defecation
6231.D38	Defectors
6231.D4	Dentistry
6231.D43	Depression, Mental
6231.D6	Dialect
	Cf. PN6231.G4 German dialect
	Cf. PN6231.J5 Jewish
6231.D62	Diaries
6231.D64	Dieting
6231.D647	Dinners and dining
6231.D65	Dinosaurs
6231.D657	Disasters
6231.D66	Disco dancing
6231.D662	Divorce. Divorced people
	Divorced people see PN6231.D662
6231.D67	Do-it-yourself
6231.D68	Dogs
6231.D7	Drinking. Drunks
6231.D73	Drive-in theaters
6231.D77	Drug traffic
6231.D79	Duct tape
6231.D8	Dueling
	Dusting see PN6231.S89
6231.E29	Eccentrics and eccentricities
6231.E295	Economics
6231.E3	Edison
6231.E35	Egoism
6231.E4	Electronic data processing. Computers
6231.E5	Elephants
6231.E58	Engineering
6231.E63	Enlightenment (Buddhism)
6231.E64	Entertainment events
6231.E65	Entrepreneur
6231.E66	Environmental protection
6231.E67	Envy
6231.E69	Epitaphs

Wit and humor
Collections on special topics, A-Z -- Continued

6231.E72	Erotica
6231.E74	Errors
6231.E75	Espionage
6231.E78	Ethnology
6231.E8	Etiquette
6231.E87	Excuses
6231.E88	Executives
6231.E9	Exercise
6231.E95	Expo 67
6231.F25	Facial expression
6231.F28	Failure
6231.F283	Fairies
6231.F285	Fairy tales
6231.F287	Faith
	Falsehood see PN6231.T74
6231.F29	Fame
6231.F3	Family
6231.F35	Farewells
6231.F37	Fathers
6231.F4	Fear
6231.F44	Feminism
6231.F45	Feng shui
6231.F47	Finance
6231.F49	Fires
6231.F5	Fishing
6231.F55	Flatulence
6231.F58	Flies
6231.F62	Fly fishing
6231.F66	Food
	Food habits see PN6231.G35
6231.F72	Forbes magazine
6231.F74	Foreigners
6231.F743	France
6231.F745	French language
6231.F748	Friendship
6231.F75	Frogs and toads
6231.G3	Gardening
6231.G35	Gastronomy. Food habits
6231.G36	Gates, Bill, 1955-
6231.G38	Genealogy
6231.G4	German dialect
6231.G42	German language
6231.G45	Ghosts
6231.G47	Ghouls and ogres
6231.G5	Girls

Wit and humor
Collections on special topics, A-Z -- Continued

6231.G65	Gnus
6231.G66	Goblins
6231.G67	Godzilla
6231.G68	Golf
6231.G74	Gorillas
6231.G76	Government consultants
6231.G8	Grandparents
6231.G84	Gravity
6231.G86	Great Britain
6231.G87	Greek language
6231.G92	Gummy bears
6231.G95	Gun control
6231.H28	Haiku
6231.H3	Hair
6231.H35	Happiness
6231.H38	Health
	Hearing impaired see PN6231.D33
6231.H42	Heaven
	Hebrew see PN6231.J5
6231.H47	History
6231.H5	Hitchhiking
6231.H53	Hobbies
6231.H54	Hockey
6231.H547	Holidays
6231.H55	Home economics
6231.H57	Homosexuality
6231.H575	Horoscopes
6231.H577	Horsemanship
6231.H58	Horseracing
6231.H59	Horses
6231.H6	Hospitality
6231.H7	Hotels
6231.H73	House buying
6231.H74	Housewives
6231.H76	Human-animal relationships
6231.H763	Human behavior
6231.H77	Hunting
6231.H8	Husbands
6231.H94	Hygiene
6231.H96	Hypochondria
6231.I44	Impotence
6231.I48	Industrial relations
6231.I5	Infants
6231.I54	Inner cities
6231.I56	Insects

Wit and humor
   Collections on special topics, A-Z -- Continued

6231.I6	Insurance
6231.I62	Internet
6231.I63	Interviews
6231.I65	Invective
6231.I67	Inventors. Inventions
6231.I7	Ireland
6231.I84	Italian language
6231.I85	Italians. Italian Americans
6231.I86	Italy
6231.J3	Jargon
6231.J4	Jewelry trade
6231.J5	Jewish
6231.J59	Job hunting
6231.J63	Jogging
6231.J68	Journalists
6231.K35	Kansas
6231.K5	Kissing
6231.K54	Knives
6231.K55	Knock-knock jokes
6231.L32	Labor. Working class
6231.L33	Laundry
6231.L35	Learning and scholarship
6231.L39	Left- and right-handedness
6231.L4	Legal (Wit and humor of the law)
6231.L43	Lesbians
6231.L44	Letter writing
6231.L47	Liberalism
6231.L48	Life
6231.L49	Life skills
6231.L5	Limericks
6231.L55	Literary periodicals
6231.L56	Lobsters
6231.L58	Lookalikes
6231.L59	Lost articles
6231.L6	Love
	Lying see PN6231.T74
6231.M15	Machismo
6231.M16	Madonna, 1958-
6231.M163	Mafia
6231.M17	Mail-order business
6231.M18	Maine
6231.M19	Malapropisms
6231.M2	Management
6231.M23	Manufactures
6231.M24	Marijuana

	Wit and humor
	Collections on special topics, A-Z -- Continued
6231.M25	Marine fauna
6231.M26	Marketing
6231.M3	Marriage
6231.M35	Matrimonial advertisements
6231.M37	Maturation (Psychology)
6231.M4	Medical
	Cf. R705 Medicine
6231.M42	Meetings
6231.M44	Memorandums
6231.M45	Men
6231.M453	Menopause
6231.M46	Mice
6231.M47	Middle age
6231.M48	Middle Ages
	Middle-finger gesture see PN6231.O26
6231.M5	Military
6231.M52	Millennium
6231.M55	Miners
6231.M57	Minnesota
	Minstrels see PN4305.N5
6231.M59	Misanthropy
6231.M65	Monasticism and religious orders
6231.M66	Money
6231.M665	Monsters
6231.M67	Moon
6231.M672	Moon Pies
6231.M675	Mormon Church. Mormons
6231.M68	Mothers
6231.M682	Mothers-in-law
6231.M7	Motion pictures
6231.M744	Motorcycling
6231.M75	Mountaineering
6231.M82	Murphy's law
6231.M85	Music
	Cf. ML65 Anecdotes, humor, etc.
6231.M87	Mustache
	Mythical animals see PN6231.A54
6231.N24	Names
6231.N27	Nasreddin Hoca (Legendary character)
6231.N3	National characteristics
6231.N35	National socialism
6231.N4	Nebraska
6231.N5	Negroes. Blacks
6231.N53	Neighbors
6231.N55	Neuroses. Neurotics

Wit and humor
　Collections on special topics, A-Z -- Continued
　　Neurotics see PN6231.N55

6231.N556	New Age movement
6231.N557	New England
6231.N558	New Jersey
6231.N559	New York (N.Y.)
6231.N56	Newfoundland
6231.N6	Newsbreaks
6231.N63	Newspapers
6231.N67	Nobility
6231.N68	Nonsense

Cf. PN6110.N6 Nonsense

6231.N69	North Dakota
6231.N693	Northeastern States
6231.N7	Norwegian-American dialect
6231.N72	Nose
6231.N73	Nostalgia
6231.N9	Nudism
6231.O23	Obesity
6231.O25	Obituaries
6231.O26	Obscene gestures

Including individual gestures, e.g. middle-finger gesture
Occupations see PN6231.P74

6231.O27	Ocean travel
6231.O58	Ontario
6231.O96	Outdoor recreation

Outer space see PN6231.S645

6231.O97	Outhouses
6231.O98	Oxymoron
6231.P16	Paranoia
6231.P2	Parents
6231.P3	Parodies

Cf. PN6110.P3 Poetry

6231.P33	Peanuts
6231.P34	Penguins
6231.P344	Penis
6231.P35	Personality tests
6231.P36	Personals
6231.P37	Personnel management
6231.P39	Peter, Saint, apostle
6231.P4	Petroleum
6231.P42	Pets
6231.P43	Pharmacy
6231.P47	Philosophy
6231.P5	Photography

Wit and humor
   Collections on special topics, A-Z -- Continued
      Pigs see PN6231.S895

6231.P55	Plants
6231.P58	Plumbing
6231.P588	Poles. Polish jokes
6231.P59	Police
6231.P6	Politics
6231.P63	Popes
6231.P64	Portmanteau words
6231.P645	Posters
6231.P65	Poverty
6231.P67	Practical jokes
6231.P68	Pregnancy
6231.P686	Premenstrual syndrome
6231.P69	Preppies
6231.P693	Presidents
6231.P696	Presley, Lisa Marie, 1968-
6231.P7	Printing
6231.P73	Procrastination
6231.P74	Professions. Occupations
6231.P75	Prohibition
6231.P78	Psychoanalysis
6231.P785	Psychology
6231.P79	Public administration
6231.P8	Puns
6231.R23	Rabbits
6231.R25	Race problems
6231.R3	Railway
6231.R35	Ranch life
6231.R36	Readers (Books)
6231.R37	Redheads
6231.R38	Rednecks
6231.R39	Rejection
6231.R397	Relaxation
6231.R4	Religion
	Religious orders see PN6231.M65
6231.R43	Restaurants
6231.R44	Retirement
6231.R45	Revenge
	Right-handedness see PN6231.L39
6231.R56	Rights and ceremonies
6231.R59	Rock music
6231.R62	Roommates
6231.R78	Rubik's Cube
6231.R79	Rugby
6231.R8	Rugs, Hooked

Wit and humor
Collections on special topics, A-Z -- Continued

6231.R85	Running
6231.R87	Rural churches
6231.S15	Sailors. Sea life
6231.S16	Saint Valentine's Day
6231.S17	Salesmen
6231.S2	Satires
	Cf. PN6110.S27 Poetry
6231.S22	Sausages
6231.S25	Scandinavians
6231.S3	Schools, professors, etc.
	Cf. LB3060 Examination humor
	Cf. LB3087 Attendance humor
6231.S4	Science
6231.S42	Science fiction
6231.S45	Scots humor
6231.S46	Scuba diving
6231.S48	Secretaries
6231.S485	Segregation
6231.S489	Self-care, Health
6231.S49	Self-defense
6231.S493	Self-interest
6231.S495	Separation (Psychology)
6231.S497	Sequels
6231.S5	Sermons (Burlesques)
6231.S53	Servants
6231.S54	Sex
6231.S542	Sex differences
6231.S545	Sharks
6231.S546	Sheep
6231.S5467	Shopping
6231.S547	Short men
6231.S548	The sick
6231.S5483	Simpson, O.J., 1947-
6231.S5484	Single parents
6231.S5485	Single women
6231.S5486	Sisters
6231.S549	Skiing
6231.S55	Sleeping customs
6231.S555	Slovenes
6231.S56	Smoking
6231.S6	Snakes
6231.S625	Snobs and snobbishness
6231.S627	Snowboarding
6231.S63	Soap bubbles
6231.S632	Soccer

PN
6010-6790

Wit and humor

Collections on special topics, A-Z -- Continued

6231.S633	Sociology
6231.S634	Socks
	Soldiers see PN6231.M5
6231.S638	South Africa
6231.S64	Southern States
6231.S643	Soviet Union
6231.S645	Space travel. Outer space
6231.S646	Spanish language
6231.S647	Spelling
6231.S649	Spoonerisms
6231.S65	Sports
	Stage see PN6231.T57
6231.S73	Stock ownership
6231.S75	Stress management
6231.S79	Subtenants
6231.S8	Suburban life
6231.S82	Subways
6231.S83	Success
6231.S86	Sufi
6231.S876	Suicide
6231.S877	Supernatural
6231.S88	Superstition
6231.S883	Surrealism (Literature)
6231.S886	Survival skills
6231.S89	Sweeping and dusting
6231.S895	Swine
6231.S93	Systems. System theory
6231.T15	Tackiness
6231.T17	Talk shows
6231.T2	Taxation
6231.T23	Taxicabs
	Teachers see PN6231.S3
6231.T3	Technocracy
6231.T35	Teddy bears
6231.T4	Telegrams
6231.T5	Telephone
6231.T53	Television
6231.T55	Tennis
6231.T56	Texas. Texans
6231.T57	Theater
6231.T6	Theology
6231.T63	Therapeutics
6231.T64	Time
6231.T642	Time, the weekly news-magazine
6231.T65	Titles of books

	Wit and humor
	Collections on special topics, A-Z -- Continued
	Toads see PN6231.F75
6231.T656	Tobacco chewing
	Toilets see PN6231.W3
6231.T66	Toronto (Ontario)
6231.T67	Tourist trade
6231.T673	Toys
6231.T677	Tractors
6231.T68	Traffic regulations
6231.T69	Tramps
6231.T694	Transportation
6231.T7	Traveling
6231.T73	Trolls
6231.T74	Truthfulness and falsehood
6231.T76	Twenty-first century
6231.T78	Typewriting
6231.T8	Typographical humor
6231.U52	Underwear
6231.U54	Unicorns
6231.U64	Upper classes
6231.V2	Vacations
	Valentine's Day see PN6231.S16
6231.V25	Valley girls
6231.V27	Vampires
6231.V4	Venice
6231.V46	Vermont
6231.V48	Veterinary medicine
6231.V53	Vikings
	Vocabulary see PN6231.W64
6231.V65	Vomiting
6231.W17	WASPs (Persons)
6231.W27	Waiters
6231.W29	Warning lables
6231.W3	Water closets. Toilets
6231.W35	WD-40 (Trademark)
6231.W37	Weddings
6231.W4	The West
6231.W44	Whales
6231.W444	Whites
6231.W45	Windsurfing
6231.W46	Wine and winemaking
6231.W48	Wishes
6231.W5	Wives
6231.W6	Women
	For suffrage see JF847+
	Wonders see PN6231.C85

Wit and humor
 Collections on special topics, A-Z -- Continued
6231.W64   Words. Vocabulary
6231.W644   Work
6231.W645   Workaholics
6231.W646   World records
6231.W648   Worry
6231.W65   Worship programs
6231.W73   Wrestling
                Yiddish see PN6231.J5
6231.Y67   York (Pa.)
                Youth see PN6231.A26
6231.Z65   Zombies
             Anacreontic literature
              General works
                 Prefer HQ450+
6233   Early through 1800
6235   1801-
              Erotic literature see HQ450+
6237   Praise of wine, drinking, etc.
6238   Pleasures of the table
                 Cf. GT2850+ Manners and customs
              Nicotiana see GT3020+
              Literary extracts. Commonplace books
                 Cf. PN245 Authorship
                 Cf. PN6080+ Quotations
6244   Polyglot
6245   English
6246.A-Z   Other, A-Z
              Miscellaneous
                 Class here collections from various authors and
                    works of individual authors who have not
                    written in other literary forms
              Ana
6249   Polyglot. Greek and Latin
                English
6250   Early through 1800
6251   1801-
6252   French
6253   German
6254   Italian
6255   Spanish
6257.A-Z   Other, A-Z
                   e. g.
6257.D8   Dutch
6257.I7   Irish
6257.L5   Lithuanian

	Miscellaneous
	Ana
	Other, A-Z -- Continued
6257.O7	Oriental (General)
6257.P6	Polish
6257.S4	Scotch
6258.A-Z	Special topics, A-Z
	Anecdotes. Table talk
6259.A2	General works
	Collections
6259.A3-Z	Polyglot. Greek and Latin
	Other language divisions
	English
6260	Early though 1800
6261	1801-
6262	French
6263	German
6264	Italian
6265	Spanish
6267.A-Z	Other, A-Z
6268.A-Z	Special topics, A-Z
6268.A35	Aeronautics
6268.A7	Aristocracy
6268.A8	Authors
6268.B3	Banks
6268.B4	Beer
6268.B6	Books
6268.C45	Children
6268.C5	Clergy
6268.D35	Death
6268.D4	Desert
6268.D5	Diplomacy
6268.D8	Dwarfs
6268.E8	Englishmen
6268.F35	Family
6268.F58	Flight attendance
6268.F74	Friendship
6268.G7	Grandmothers
6268.H6	Home
6268.H76	Hospitality
6268.H8	Hotels, taverns, etc.
6268.J4	Jews
6268.L4	Legal
6268.L7	Love
6268.M4	Medical
	Cf. R705 Medicine
6268.M45	Mentally ill

Miscellaneous
Anecdotes. Table talk
Special topics, A-Z -- Continued

6268.M48	Military art and science
6268.M5	Miners
6268.M6	Money
6268.M65	Mothers
6268.O4	Old age
6268.P3	Patriotism
6268.P6	Politics
6268.R4	Religious
6268.S4	Sea
6268.S47	Sex
6268.S55	Sisters
6268.S6	Soldiers
6268.S7	Stonemasons
6268.S73	Stress
6268.T3	Taxicabs
6268.T7	Traveling
6268.T77	Truck drivers
6268.W4	West Indians
6268.W5	Wives
6268.W6	Women

Aphorisms. Apothegms
6269.A2	General works

Collections
6269.A3-Z	Polyglot. Greek and Latin
	Including classical and medieval

Other language divisions
English
6270	Early through 1800
6271	1801-
6272	French
6273	German
6274	Italian
6275	Spanish
6277.A-Z	Other, A-Z
6278.A-Z	Special topics, A-Z
6278.A28	Acting
6278.A77	Art
6278.A87	Aunts
6278.B6	Books
6278.C36	Cats
6278.C6	Cowboys
6278.E78	Ethics
6278.E8	Etiquette
6278.F66	Food

	Miscellaneous
	Aphorisms. Apothegms
	Special topics, A-Z -- Continued
6278.F7	Friendship
6278.H3	Happiness
6278.H67	Horses
6278.I68	Islands
6278.K68	Kosovo Civil War, 1998-
6278.L6	Love
6278.M35	Marriage
6278.M4	Men
6278.M54	Military art and science
6278.P3	Patriotism
6278.P64	Political science
6278.P68	Power
6278.P8	Public officers
6278.S55	Sisters
6278.T5	Time
6278.U52	Uncles
6278.W35	War
6278.W6	Women
6278.W63	Work
	Epigrams
	Cf. PN1441 Poetry
6279.A2	General works
	Collections
6279.A3-Z	Polyglot. Greek and Latin
	Other language divisions
	English
6280	Early to 1800
6281	1801-
6282	French
6283	German
6284	Italian
6285	Spanish
6287.A-Z	Other, A-Z
6288.A-Z	Special topics, A-Z
6288.H8	Hunting
6288.L6	Love
6288.M3	Marriage
6288.M4	Men
6288.P6	Politics
6288.W6	Women
	Epitaphs
6288.5	Epitaphs as a literary form
6289	Polyglot. Greek and Latin
	Other language divisions

PN
6010-6790

	Miscellaneous
	Epitaphs
	Other language divisions -- Continued
	English
6290	Early through 1800
6291	1801-
6292	French
6293	German
6294	Italian
6295	Spanish
6297.A-Z	Other, A-Z
6298.A-Z	Special topics, A-Z
6298.C5	Children
6298.S4	Servants
6298.S64	Soldiers
	Exempla see BV4224+
	Maxims
6299.A2	General works
	Collections
6299.A3-Z	Polyglot. Greek and Latin
	Other language divisions
	English
6300	Early through 1800
6301	1801-
6302	French
6303	German
6304	Italian
6305	Spanish
6307.A-Z	Other, A-Z
	e. g.
6307.D8	Dutch
6307.I7	Irish
6307.L5	Lithuanian
6307.O7	Oriental (General)
6307.P6	Polish
6307.S4	Scotch
6308.A-Z	Special topics, A-Z
6308.C5	Chance
6308.C6	Conversation
6308.D4	Delphic maxims
6308.D5	Diplomacy
6308.F6	Food
6308.F7	Friendship
6308.H66	Hope
6308.M3	Marriage
6308.M6	Money
6308.S58	Social service

	Miscellaneous
	Maxims
	Collections
	Special topics, A-Z -- Continued
6308.S6	Sports
6308.W4	Weather
6308.W6	Maxims for women
	Mottoes
	Cf. CR73+ Heraldry
6309	Polyglot. Greek and Latin
6310-6317	Other language divisions (Table PN9)
6318.A-Z	Special classes, A-Z
	Sayings, bon mots, etc.
6319	Polyglot. Greek and Latin
6320-6327	Other language divisions (Table PN9)
6328.A-Z	Special classes, A-Z
6328.C5	Children's sayings
6328.L3	Last words
6328.M67	Mothers' sayings
6328.P3	Parents' sayings
6328.S78	Students' sayings
	Thoughts
6329	Polyglot. Greek and Latin
6330-6337	Other language divisions (Table PN9)
6338.A-Z	Special topics, A-Z
6338.A78	Arts
6338.C5	Children
6338.D5	Death
	Falsehood see PN6338.T7
6338.F7	Friendship
6338.H35	Happiness
6338.H64	Holidays
6338.K58	Kissing
6338.L6	Love
6338.O6	Optimism
6338.P45	Photography
6338.R4	Reformers
6338.S4	Science
6338.T7	Truthfulness and falsehood
6338.W6	Women
	Toasts
	English
6340	Early through 1800
6341	1801-
6342	French
6343	German
6344	Italian

PN
6010-6790

	Miscellaneous
	Toasts -- Continued
6345	Spanish
6347.A-Z	Other divisions, A-Z
	e. g.
6347.I7	Irish
6347.S4	Scotch
6348.A-Z	Special topics, A-Z
6348.L88	Lutefisk
6348.W4	Weddings
	Emblems, devices
	For collections illustrated with engravings, see subclass NE
	For works of individual authors, see PA - PT
	Cf. N7740+ Art
6348.5	General works
	Collections
6349	Polyglot. Greek and Latin
6350	Dutch
6351	English
6352	French
6353	German
6354	Italian
6355	Spanish
6357.A-Z	Other, A-Z
6358.A-Z	Special topics, A-Z
	Paradoxes (Collections)
6361	General
	Rhetoric see PN228.P2
	Logic see BC199.P2
	Riddles, acrostics, charades, conundrums, palindromes, etc.
	Including folk riddles
6366	Collected works
	Including pamphlets, etc.
6367	General works
	Collections
	Including works of individual authors
6369	Polyglot. Greek and Latin
	English
6370	Early through 1800
	1801-
6371	General works
6371.5	Juvenile works
6372	French
6373	German
6374	Italian

Miscellaneous
Riddles, acrostics, charades, conundrums,
palindromes, etc.
Collections -- Continued

6375	Spanish
6377.A-Z	Other languages, A-Z
6377.A35	Ainu
6377.A8	Arabic
6377.A87	Assamese
6377.A9	Azerbaijani
6377.B37	Belarusian
6377.B4	Bengali
6377.B53	Bihari
6377.B8	Bulgarian
6377.B82	Buriat
6377.C35	Cape Verde Creole
6377.C37	Catalan
6377.C5	Chinese
6377.C65	Comorian
	Croatian see PN6377.S4
6377.D45	Dena'ina
6377.D76	Dusun
6377.D8	Dutch
6377.E76	Estonian
6377.F5	Finnish
6377.F8	Fulah
6377.H4	Hebrew
6377.H5	Hindi
6377.H54	Hmong
6377.I48	Indian
6377.J3	Japanese
6377.J38	Javanese
6377.K3	Kannada
6377.K36	Karelian
6377.K39	Kazakh
6377.K58	Komi
6377.K6	Korean
6377.L4	Latvian
6377.L5	Lithuanian
6377.M27	Makasar
6377.M29	Malay
6377.M3	Malayalam
6377.M35	Mari
6377.M37	Masikoro
6377.M39	Maya
6377.N24	Nahuatl
6377.N3	Ndonga

Miscellaneous
Riddles, acrostics, charades, conundrums,
palindromes, etc.
Collections
Other languages, A-Z -- Continued

6377.O75	Oriya
6377.O78	Ossetic
6377.P47	Persian
6377.P49	Philippine
6377.P67	Polish
6377.P7	Portuguese
6377.Q42	Quechua
6377.R34	Rajasthani
6377.R7	Romanian
6377.R8	Ruanda
6377.R9	Russian
6377.S25	Sanskrit
6377.S4	Serbo-Croatian
6377.S42	Shona
6377.S45	Sindhi
6377.S49	Slovak
6377.S5	Slovenian
6377.S85	Sundanese
6377.T23	Tagalog
6377.T24	Tajik
6377.T246	Tamazight
6377.T25	Tamil
6377.T32	Tay-Nung
6377.T4	Telugu
6377.T8	Turkish
6377.T87	Tusia
6377.U26	Udmurt
6377.U4	Ukrainian
6377.U7	Urdu
6377.U9	Uzbek
6377.V53	Vietnamese
6377.V66	Votic
6377.W64	Woisika
6377.Y34	Yakut
6377.Y5	Yiddish
6381	Miscellanea

Including Carmel, Blottentots and how to make
them
Proverbs
Cf. GR, Folklore
General works. History. Philosophy

6400	Early works through 1800

	Proverbs
	General works. History. Philosophy -- Continued
6401	1801-
	Collections
	General. Proverbs of all nations
6403	Early through 1800
	1801-
6404	Polyglot
6405	English
6406	French
6407	German
6408	Italian
6409.A-Z	Other languages, A-Z
	Ancient
6410	General works
6413	Greek
	Including original texts
	For modern Greek see PN6505.G7
6414	Hebrew, Jewish
	Including original and medieval texts
	Cf. PN6519.J5 Modern proverbs
	Latin
	Including original texts
6416	Classical
6418	Medieval and modern
6418.5.A-Z	Other, A-Z
	Class here translations and criticism only
	For original texts, see the language in P
	- PM
6418.5.A8	Assyro-Babylonian
6418.5.E35	Egyptian
	For modern Egyptian see PN6519.E35
6418.5.S3	Sanskrit
6418.5.S8	Sumerian
6419	Romance languages
	Class here general works only
6419.5	Germanic languages
	Class here general works only
	Modern
	English and American proverbs
	General works. Collections
6420	Early through 1800
6421	1800-
	Local divisions
	For special subjects see PN6427.A+

	Proverbs
	Modern
	English and American proverbs
	Local divisions -- Continued
	Great Britain
	Cf. PN6505.C3+ Proverbs in Celtic languages
	General see PN6420+
6425.A-Z	Local, A-Z
	United States
6426	General
6426.3.A-Z	Local, A-Z
6426.6.A-Z	Other English-speaking countries, A-Z
6427.A-Z	Special topics, A-Z
6429	Miscellaneous
6429.5	European (General)
	Dutch. Flemish
	General works. Collections
6430	Early through 1800
6431	1801-
6435.A-Z	Local, A-Z
	For special topics see PN6437.A+
6437.A-Z	Special topics, A-Z
6439	Miscellaneous
	French
	General works. Collections
6450	Early through 1800
6451	1801-
6455.A-Z	Local, A-Z
6457.A-Z	Special topics, A-Z
6459	Miscellaneous
	German
	Cf. PN6505.L68 Low German
	General works. Collections
6460	Early through 1800
6461	1801-
6465.A-Z	Local, A-Z
6467.A-Z	Special topics, A-Z
6469	Miscellaneous
	Italian
	General works. Collections
6470	Early through 1800
6471	1801-
6475.A-Z	Local, A-Z
6477.A-Z	Special topics, A-Z
6479	Miscellaneous
	Scandinavian

	Proverbs
	Modern
	Scandinavian -- Continued
	General works. Collections
6480	Early through 1800
6481	1801-
	Local divisions
	For special topics see PN6488.A+
	Danish
6484.A2	General works
6484.A3-Z	Local
6485	Icelandic
	Norwegian
6486.A2	General works
6486.A3-Z	Local
	Swedish
6487.A2	General works
6487.A3-Z	Local
6488.A-Z	Special topics, A-Z
6489	Miscellaneous
	Spanish and Portuguese
	General works. Collections
6490	Early through 1800
6491	1801-
6495.A-Z	Local, A-Z
	For special topics see PN6497.A+
6497.A-Z	Special topics, A-Z
6499	Miscellaneous
	Swiss
	see PN6455.S9 PN6465.S9 PN6475.S9
6505.A-Z	Other European, A-Z
6505.A38	Adygei
6505.A42	Albanian
6505.B17	Balkan (General)
6505.B18	Baltic
6505.B19	Baltic-Finnic
6505.B2	Basque
6505.C2	Catalan
	Celtic
6505.C3	General works
6505.C33	Breton
(6505.C37)	Cornish
6505.C4	Gaelic (Scottish)
6505.C5	Irish
(6505.C6)	Manx
(6505.C7)	Welsh
6505.C75	Circassian

	Proverbs
	Modern
	Other European, A-Z -- Continued
6505.D34	Daghestan
6505.E73	Estonian
6505.F5	Finnish
6505.F7	Frisian
6505.G34	Gallegan
6505.G45	Georgian
6505.G7	Greek, Modern
6505.H8	Hungarian
6505.K3	Karelian
6505.K34	Kashubian
6505.K65	Komi
6505.L28	Langue d'oc
6505.L3	Lapp
6505.L5	Lithuanian. Latvian
6505.L56	Livonian
6505.L68	Low German
6505.M34	Maltese
6505.M37	Mari
6505.M64	Moldavian
6505.P6	Provençal
6505.R33	Raeto-Romance
6505.R7	Romanian
6505.S15	Sardinian
	Slavic
6505.S2	General works
6505.S3	Bohemian. Czech
6505.S33	Bulgarian
	Byelorussian see PN6505.S78+
6505.S35	Croatian
6505.S37	Macedonian
6505.S4	Polish
6505.S5	Russian
	Ruthenian see PN6505.S76
6505.S6	Serbian. Montenegrin
6505.S7	Slovak
6505.S75	Slovenian
	Sorbian see PN6505.S77
6505.S76	Ukrainian. Ruthenian
6505.S77	Wendic. Sorbian
	White Russian. Byelorussian
6505.S78	Collections
6505.S79	History and criticism
6505.U34	Udmurt
6505.V63	Votic

	Proverbs
	Modern -- Continued
6511	Oriental (General)
6519.A-Z	Other special, A-Z
	Prefer classification by language
6519.A24	Abidji
6519.A25	Achinese
6519.A3	Acoli
6519.A4	Adangme
6519.A6	African
6519.A625	Akan
6519.A627	Alur
6519.A63	Amharic
6519.A66	Angika
	Annamese see PN6519.V5
6519.A7	Arabic
6519.A75	Armenian
6519.A8	Ashanti
6519.A85	Assamese
6519.A87	Asu
6519.A88	Awadhi
6519.A9	Azerbaijani
6519.B26	Bakundu
6519.B27	Balinese
6519.B28	Baluchi
6519.B3	Bambara
6519.B315	Bamileke
6519.B32	Bamun
6519.B326	Bangaru
6519.B33	Bantu
6519.B34	Baoulé. Baule
6519.B36	Bartang
6519.B37	Bashkir
6519.B374	Batak
6519.B375	Bati
	Baule see PN6519.B34
6519.B4	Bemba
6519.B42	Bengali
6519.B44	Berber
6519.B48	Bhili
6519.B5	Bhojpuri
6519.B55	Biak
6519.B57	Biharii
6519.B59	Bini
6519.B7	Brahui
6519.B77	Buginese
6519.B8	Burmese

Proverbs
Modern
Other special, A-Z -- Continued

6519.B86	Buryat
6519.C44	Chakma
6519.C444	Cham
6519.C47	Chewa
6519.C5	Chinese
6519.C53	Chokwe
6519.C55	Chuvash
	Congo see PN6519.K59
6519.C62	Congo (Brazzaville)
6519.C8	Creole
6519.D56	Diola
6519.D6	Dogri
6519.D7	Dravidian
6519.D8	Duala
6519.E33	Efik
6519.E35	Egyptian
6519.E76	Etsako
6519.E9	Ewe
6519.E96	Ewondo
6519.F36	Fang
6519.F54	Fijian
6519.F8	Fulah
6519.G23	Gambai
6519.G25	Ganda
6519.G27	Garhwali
6519.G3	Gayo
6519.G6	Goajiro
6519.G8	Guarani
6519.G85	Gujarati
6519.H3	Haitian
6519.H35	Hausa
6519.H4	Hawaiian
	Hebrew see PN6519.J5
6519.H55	Hindi
6519.H57	Hindko
6519.H58	Hindustani
6519.H64	Hmong
6519.H85	Hunde
6519.I33	Igbo
6519.I35	Ikwere
6519.I39	Indian
6519.I4	Indic
	Cf. PN6418.5.S3 Sanskrit
6519.I5	Indonesian

Proverbs
   Modern
      Other special, A-Z -- Continued

6519.I75	Itsekiri
6519.I855	Ivory Coast
6519.J15	Jabo
6519.J2	Jamaican
6519.J3	Japanese
6519.J38	Javanese
6519.J5	Jewish
	Cf. PN6519.L3 Ladino
6519.J83	Judeo-Arabic
6519.J84	Judeo-Tat
6519.K22	Kabardian
6519.K223	Kabre
6519.K226	Kaili
6519.K23	Kalanga
6519.K24	Kamba
6519.K25	Kannada
6519.K27	Karaim
6519.K28	Karo-Batak
6519.K29	Kasem
6519.K3	Kashmiri
6519.K38	Kazakh
6519.K44	Kenga
6519.K5	Kikuyu
6519.K53	Kilega
6519.K55	Kimbundu
6519.K57	Kirghiz
6519.K59	Kongo
6519.K593	Konkani
6519.K6	Korean
6519.K75	Krio
6519.K8	Kuanyama
6519.K83	Kukwa
6519.K84	Kuo
6519.K85	Kurdish
6519.L27	Ladakhi
6519.L3	Ladino (Judeo-Spanish)
	Cf. PN6519.J5 Jewish
6519.L35	Lambadi
6519.L39	Lao
	Lega see PN6519.W3
6519.L47	Liberian
6519.L56	Limbum
6519.L73	Luba-Lulua
6519.L74	Lucazi

Proverbs
   Modern
      Other special, A-Z -- Continued

6519.L76	Lugbara
6519.L8	Luvale
6519.M22	Majingai
6519.M225	Makasar
6519.M23	Makua
6519.M24	Malagasy
6519.M26	Malay
6519.M28	Malayalam
6519.M29	Mampruli
6519.M3	Manchu
6519.M313	Mandailing
6519.M316	Mandingo
6519.M32	Manipuri
6519.M35	Maori
6519.M36	Marathi
6519.M37	Masai
6519.M375	Masikoro
6519.M39	Mbai (Moissala)
6519.M44	Medumba
6519.M54	Minangkabau
6519.M55	Minianka
6519.M57	Moba
6519.M58	Mongo
6519.M6	Mongolian
6519.M64	Moré
6519.M85	Mundari
6519.M87	Mungaka
6519.N38	Ndebele (Zimbabwe)
6519.N385	Ndonga
6519.N387	Ndumu
6519.N39	Near Eastern
6519.N4	Nepali
6519.N5	Newari
6519.N52	Ngaju
6519.N53	Nias
6519.N55	Nigerian
6519.N58	Nomaante
6519.N6	Northern Sotho
6519.N9	Nyaneka
6519.N93	Nyanja
6519.N95	Nzima
6519.O7	Oriya
6519.O75	Oromo
6519.O85	Ossetic

Proverbs
 Modern
  Other special, A-Z -- Continued

6519.P3	Panjabi
6519.P36	Papiamento
6519.P5	Persian
6519.P55	Philippine
6519.P6	Pidgin English
6519.P8	Pushto
6519.Q45	Quechua
6519.R35	Rajasthani
6519.R46	Rendille
6519.R8	Ruanda
6519.R84	Rundi
6519.R98	Ryukyu
6519.S23	Sabaot
6519.S3	Samoan
6519.S36	Senari
6519.S38	Serer
6519.S43	Shi
6519.S45	Shona
6519.S48	Simelungun
6519.S49	Sindhi
6519.S5	Sinhalese
6519.S55	Siraiki
6519.S58	Somali
6519.S67	Sranan
6519.S8	Sudanese
6519.S83	Sukuma
6519.S85	Sundanese
6519.S87	Svan
6519.S9	Swahili
6519.T2	Tagalog
6519.T28	Tajik
6519.T29	Tamashek
6519.T3	Tamil
6519.T32	Tamu
6519.T33	Tanzanian
6519.T35	Tatar
6519.T36	Tay-Nung
	Tebele see PN6519.N38
6519.T4	Telugu
6519.T45	Thai
6519.T55	Tibetan
6519.T57	Toba-Batak
6519.T58	Tobote
6519.T62	Toraja

	Proverbs
	Modern
	Other special, A-Z -- Continued
6519.T7	Tshi
6519.T74	Tsonga
6519.T75	Tswana
6519.T76	Tugen
6519.T77	Tulu
6519.T78	Turkic
6519.T79	Turkish
6519.T8	Turkmen
6519.T84	Tuvinian
6519.U5	Uighur
6519.U54	Umbundu
6519.U7	Urdu
6519.U9	Uzbek
6519.V5	Vietnamese
6519.W3	Warega. Lega
6519.W62	Wobe
6519.X6	Xosa
6519.Y19	Yaka (Zaire and Angola)
6519.Y2	Yakut
6519.Y25	Yay
	Yiddish see PN6519.J5
6519.Y55	Yombe
6519.Y6	Yoruba
6519.Z27	Zambian
6519.Z3	Zapotec
6519.Z35	Zarma
6519.Z8	Zulu
6525.A-Z	Special topics, A-Z
	Class here general collections only
6525.A6	Animals. Bestiaries
6525.A8	Atheism
	Bestiaries see PN6525.A6
6525.B73	Bread
6525.D49	Devil
6525.E3	Education
6525.G35	Gardens
6525.G6	God
6525.H9	Hygiene
6525.L68	Love
6525.M55	Milk
6525.S36	Sea
6525.S4	Sex
6525.W4	Weather
	Comic books, strips, etc.

Comic books, strips, etc. -- Continued

6700	Periodicals. Societies. Serials
6702	Congresses
	Exhibitions, museums, etc.
6705.A1	General works
6705.A2-Z	By region or country, A-Z

       Individual institutions are classed by
         country without further subdivision

6707	Encyclopedias. Dictionaries
6710	General works

     Including history
     For collective biography of cartoonists see
       NC1305

Special topics
     Cf. HQ784.C6 Comic books and children
     Cf. HV9076.5 Juvenile delinquency

6712	Moral and religious aspects
6714	Other special (not A-Z)
6720	General collections
	By region or country
6725-6728	United States (Table PN11)
6731-6734	Canada (Table PN11)
6735-6738	Great Britain (Table PN11)
6745-6748	France (Table PN11 modified)
6747.A-Z	Individual authors or works, A-Z

     Subarrange individual authors by Table
       P-PZ40
     Subarrange individual works by Table P-PZ43

6747.G5	Gir, 1938- (Table P-PZ40)

     Giraud, Jean see PN6747.G5
     Moebius, 1938- see PN6747.G5

6755-6758	Germany (Table PN11)
6765-6768	Italy (Table PN11)
6775-6778	Spain (Table PN11)
6790.A-Z	Other regions or countries, A-Z

    Under each country:

.x	*History*
.x2	*Collections*
.x3	*Individual authors or works, A-Z*

          *Prefer classification
          of comic strips by
          title*

.x4	*Individual comic strips. By title, A-Z*

	Periodicals
	see PN4699+
	Societies, conferences, collections
1	Societies
2	Conferences. Congresses
3	Collections
	History and other general works
4	Comprehensive
5	Early
	Recent
6	18th century
7	19th century
8	20th century
9	21st century
	Biography of editors, journalists, etc.
	For historical characters, see classes D-F
12	Collective
13.A-Z	Individual, A-Z
	Subarrange each by Table P-PZ50
14.A-Z	Special topics, A-Z
	For press coverage of specific events or
	organizations, see the event or organization
	in classes B-Z
14.A39	Advice columns
14.A397	Africa
14.A4	Agricultural journalism
14.A44	AIDS (Disease)
14.A53	Anarchist press
14.A75	Arts
14.A78	Astronautics
14.A83	Australian aborigines
14.A84	Austria
14.A85	Authorship
14.A87	Awards
14.B42	Beauty, Personal
14.B55	Black press
14.B75	Broadcast journalism
14.C35	Canards
14.C4	Catholic press
	Children's periodicals see PN1 14.J8
14.C5	Circulation. Marketing
14.C57	Commercial journalism
14.C6	Communist press
14.C63	Community newspapers
14.C64	Conservatism
14.C65	Correction articles

	Special topics, A-Z -- Continued
14.C67	Country newspapers. Rural journalism
14.C74	Crime journalism
14.D38	Data processing
14.D48	Developing countries
14.D58	Disaster reporting
14.E34	Editing
14.E38	Educational journalism
14.E6	Employees
14.E64	Environmental protection
14.E8	Ethics of journalism
14.E84	Ethnic press
14.E87	European Union
14.E94	Extra editions
14.F35	Fanzines
14.F37	Fashion
14.F45	Fiction
14.F5	Finance
	Foreign language press
14.F6	General works
14.F62A-.F62Z	By language, A-Z
14.F67	Foreign news
14.F74	Freemasonry
14.G35	Gangs
14.H4	Headlines
14.H55	Homosexuality
14.H58	Hours of labor
14.H8	Humorous periodicals
14.I44	Illustrated periodicals
14.I55	Immigration
14.I78	Islam
14.I8	Islamic press
14.J34	Japan
14.J48	Jews
14.J8	Juvenile periodicals
14.L3	Labor
14.L34	Legal journalism
14.L4	Letters to the editor. Readers' opinion
14.L6	Literature
14.L62	Little magazines
14.L65	Local editions
14.L8	Lutheran press
	Marketing see PN1 14.C5
14.M43	Medical journalism
14.M45	Men's magazines
14.M5	Military journalism

TABLES

	Special topics, A-Z -- Continued
14.M53	Minorities
14.M68	Motion picture journalism
14.O24	Objectivity
14.O9	Ownership
14.P4	Periodicals. Magazines (other than newspapers)
14.P54	Poland
14.P58	Police
14.P6	Politics
14.P65	Prices
14.P67	Prison journalism
14.P7	Propaganda
14.P73	Prostitution
14.P74	Protestant press
14.P82	Public opinion
14.R28	Race problems
14.R29	Racism
14.R3	Radio journalism
14.R43	Readership surveys
14.R44	Regional journalism
14.R45	Religious journalism
14.R5	Reporters and reporting
14.R55	Reviews. Critical writing
	Rural journalism see PN1 14.C67
14.S34	Scholarly periodicals
14.S35	Scientific journalism
14.S4	Sections, columns, etc. (General)
14.S45	Sensationalism
14.S47	Sex crimes in the press
14.S6	Social aspects
14.S63	Socialist journalism
14.S65	Sports journalism
14.S75	Strikes and lockouts
14.T37	Technical journalism
14.T4	Television journalism
14.T43	Television program guides
14.T46	Terrorism
14.U5	Underground literature
14.U53	Underground press
14.V56	Violence
14.W25	Wages
14.W3	Wall newspapers
14.W36	War
14.W45	Wholesalers
14.W58	Women
14.W6	Women's magazines

	Local
16.A-Z	By region, A-Z
17.A-Z	By state, province, etc., A-Z
19.A-Z	By place, A-Z

Under each, using successive cutter numbers:

.x	*Collections*
.x2	*General works. History*
.x3A-.x3Z	*Special newspapers, A-Z*

20.A-Z	Special magazines and other periodicals, A-Z

For newspapers see PN1 19.A+

TABLES

	Periodicals
	see PN4699+
1	Societies, conferences, collections
	History and other general works
2	Comprehensive
3	Early
4	Recent
	Biography of editors, journalists, etc.
	For historical characters, see classes D-F
6.A1-.A5	Collective
6.A6-Z	Individual, A-Z
	Subarrange each by Table P-PZ50
7.A-Z	Special topics, A-Z
	For list of Cutter numbers, see Table PN1 14
	For press coverage of specific events, see the event in classes B-Z
	Local
8.A-Z	By state, province, etc., A-Z
9.A-Z	By place, A-Z

Under each, using successive cutter numbers:

.x	Collections
.x2	General works. History
.x3A-.x3Z	Special newspapers, A-Z

10.A-Z	Special magazines and other periodicals, A-Z
	For newspapers see PN2 9.A+

1	Societies, conferences, collections
2	History and other general works
	Biography
3.A1-.A5	Collective
3.A6-Z	Individual
4.A-Z	Local, A-Z
5.A-Z	Special journals, A-Z

	Periodicals
	see PN4705
.xA1-.xA5	Societies, conferences, collections
.xA6-.xZ5	History and other general works
	Biography
.xZ6-.xZ69	Collective
.xZ7-.xZ79	Individual
.xZ8-.xZ89	Local
.xZ9-.xZ99	Special newpapers, periodicals, etc.

0	Early through 1800
	1801-
0.5	Polyglot
1	American and English
2	Dutch
3	French
4	German
5	Italian
6	Scandinavian
7	Slavic
8	Spanish and Portuguese
9.A-Z	Other, A-Z

TABLES

0	Collections
	History
1	General works
2	Early to 1800
3	19th century
4	20th century
4.2	21st century
5.A-Z	States, provinces, etc., A-Z
6.A-Z	Cities, A-Z
	Subarrange each by Table PN8a
	Biography
7	Collective
8.A-Z	Individual, A-Z
	Subarrange each by Table P-PZ50
8.5	Directories. Guidebooks, etc.
	For local see PN6 5.A+

0	Periodicals. Serials
	History
1	General works
1.5	General special
2	Early to 1800
3	19th century
4	20th century
4.2	21st century
5.A-Z	States, provinces, etc., A-Z
6.A-Z	Cities, A-Z
	Subarrange each by Table PN8a
	Biography
7	Collective
8.A-Z	Individual, A-Z
	Subarrange each by Table P-PZ50

TABLES

0	Collections
	History
1	General works
2.A-Z	Local, A-Z
	Subarrange each by Table PN8a
	Biography
3	Collective
4.A-Z	Individual, A-Z
	Subarrange each by Table P-PZ50

0	Periodicals. Serials
	History
0.1	General works
0.2	Early to 1800
0.3	19th century
0.4	20th century
0.42	21st century
0.5.A-Z	States, provinces, etc., A-Z
0.6.A-Z	Cities, A-Z
	Biography
0.7	Collective
0.8.A-Z	Individual, A-Z
	Subarrange each by Table P-PZ50

.x	General works
.x2A-.x2Z	Individual theaters. By conventional name, A-Z

	English
0	Early through 1800
1	1801-
2	French
3	German
4	Italian
5	Spanish
7.A-Z	Other, A-Z
	e.g.
7.D8	Dutch
7.I7	Irish
7.L5	Lithuanian
7.O7	Oriental (General)
7.P6	Polish
7.S4	Scots

TABLES

1	Series
2	General works
3.A-Z	Special, A-Z
3.D5	Dialogues
3.H8	Humorous
3.J8	Juvenile
3.M6	Monologues
3.P3	Patriotic
3.R4	Religious

1	History
2	Collections
3.A-Z	Individual authors or works, A-Z
	Subarrange individual authors by Table P-PZ40
	Subarrange individual works by Table P-PZ43
	Prefer classification of comic strips by title
4.A-Z	Individual comic strips. By title, A-Z

A

Abidji proverbs: PN6519.A24
Abjection in literature
  General
    Literary history: PN56.A23
Aboriginal Australians in motion
  pictures: PN1995.9.A835
Abortion
  Journalism: PN4784.A18
    United States: PN4888.A2
Absurdity in literature
  General
    Collections
      Quotations
        French: PN6089.A2
    Literary history: PN56.A24
      Prose: PN3352.A34
Accidents in literature
  General
    Collections
      Wit and humor: PN6231.A22
Accounting in literature
  General
    Collections
      Wit and humor: PN6231.A24
Achinese proverbs: PN6519.A25
Acoli proverbs: PN6519.A3
Acronyms in literature
  General
    Collections
      Wit and humor: PN6231.A25
Acrostics
  General
    Collections: PN6366+
Acting
  Radio broadcasts: PN1991.8.A32
Acting in literature
  General
    Collections
      Aphorisms: PN6278.A28
Actors, actresses, and acting
  Acting as a profession: PN2055
  African American actors and
    actresses: PN2286
  Asian American actors and
    actresses: PN2286.2

Actors, actresses, and acting
  Gay actors and actresses:
    PN2286.5
  Psychology: PN2058
Actors, actresses, and acting in
  literature
  General
    Collections
      Quotations
        English: PN6084.A25
Actors, actresses, and acting in
  motion pictures: PN1995.9.A26
Actors, actresses, and acting in
  television broadcasts:
  PN1992.8.A3
Adalbert, Saint, Bp. of Prague,
  in literature
  General
    Literary history
      Legends: PN687.A3
Adangme: PN6519.A4
Adaptations
  Film: PN1997.85
  Video: PN1997.85
Adolescence and motion pictures:
  PN1995.9.C45
Adolescence in literature
  General
    Collections: PN6071.A3
      Wit and humor: PN6231.A26
Adolescent girls in literature
  General
    Literary history: PN56.5.A35
Adoption in literature
  General
    Collections
      Quotations
        English: PN6084.A3
Adultery in literature
  General
    Collections: PN6071.A35
      Wit and humor: PN6231.A28
    Literary history
      Prose: PN3352.A38
Adulthood in literature
  General
    Collections: PN6071.A36

Adventure films: PN1995.9.A3
Adventure in literature
  General
    Literary history: PN56.A3
Adventure programs
  Television broadcasts:
    PN1992.8.A317
Adventure stories
  General
    Collections: PN6071.A38
    Literary history: PN3448.A3
      Technique: PN3377.5.A37
Adventuriers: PN3432
Advertising in literature
  General
    Collections
      Wit and humor: PN6231.A3
Advertising of television
  programs: PN1992.8.A32
Advice columns
  Journalism: PN1 14.A39
Adygei proverbs: PN6505.A38
Aeronautical journalism:
  PN4784.A26
  United States: PN4888.A4
Aeronautics in literature
  General
    Collections: PN6071.A4
      Anecdotes: PN6268.A35
      Poetry: PN6110.A2
      Wit and humor: PN6231.A4
    Literary history: PN56.A4
Aeronautics in motion pictures:
  PN1995.9.F58
Aesthetics in literature
  General
    Collections
      Quotations
        German: PN6093.A3
    Literary history
      Juvenile literature:
        PN1009.5.A34
Aesthetics of literature
  General
    Literary history: PN45+
      Drama: PN1631+
      Prose: PN3335

Affirmations in literature
  General
    Collections
      Wit and humor: PN6231.A42
Africa
  Journalism: PN1 14.A397
Africa in literature
  General
    Collections: PN6071.A45
    Literary history: PN56.3.A39
Africa in motion pictures:
  PN1995.9.A43
Africa, North, Literature of
  Literary history: PN849.A355+
African American actors and
  actresses: PN2286
African American press: PN4882.5
African American theater:
  PN2270.A35
African Americans in radio
  broadcasts: PN1991.8.A35
African Americans in television
  broadcasts: PN1992.8.A34
African proverbs: PN6519.A6
Africans in literature
  General
    Literary history
      Juvenile literature:
        PN1009.5.A47
Afrikaans quotations: PN6095.A35
After-dinner speeches: PN4193.O4
  English recitations: PN4305.O4
Agamemnon in literature
  General
    Literary history: PN57.A33
Age in literature
  General
    Collections
      Quotations
        English: PN6084.A35
Agents, Literary: PN163
Aging in literature
  General
    Collections: PN6071.A48
      Wit and humor: PN6231.A43
Agitprop theater: PN3305+

Agricultural journalism:
PN4784.A3, PN1 14.A4
United States: PN4888.A43
Agriculture in literature
General
Collections
Wit and humor: PN6231.A44
AIDS (Disease)
Journalism: PN1 14.A44
AIDS (Disease) in motion
pictures: PN1995.9.A435
Ainu riddles: PN6377.A35
Air Force newspapers
United States: PN4888.M54
Air in literature
General
Collections: PN6071.A56
Air travel in literature
General
Collections
Wit and humor: PN6231.A445
Airships in literature
General
Collections: PN6071.A57
Akan proverbs: PN6519.A625
Alamo (San Antonio, Tex.) in
motion pictures: PN1995.9.A44
Alarcos in literature
General
Literary history: PN57.A35
Albanian proverbs: PN6505.A42
Albanian quotations: PN6095.A42
Albanian-American newspapers:
PN4885.A4
Album verses
General
Collections: PN6110.A4
Alcestis in literature
General
Collections
Drama: PN6120.A3
Literary history: PN57.A37
Alchemy in literature
General
Literary history: PN56.A44
Drama: PN1650.A42

Alcoholics in literature
General
Collections
Wit and humor: PN6231.A448
Alcoholism in motion pictures:
PN1995.9.A45
Alexander, the Great, in
literature
General
Literary history: PN57.A4
Legends: PN687.A5
Alexandrian literature: PN640+
Algeria in literature
General
Literary history: PN56.3.A43
Alien films: PN1995.9.A457
Alien labor in motion pictures:
PN1995.9.A46
Alienation (Social psychology)
in literature
General
Collections: PN6071.A6
Literary history: PN56.A45
Alienation (Social psychology)
in motion pictures:
PN1995.9.A47
Aliens in motion pictures:
PN1995.9.A48
Allegory in literature
General
Literary history: PN56.A5
Epic poetry: PN1329
Medieval: PN682.A5
Alphabet in literature
General
Collections
Wit and humor: PN6231.A45
Alphabet rhymes
General
Collections
Poetry: PN6110.A44
Alternative theater: PN2193.E86
Altruism in literature
General
Collections
Poetry: PN6110.A5
Alur proverbs: PN6519.A627

Amateur drama: PN6119.9
Amateur journalism: PN4825+
Amateur motion pictures:
 PN1995.8
Amateur radio in literature
 General
  Collections
   Wit and humor: PN6231.A47
Amateur theatricals: PN3151+
Amateur writers: PN159
Ambiguity in literature
 General
  Literary history: PN56.A55
America in literature
 General
  Literary history: PN56.3.A45
  Poetry: PN1083.A48
American Indian press: PN4883
American Indians
 Authors
  General
   Collections: PN6069.I53
American Indians and broadcasting
 Radio: PN1991.8.I53
American Indians in literature
 General
  Collections
   Drama: PN6120.I6
  Literary history: PN56.3.I6
  Recitations: PN4305.I6
American Indians in motion
 pictures: PN1995.9.I48
American literature
 Literary history: PN843+
Amharic proverbs: PN6519.A63
Amphitryon in literature
 General
  Collections
   Drama: PN6120.A6
  Literary history: PN57.A43
Amplification
 Literary style: PN225

Amvrosil, Metropolitan of
 Novgorod and St. Petersburg,
 in literature
 General
  Collections
   Poetry: PN6110.A58
Ana: PN6249+
Anacreontic literature: PN6233+
Anagnorisis in literature
 General
  Literary history: PN56.R33
Anagrams: PN1525
Anarchism in motion pictures:
 PN1995.9.A487
Anarchist press: PN1 14.A53
Ancient drama: PN1741
Ancient theater: PN2131+
Androgyny (Psychology) in
 literature
 General
  Literary history: PN56.A57
Angélique films: PN1995.9.A49
Angels in literature
 General
  Collections: PN6071.A65
   Poetry: PN6110.A59
  Quotations
   English: PN6084.A55
  Literary history: PN56.A59
Angels in motion pictures:
 PN1995.9.S8
Anger in literature
 General
  Literary history: PN56.A6
Angika proverbs: PN6519.A66
Angling in literature
 General
  Collections
   Poetry: PN6110.A6
Animals
 Performing arts: PN1590.A54
Animals in literature
 General
  Collections: PN6071.A7
   Drama: PN6120.A7
   Poetry: PN6110.A7
   Proverbs: PN6525.A6

Animals in literature
General
Collections
Quotations
English: PN6084.A57
German: PN6093.A5
Wit and humor: PN6231.A5
Literary history: PN56.A64
Epics: PN1333.A6
Medieval: PN690.A6
Medieval: PN682.A57
Poetry: PN1083.A5
Prose: PN3352.A55
Animals in motion pictures:
PN1995.9.A5
Animals in television
broadcasts: PN1992.8.A58
Animals in the theater:
PN2270.A54
Animals, Mythical, in literature
General
Collections
Wit and humor: PN6231.A54
Animated programs
Television broadcasts:
PN1992.8.A59
Annamese proverbs: PN6519.V5
Anne of Brittany in literature
General
Literary history: PN57.A45
Anniversary editions
Journalism: PN4784.A5
Announcing
Broadcasting: PN1990.9.A54
Announcing (Broadcasting)
Radio broadcasts: PN1991.8.A6
Television broadcasts:
PN1992.8.A6
Anonymity
Authorship: PN171.A6
Anthologies
English: PN6014
General: PN4397
Anthropology
Performing arts: PN1590.A58

Anthropology in literature
General
Literary history
Drama: PN2041.A57
Anti-clericalism in literature
General
Collections: PN6071.A75
Antigone in literature
General
Collections
Drama: PN6120.A75
Literary history: PN57.A47
Antiquities in literature
General
Literary history: PN56.A67
Antisemitism in motion pictures:
PN1995.9.A55
Antoinette Perry awards:
PN2270.A93
Apartheid in literature
General
Collections: PN6071.A775
Aphorisms: PN6269+
Apocalyptic literature
General
Collections: PN6071.A78
Literary history: PN56.A69
Apollo (Greek deity) in
literature
General
Literary history: PN57.A49
Apollonius of Tyre in literature
General
Literary history: PN57.A5
Apostles in literature
General
Collections: PN6071.A79
Apothegms: PN6269+
Appalachian Region in literature
General
Collections
Wit and humor: PN6231.A65
Appalachians (People) in motion
pictures: PN1995.9.M67
Appearance, Personal
Television: PN1992.8.P4

Apprentices in literature
General
Literary history: PN56.5.A64
Arab countries in literature
General
Collections
Wit and humor: PN6231.A68
Arab influences in literature
General
Literary history
Medieval: PN682.A67
Arabic proverbs: PN6519.A7
Arabic quotations: PN6095.A7
Arabic riddles: PN6377.A8
Arabic-American newspapers:
PN4885.A73
Arabs in literature
General
Collections
Wit and humor: PN6231.A68
Arabs in motion pictures:
PN1995.9.A68
Arabs in television broadcasts:
PN1992.8.A7
Arabs in the press
United States: PN4888.A67
Archaeology in motion pictures:
PN1995.9.A69
Archers and archery in literature
General
Collections: PN6071.A8
Archetypes in literature
General
Literary history: PN56.A72
Architects
Oratory: PN4192.A72
Architects in motion pictures:
PN1995.9.A695
Architecture in literature
General
Collections
Drama: PN6120.A77
Quotations
English: PN6084.A75
Literary history: PN56.A73
Poetry: PN1083.A72

Architecture in literature
General
Literary history
Romance literatures:
PN810.A7
Arena stage: PN2081.A7
Argentina in motion pictures:
PN1995.9.A7
Argonauts (Greek mythology) in
literature
General
Literary history
Legends: PN687.A73
Argumentation
Authorship: PN207
Aristocracy in literature
General
Collections
Anecdotes· PN6268.A7
Arizona in literature
General
Collections
Wit and humor: PN6231.A69
Armed Forces in motion pictures:
PN1995.9.A72
Armed Forces newspapers
United States: PN4888.M54
Armenian proverbs: PN6519.A75
Armenian quotations: PN6095.A75
Armenian-American newspapers:
PN4885.A75
Armenians in literature
General
Literary history
Fiction: PN3426.A75
Arminius, Prince of the
Cherussi, in literature
General
Literary history: PN57.A55
Army newspapers
United States: PN4888.M54
Art and journalism: PN4762
Art and literature: PN53
General
Literary history
Poetry: PN1069
Prose: PN3342

Art direction
  Motion pictures: PN1995.9.A74
  Television broadcasts:
    PN1992.8.A76
Art in literature
  General
    Collections: PN6071.A83
      Aphorisms: PN6278.A77
      Poetry: PN6110.A77
      Quotations
        English: PN6084.A8
        German: PN6093.A8
    Literary history
      Medieval: PN682.A7
Art in television broadcasts:
  PN1992.8.A75
Arthur and Arthurian legends in
  literature
  General
    Collections: PN6071.A84
    Literary history: PN57.A65
      Medieval: PN685+
Arthur and Arthurian legends in
  motion pictures: PN1995.9.A75
Arthur, King, in literature
  General
    Collections: PN6071.A84
    Literary history
      Legends: PN686.A7
Arthurian romances in literature
  General
    Collections
      Quotations
        English: PN6084.A83
Artisans in literature
  General
    Collections: PN6071.A85
      Wit and humor: PN6231.A7
Artists in literature
  General
    Literary history: PN56.5.A78
      Fiction: PN3426.A77
Arts
  Journalism: PN1 14.A75

Arts in literature
  General
    Collections
      Thoughts: PN6338.A78
Arts in motion pictures:
  PN1995.9.A73
Ashanti proverbs: PN6519.A8
Ashurbanipal, King of Assyria,
  in literature
  General
    Literary history: PN57.A74
Asian American actors and
  actresses: PN2286.2
Asian Americans in motion
  pictures: PN1995.9.A77
Asian Americans in television
  broadcasts: PN1992.8.A78
Asians in motion pictures:
  PN1995.9.A78
Assamese proverbs: PN6519.A85
Assamese riddles: PN6377.A87
Assertiveness (Psychology) in
  literature
  General
    Collections
      Wit and humor: PN6231.A72
Assyro-Babylonian proverbs:
  PN6418.5.A8
Astrology in literature
  General
    Collections
      Wit and humor: PN6231.A73
    Literary history: PN56.A77
Astronautics
  Journalism: PN1 14.A78
Astronautics in literature
  General
    Collections
      Poetry: PN6110.A88
    Literary history: PN56.A8
Astronomy in literature
  General
    Literary history: PN56.A82
Asu proverbs: PN6519.A87
Atheism in literature
  General
    Collections: PN6071.A87

Atheism in literature
  General
    Collections
      Proverbs: PN6525.A8
Attila in literature
  General
    Literary history: PN57.A8
Audiences
  Children: PN3157
  Motion pictures: PN1995.9.A8
  Oratory: PN4135
  Performing arts: PN1590.A9
  Theater: PN2193.A8
    French: PN2622.A8
    German: PN2642.A84
    United States: PN2270.A89
Audiovisual aids
  Journalism: PN4788
  Literature: PN61.5
    Drama: PN1701.5
  Motion pictures: PN1993.75
  Oratory: PN4088
Auditions and auditioning
  Acting: PN2071.A92
Auditions and auditioning
  (Acting)
  Motion pictures: PN1995.9.A26
  Television: PN1992.8.A3
Aunts in literature
  General
    Collections
      Aphorisms: PN6278.A87
    Literary history: PN56.A85
Australia in literature
  General
    Collections
      Wit and humor: PN6231.A76
    Literary history: PN56.3.A9
Australia, Literature of
  Literary history: PN849.A95+
Australian aborigines
  Journalism: PN1 14.A83
Australian football in literature
  General
    Collections
      Wit and humor: PN6231.A762

Austria
  Journalism
    By region or country: PN1
      14.A84
Austria in literature
  General
    Collections
      Wit and humor: PN6231.A764
Auteur theory in motion
  pictures: PN1995.9.A837
Authority in literature
  General
    Literary history: PN56.A87
    Juvenile literature:
      PN1009.5.A94
Authors and publishers
  General
    Literary history: PN155
Authors in literature
  General
    Collections: PN6071.A9
      Anecdotes: PN6268.A8
    Literary history: PN56.5.A84
      Medieval: PN682.A88
Authors in motion pictures:
  PN1995.9.A84
Authorship
  Broadcasting: PN1990.9.A88
    Radio broadcasts: PN1991.7+
    Television broadcasts:
      PN1992.7
  Journalism: PN1 14.A85
  Literature
    General
      Collections
        Wit and humor: PN6231.A77
      Literary history: PN101+
        Children's literature:
          PN497
        Poetry: PN1059.A9
        Prose: PN3355+
        Wit and humor: PN6149.A88
  Motion pictures: PN1996
Autobiographical fiction
  General
    Literary history: PN3448.A8

Autobiography in literature
  General
    Literary history: PN56.A89
Automata in literature
  General
    Collections: PN6071.A94
    Literary history: PN56.A9
Automobile travel in literature
  General
    Collections
      Wit and humor: PN6231.A8
Automobiles in literature
  General
    Collections: PN6071.A95
      Quotations
        German: PN6093.A9
      Wit and humor: PN6231.A8
Automobiles in motion pictures:
  PN1995.9.A85
Automotive journalism:
  PN4784.A94
Autumn in literature
  General
    Collections: PN6071.A97
Avant-garde films: PN1995.9.E96
Avant-garde poetry: PN1059.E94
Avant-garde theater: PN2193.E86
Avarice in literature
  General
    Collections
      Drama: PN6120.A9
Awadhi proverbs: PN6519.A88
Awards, prizes, etc.
  Journalism: PN1 14.A87
    United States: PN4888.A87
  Motion pictures: PN1993.9+
  Theater
    Great Britain: PN2595.15
    United States: PN2270.A93
Azerbaijani proverbs: PN6519.A9
Azerbaijani quotations:
  PN6095.A9
Azerbaijani riddles: PN6377.A9

B

Babel, Tower of, in literature
  General
    Collections: PN6071.B23
    Literary history: PN56.B23
Baby boom generation in
  literature
  General
    Collections
      Wit and humor: PN6231.B22
Baby sitters in literature
  General
    Collections
      Wit and humor: PN6231.B24
Bachelors in literature
  General
    Collections
      Wit and humor: PN6231.B25
Bahai authors
  General
    Collections
      Poetry: PN6109.95.B34
Bahamas in literature
  General
    Collections
      Wit and humor: PN6231.B26
Bahamians in literature
  General
    Collections
      Wit and humor: PN6231.B26
Bakundu proverbs: PN6519.B26
Baldness in literature
  General
    Collections
      Wit and humor: PN6231.B27
Balgansang (Legendary
  character) in literature
  General
    Collections
      Wit and humor: PN6231.B28
Balin and Balan in literature
  General
    Literary history
      Legends: PN686.B3
Balinese proverbs: PN6519.B27

Balkan Peninsula, Literature of
  Literary history: PN849.B3+
Balkan proverbs: PN6505.B17
Ballads: PN1471
  General
    Collections: PN6110.B2
    Literary history: PN1376
Ballets in literature
  General
    Collections
      Drama: PN6120.B3
Balloons in literature
  General
    Literary history: PN56.B27
Baltic proverbs: PN6505.B18
Baltic-Finnic proverbs:
  PN6505.B19
Baluchi proverbs: PN0510.B28
Bambara proverbs: PN6519.B3
Bamileke proverbs: PN6519.B315
Bamun proverbs: PN6519.B32
Bangaru proverbs: PN6519.B326
Banks and banking in literature
  General
    Collections
      Wit and humor: PN6231.B3
Banks in literature
  General
    Collections
      Anecdotes: PN6268.B3
Banquet quotations
  General
    Collections
      English: PN6084.B3
Bantu proverbs: PN6519.B33
Baoulé proverbs: PN6519.B34
Barbers in literature
  General
    Collections
      Wit and humor: PN6231.B32
Barbie dolls in literature
  General
    Collections
      Wit and humor: PN6231.B324
Barlaam and Joasaph in literature
  General
    Literary history: PN57.B25

Barn theater
  United States: PN2269
Baroque literature
  General
    Literary history: PN56.B3
Barrel organs in literature
  General
    Collections: PN6071.B3
      Poetry: PN6110.B25
Bartang proverbs: PN6519.B36
Bartenders in literature
  General
    Collections
      Wit and humor: PN6231.B33
Baseball films: PN1995.9.B28
Baseball in literature
  General
    Collections
      Quotations
        English: PN6084.B35
      Wit and humor: PN6231.B35
Bashkir proverbs: PN6519.B37
Basque proverbs: PN6505.B2
Basque provinces in literature
  General
    Literary history: PN56.3.B3
Basques in literature
  General
    Literary history: PN56.3.B3
    Romance literatures:
      PN810.B3
Basques in motion pictures:
  PN1995.9.B29
Bassari (Togo and Ghana)
  proverbs: PN6519.T58
Batak proverbs: PN6519.B374
Bathing in literature
  General
    Collections
      Wit and humor: PN6231.B38
Baths in motion pictures:
  PN1995.9.B3
Bati proverbs: PN6519.B375
Baule proverbs: PN6519.B34

Bavaria in literature
  General
    Collections
      Wit and humor: PN6231.B39
Beads in literature
  General
    Collections
      Wit and humor: PN6231.B396
Beans in literature
  General
    Collections: PN6071.B34
Beards in literature
  General
    Collections
      Wit and humor: PN6231.B4
Bears in literature
  General
    Collections
      Wit and humor: PN6231.B42
Beatrix Sacrista in literature
  General
    Literary history: PN57.B3
Beauty in literature
  General
    Collections: PN6071.B36
Beauty, Personal
  Journalism: PN1 14.B42
Beauty, Personal, in motion
  pictures: PN1995.9.B42
Beds in literature
  General
    Collections: PN6071.B38
Beer in literature
  General
    Collections
      Anecdotes: PN6268.B4
      Wit and humor: PN6231.B43
Bees in literature
  General
    Collections
      Poetry: PN6110.B28
Belarusian riddles: PN6377.B37
Belisarius in literature
  General
    Literary history: PN57.B4

Bells in literature
  General
    Collections
      Poetry: PN6110.B3
Belly and the members
  General
    Literature: PN995.B44
Bemba proverbs: PN6519.B4
Benefit performances
  Theater
    Great Britain: PN2582.B4
Bengali proverbs: PN6519.B42
Bengali quotations: PN6095.B3
Bengali riddles: PN6377.B4
Bengbengxi (Folk dramas):
  PN2874.5.P56
Berber proverbs: PN6519.B44
Berenice in literature
  General
    Literary history: PN57.B47
Berlin (Germany) in literature
  General
    Collections: PN6071.B42
    Literary history: PN56.3.B4
Berlin (Germany) in motion
  pictures: PN1995.9.B47
Bestiaries in literature
  General
    Collections
      Proverbs: PN6525.A6
Beti proverbs: PN6519.E96
Beverages in literature
  General
    Collections: PN6071.B43
Bhili proverbs: PN6519.B48
Bhojpuri proverbs: PN6519.B5
Biak proverbs: PN6519.B55
Bible films: PN1995.9.B53
Bible in literature
  General
    Collections: PN6071.B5
      Poetry: PN6110.B38
      Wit and humor: PN6231.B45
    Literary history: PN56.B5
      Drama: PN1650.B53
      Prose: PN3352.B53

Bibliographical citations
  Authorship citations:
   PN171.F56
Bicycles in literature
  General
    Collections: PN6071.C95
      Wit and humor: PN6231.C92
Bicycling in literature
  General
    Collections
      Poetry: PN6110.B4
Bihari proverbs: PN6519.B57
Bihari riddles: PN6377.B53
Biker films: PN1995.9.M66
Bildungsroman
  General
    Literary history: PN3448.B54
Bilingualism
  authorship: PN171.M93
Bini proverbs: PN6519.B59
Biographical films: PN1995.9.B55
Biographical speeches: PN4193.B6
Biographies in literature
  General
    Collections
      Wit and humor: PN6231.B457
Birds in literature
  General
    Collections: PN6071.B55
      Poetry: PN6110.B6
      Quotations
        English: PN6084.B48
      Wit and humor: PN6231.B46
    Literary history: PN56.B56
      Poetry: PN1083.B5
Birth control
  Journalism
    United States: PN4888.B57
Birthdays in literature
  General
    Collections
      Poetry: PN6110.B65
      Quotations
        English: PN6084.B5
        German: PN6093.B5
Bisexuality in motion pictures:
  PN1995.9.B57

Black authors
  General
    Collections: PN6068
      Drama: PN6119.7
      Fiction: PN6120.92.B45
      Poetry: PN6109.7
      Quotations
        English: PN6081.3
    Literary history
      Biography: PN490
Black box theaters: PN1979.B57
Black literature (General):
  PN841
Black poetry
  Indexes: PN1025
Black press: PN1 14.B55
Black recitations: PN4305.N5
Blackface
  Acting: PN2071.B58
Blacklisting of entertainers
  Performing arts: PN1590.B5
Blacks in literature
  General
    Collections: PN6071.B57
      Drama: PN6120.N4
      Wit and humor: PN6231.N5
    Literary history: PN56.3.B55
      Poetry: PN1083.B55
      Prose: PN3423
      Recitations: PN4305.N5
Blacks in motion pictures:
  PN1995.9.N4
Blacks in radio broadcasts:
  PN1991.8.A35
Blacks in television broadcasts:
  PN1992.8.A34
Blacks in the performing arts:
  PN1590.B53
Blind authors
  General
    Literary history: PN491
Blindness in literature
  General
    Collections
      Poetry: PN6110.B68
    Literary history: PN56.B6

Blood in literature
  General
    Literary history
      Medieval: PN682.B56
Blue glass in literature
  General
    Collections
      Wit and humor: PN6231.B5
Bluebeard in literature
  General
    Literary history: PN57.B55
Blunders
  Authorship: PN171.E8
Boastfulness in comedies:
  PN1929.B6
Boats and boating in literature
  General
    Collections: PN6071.B65
      Quotations
        German: PN6093.B6
      Wit and humor: PN6231.B6
Body and soul in literature
  General
    Literary history
      Legends: PN687.B6
      Medieval: PN682.B63
Body, Human, in literature
  General
    Collections: PN6110.B75
Body, Human, in motion pictures:
  PN1995.9.B62
Body, Human, in television
  broadcasts: PN1992.8.B64
Bogotá (Colombia) in motion
  pictures: PN1995.9.B63
Bohemian Club of San Francisco:
  PN3166.S3
Bohemian proverbs: PN6505.S3
Bon mots: PN6319+
Bondage (Sexual behavior) in
  motion pictures: PN1995.9.B64
Book review programs
  Radio broadcasts: PN1991.8.B66
Book reviewing: PN98.B7

Books and reading in literature
  General
    Literary history
      Medieval: PN682.B65
Books in literature
  General
    Collections: PN6071.B7
      Anecdotes: PN6268.B6
      Aphorisms: PN6278.B6
      Quotations
        English: PN6084.B65
      Wit and humor: PN6231.B62
    Literary history: PN56.B64
Boredom in literature
  General
    Collections
      Wit and humor: PN6231.B63
    Literary history: PN56.B7
Borges, Jorge Luis, in literature
  General
    Collections: PN6071.B72
Boundaries in literature
  General
    Literary history: PN56.B74
Bowery Boys films: PN1995.9.B68
Bowling in literature
  General
    Collections
      Wit and humor: PN6231.B65
Boxing in literature
  General
    Collections: PN6071.B73
    Poetry: PN6110.B66
Boy actors
  Great Britain
    Renaissance theater:
      PN2590.B6
Boys in literature
  General
    Collections
      Poetry: PN6110.B8
Brahui proverbs: PN6519.B7
Bran, son of Llyr, in literature
  General
    Literary history
      Legends: PN686.B65

Brancusi, Constantin, in
   literature
   General
      Collections: PN6071.B75
Brazil in motion pictures:
   PN1995.9.B72
Bread in literature
   General
      Collections
         Proverbs: PN6525.B73
Breasts in literature
   General
      Collections
         Wit and humor: PN6231.B67
Breathing
   Acting: PN2071.B74
Brigands and robbers in
   literature
   General
      Collections: PN6071.B76
Broadcast journalism:
   PN4784.B75, PN1 14.B75
   United States: PN4888.B74
Broadcasting: PN1990+
Broadcasts, Television
   Communication: PN1992+
Brocêliande in literature
   General
      Literary history
         Legends: PN686.B68
Brooklyn in motion pictures:
   PN1995.9.B76
Brotherhood in literature
   General
      Collections
         Poetry: PN6110.B85
Brotherliness in literature
   General
      Collections
         Quotations
            English: PN6084.B7
Brothers and sisters in
   literature
   General
      Collections
         Wit and humor: PN6231.S5486
      Literary history: PN56.5.B74

Brothers in literature
   General
      Collections: PN6071.B78
Bruges (Belgium) in literature
   General
      Collections: PN6071.B8
Bubble wrap in literature
   General
      Collections
         Wit and humor: PN6231.B69
Bucolic poetry
   General
      Literary history: PN1421
Buginese proverbs: PN6519.B77
Building in literature
   General
      Collections
         Wit and humor: PN6231.B7
Bulgaria in literature
   General
      Literary history: PN56.3.B84
Bulgarian proverbs: PN6505.S33
Bulgarian quotations: PN6095.B8
Bulgarian riddles: PN6377.B8
Bullfights in literature
   General
      Collections: PN6071.B84
         Poetry: PN6110.B88
         Wit and humor: PN6231.B78
Bullfights in motion pictures:
   PN1995.9.B8
Bulls and blunders in literature
   General
      Collections
         Wit and humor: PN6231.B8
Bulls in literature
   General
      Collections
         Poetry: PN6110.B88
Bundling in literature
   General
      Collections
         Wit and humor: PN6231.B83
Bungee jumping in literature
   General
      Collections
         Wit and humor: PN6231.B834

Bureaucracy in motion pictures:
  PN1995.9.B85
Buriat riddles: PN6377.B82
Burlesque
  General
    Collections: PN6149.B8
      Wit and humor: PN6231.B84
    Literary history: PN1942+
Burmese proverbs: PN6519.B8
Burmese quotations: PN6095.B86
Buryat proverbs: PN6519.B86
Business in literature
  General
    Collections: PN6071.B86
      Poetry: PN6110.B9
      Quotations
        English: PN6084.B87
      Wit and humor: PN6231.B85
Business in motion pictures:
  PN1995.9.B87
Business journalism: PN4784.C7
Business speeches: PN4193.B8
Businessmen in literature
  General
    Literary history: PN56.5.B88
Businessmen in television
  broadcasts: PN1992.8.B87
Businesspeople
  Oratory: PN4192.B87
Butterflies in literature
  General
    Collections: PN6071.B88
Buttocks in literature
  General
    Collections
      Wit and humor: PN6231.B87

C

Cabaret shows: PN1969.C3
Cabbage Patch Kids dolls in
  literature
  General
    Collections
      Wit and humor: PN6231.C14

Cable dispatches
  Journalism
    United States: PN4888.C4
Caesar in literature
  General
    Literary history: PN57.C2
Café chantant shows: PN1969.C34
Cain in literature
  General
    Literary history: PN57.C25
Calabria (Italy) in motion
  pictures: PN1995.9.C32
California in literature
  General
    Collections
      Wit and humor: PN6231.C16
Callisto in literature
  General
    Literary history: PN57.C27
Camp (Army) newspapers:
  PN4888.M54
Camping and amateur theater:
  PN3160.C34
Camping in literature
  General
    Collections
      Drama: PN6120.C3
Camps in literature
  General
    Collections
      Wit and humor: PN6231.C18
Canada in literature
  General
    Collections
      Quotations
        English: PN6084.C15
      Wit and humor: PN6231.C19
Canada in motion pictures:
  PN1995.9.C33
Canada, Literature of
  Literary history: PN849.C28+
Canards: PN1 14.C35
Cannibalism in literature
  General
    Literary history: PN56.C34
Cannibalism in motion pictures:
  PN1995.9.C332

Cantos: PN1475
Cape Cod (Mass.) in literature
General
Collections
Quotations
English: PN6084.C17
Cape Verde Creole riddles:
PN6377.C35
Capitalism in literature
General
Collections
Wit and humor: PN6231.C195
Captivity in motion pictures:
PN1995.9.C333
Card games in literature
General
Collections
Wit and humor. PN6231.C2
Cards, Greeting
Authorship: PN171.G74
Caribbean Area
Journalism
United States: PN4888.C47
Caribbean Area in literature
General
Collections: PN6071.C27
Caribbean Area, Literature of
Literary history: PN849.C3+
Caricatures and cartoons in
French theater: PN2622.C37
Carlos, Prince of Asturias, in
literature
General
Literary history: PN57.C3
Carmen in literature
General
Literary history: PN57.C33
Carnival in literature
General
Literary history
Prose: PN3352.C37
Carols in literature
General
Collections
Poetry: PN6110.C28
Carry on films: PN1995.9.C335

Carter family in literature
General
Collections
Wit and humor: PN6231.C215
Cartoon captions
Authorship: PN171.C3
Cartoons, Motion picture
Plays, scenarios, etc.:
PN1997.5
Cassandra in literature
General
Literary history: PN57.C38
Casting
Broadcasting
Television: PN1992.8.C36
Motion pictures: PN1995.9.C34
The theater: PN2293.C38
Castles in literature
General
Literary history
Medieval: PN682.C3
Castration in literature
General
Literary history: PN56.C36
Castro, Ines de, in literature
General
Literary history: PN57.C39
Catalan proverbs: PN6505.C2
Catalan quotations: PN6095.C37
Catalan riddles: PN6377.C37
Catholic authors
General
Collections
Fiction: PN6120.92.C38
Poetry: PN6109.3
Literary history: PN485
Catholic Church in motion
pictures: PN1995.9.C35
Catholic influence in
literature: PN605.C2
Medieval literature: PN682.C2
Catholic press: PN4784.C3, PN1
14.C4
United States: PN4888.C5

Catholics and Catholicism in
  literature
  General
    Collections
      Quotations
        English: PN6084.C2
      Wit and humor: PN6231.C22
    Recitations: PN4305.C3
Catholics in motion pictures:
  PN1995.9.C35
Cats in literature
  General
    Collections: PN6071.C3
      Aphorisms: PN6278.C36
      Poetry: PN6110.C3
      Quotations
        English: PN6084.C23
      Wit and humor: PN6231.C23
    Literary history: PN56.C37
Cattle in literature
  General
    Collections
      Wit and humor: PN6231.C24
Causation in literature
  General
    Literary history: PN56.C38
Caves in literature
  General
    Literary history: PN56.C39
Celebrities in literature
  General
    Collections
      Quotations
        English: PN6084.C44
      Wit and humor: PN6231.C25
Cellular telephones in literature
  General
    Collections
      Wit and humor: PN6231.C255
Celtic proverbs: PN6505.C3+
Censorship in literature
  General
    Collections
      Wit and humor: PN6231.C265
    Literary history: PN156
Censorship in motion pictures:
  PN1995.6+

Censorship in the theater:
  PN2042+
Centers for the performing arts:
  PN1585+
Central America in literature
  General
    Collections: PN6071.C37
Chairs in literature
  General
    Collections: PN6071.C43
Chakma proverbs: PN6519.C44
Cham proverbs: PN6519.C444
Chamber theater
  Oratory: PN4148
Champagne (Wine) in literature
  General
    Collections: PN6071.C437
Chan, Charlie, films:
  PN1995.9.C37
Chance in literature
  General
    Collections
      Maxims: PN6308.C5
    Literary history: PN56.C43
Change in literature
  General
    Literary history: PN56.C44
Chant royal: PN1479
Chapbooks
  General
    Literary history: PN970+
Character sketches
  General
    Collections: PN6071.C44
Characters and characteristics
  in literature
  General
    Literary history: PN56.4+
      Drama: PN1689
        Comedies: PN1929.C4
      Invention of: PN218
      Juvenile literature:
        PN1009.5.C43
      Medieval: PN682.C5
      Poetry: PN1103
      Prose: PN3383.C4

Characters and characteristics
  in motion pictures:
  PN1995.9.C36
Charades
  General
    Collections: PN6366+
Charadrius in literature
  General
    Literary history: PN57.C45
Charity in literature
  General
    Collections
      Quotations
        English: PN6084.C46
Charlemagne in literature
  General
    Literary history: PN57.C48
      Legends: PN687.C5
Charlie Chan films: PN1995.9.C37
Cheating (Education) in
  literature
  General
    Collections
      Wit and humor: PN6231.C28
Cheerfulness in literature
  General
    Collections
      Poetry: PN6110.C36
Cheese in literature
  General
    Collections
      Wit and humor: PN6231.C284
Chess in literature
  General
    Collections: PN6071.C45
    Literary history: PN56.C47
Chewa proverbs: PN6519.C47
Chiasm (Rhetoric)
  Literary style: PN228.C45
Chiasmus
  Literary style: PN228.C45
Chicano theater: PN2270.M48
Chickens in literature
  General
    Collections
      Wit and humor: PN6231.C29

Child authors
  General
    Collections: PN6066
    Literary history: PN171.C5
Child care in literature
  General
    Collections
      Wit and humor: PN6231.C3
Child rearing in literature
  General
    Collections
      Quotations
        English: PN6084.C48
      Wit and humor: PN6231.C315
Child sexual abuse in motion
  pictures: PN1995.9.C39
Childbirth in literature
  General
    Literary history: PN56.C49
Childhood in literature
  General
    Collections
      Quotations
        English: PN6084.C49
Childhood in motion pictures:
  PN1995.9.C4
Children and adolescents in
  motion pictures: PN1995.9.C45
Children and motion pictures:
  PN1995.9.C45
Children and poetry: PN1085
Children and the performing
  arts: PN1590.C45
Children in literature
  General
    Collections: PN6071.C5
      Anecdotes: PN6268.C45
      Poetry: PN6110.C4
      Quotations
        English: PN6084.C5
        German: PN6093.C5
      Thoughts: PN6338.C5
      Wit and humor: PN6231.C32
    Literary history: PN56.5.C48
      Fiction: PN3426.C5

Children of Paul's
  Renaissance theater:
    PN2590.C45
Children, Plays for
  General
    Collections: PN6119.9
Children with disabilities in
  literature
  General
    Literary history
      Juvenile literature:
        PN1009.5.C44
Children's epitaphs: PN6298.C5
Children's periodicals: PN4835,
  PN1 14.J8
Children's plays, Presentation
  of: PN3157+
Children's poetry: PN6109.97
  Indexes: PN1023
Children's programs
  Broadcasting: PN1990.9.C45
    Radio broadcasts:
      PN1991.8.C45
    Television: PN1992.8.C46
Children's sayings
  General: PN6328.C5
Children's theater
  General: PN3157+
Children's voices
  Oratory: PN4163.C5
China
  Journalism
    United States: PN4888.C54
China in literature
  General
    Collections: PN6071.C54
China in motion pictures:
  PN1995.9.C47
Chinese proverbs: PN6519.C5
Chinese quotations: PN6095.C4
Chinese riddles: PN6377.C5
Chinese-American newspapers:
  PN4885.C5
Chivalry in literature
  General
    Literary history: PN56.C53
      Medieval: PN682.C53

Chocolate in literature
  General
    Collections
      Wit and humor: PN6231.C33
Chokwe proverbs: PN6519.C53
Choral recitations: PN4305.C4
Choral speaking: PN4193.C5
Christian literature
  General
    Literary history
      Early: PN640+
      Fiction: PN3448.C48
      Prose
        Technique: PN3377.5.C47
Christian symbolism in literature
  General
    Literary history
      Drama: PN1650.C48
Christianity in literature
  General
    Collections
      Wit and humor: PN6231.C35
    Literary history
      Juvenile literature:
        PN1009.5.C45
Christmas entertainments
  Pantomime: PN1988.C57
Christmas in literature
  General
    Collections: PN6071.C6
      Drama: PN6120.C5
        Pantomimes: PN6120.P4
      Poetry: PN6110.C5
      Quotations
        English: PN6084.C52
      Wit and humor: PN6231.C36
    Literary history: PN1431
Christmas in motion pictures:
  PN1995.9.C5113
Christmas letters: PN6140.C5
Christmas recitations: PN4305.C5
Church and drama: PN1649
Church leaders
  Oratory: PN4192.C45

Church of England in literature
  General
    Collections
      Wit and humor: PN6231.C367
Church year in literature
  General
    Collections
      Wit and humor: PN6231.C37
Chuvash proverbs: PN6519.C55
Cid in literature
  General
    Collections: PN6071.C62
    Literary history: PN57.C5
    Legends: PN687.C55
Cigars in literature
  General
    Collections
      Quotations
        English: PN6084.C524
Circassian proverbs: PN6505.C75
Circe in literature
  General
    Literary history: PN57.C52
Circuits, Theater: PN2291
Circulation
  Journalism: PN4784.C6, PN1
  14.C5
    United States: PN4888.C56
Circus
  Theater: PN2193.C57
Circus in literature
  General
    Collections: PN6071.C63
      Wit and humor: PN6231.C45
Circus in motion pictures:
  PN1995.9.C512
Cisco Kid in motion pictures:
  PN1995.9.C5125
Cities and towns in literature
  General
    Literary history: PN56.C55
    Drama: PN1650.C57
    Medieval: PN682.C54
    Prose: PN3352.C5
Cities and towns in motion
  pictures: PN1995.9.C513

City and town life in literature
  General
    Collections
      Poetry: PN6110.C55
      Wit and humor: PN6231.C455
City editor
  Journalism: PN4784.C62
Civil service in literature
  General
    Collections
      Quotations
        English: PN6084.C53
Civilization in literature
  General
    Collections
      Wit and humor: PN6231.C46
Classicism in literature
  General
    Literary history: PN56.C6
Cleopatra in literature
  General
    Literary history: PN57.C55
Clergy in literature
  General
    Collections
      Anecdotes: PN6268.C5
      Wit and humor: PN6231.C5
    Literary history: PN56.5.C5
Clergy in motion pictures:
  PN1995.9.C52
Climate in literature
  General
    Literary history: PN56.C612
Clinton, Chelsea, in literature
  General
    Collections
      Wit and humor: PN6231.C53
Clocks and watches in literature
  General
    Collections
      Poetry: PN6110.C57
Closings (Rhetoric) in literature
  General
    Collections
      Quotations
        German: PN6093.C56

Closure in literature
General
Literary history
Prose: PN3383.C55
Closure (Rhetoric) in comedies:
PN1929.C5
Clothing and dress in literature
General
Collections
Poetry: PN6110.C59
Quotations
English: PN6084.C535
Clothing on television:
PN1992.8.P4
Clothing trade in literature
General
Collections
Wit and humor: PN6231.C55
Clowns
Drama: PN1955
Clowns in literature
General
Collections
Wit and humor: PN6231.C554
Literary history
Drama: PN1650.C59
Club recitations: PN4305.C6
Clytemnestra in literature
General
Literary history: PN57.C57
Coach, The
Journalism: PN4784.C63
Coaches
Oratory: PN4192.C63
Coaching (Athletics) in
literature
General
Collections
Quotations
English: PN6084.C54
Cockaigne in literature
General
Literary history: PN56.C614
Cockayne in literature
General
Literary history: PN56.C614

Cockroaches in literature
General
Collections
Wit and humor: PN6231.C56
Codependency in literature
General
Collections
Wit and humor: PN6231.C563
Codfish in literature
General
Collections: PN6071.C66
Coffee in literature
General
Collections
Wit and humor: PN6231.C565
Colds in literature
General
Collections
Wit and humor: PN6231.C57
Collectibles
Motion pictures: PN1995.9.C53
Television broadcasts:
PN1992.8.C64
Collectors and collecting
Journalism
United States: PN4888.C57
Collectors and collecting in
literature
General
Collections
Wit and humor: PN6231.C58
Collectors and collecting of
motion pictures: PN1995.9.C54
Collectors and collecting of
theatrical paraphernalia:
PN1590.C6
College in literature
General
Collections
Wit and humor: PN6231.C6
College life films:
PN1995.9.C543
College plays
General
Collections: PN6120.C6
College recitations: PN4305.C7
College theatricals: PN3175+

College verse
  General
    Collections: PN6110.C7
Colombia
  Journalism: PN4784.C64
Colonies in literature
  General
    Literary history: PN56.C63
Color in literature
  General
    Literary history: PN56.C65
Columbus, Christopher, in
  literature
  General
    Collections
      Wit and humor: PN6231.C6114
    Literary history: PN57.C6
      Poetry: PN1083.C64
Column writing
  Journalism: PN4784.C65
Comedy
  Acting: PN2071.C57
Comedy acts: PN1969.C65
Comedy in literature
  General
    Literary history
      Drama: PN1922+
Comedy in motion pictures:
  PN1995.9.C55
Comedy programs
  Radio broadcasts: PN1991.8.C65
  Television broadcasts:
    PN1992.8.C66
Comic books, strips, etc.
  General
    Collections: PN6700+
Comic characters in literature
  General
    Literary history: PN56.5.C65
Comic, The, in literature
  General
    Literary history: PN56.C66
      Prose: PN3352.C6
Command performances
  Theater
    Great Britain: PN2582.K55

Commencement addresses
  General
    Collections: PN4305.C7
Commercial journalism:
  PN4784.C7, PN1 14.C57
  United States: PN4888.C59
Committees in literature
  General
    Collections
      Wit and humor: PN6231.C6117
Commonplace books: PN6244+
Commonwealth of Nations,
  Literature of
    Literary history: PN849.C5+
Communication in journalism:
  PN4729+
Communication in literature
  General
    Literary history: PN56.C662
Communism in literature
  General
    Collections
      Poetry: PN6110.C75
      Wit and humor: PN6231.C612
    Literary history
      Juvenile literature:
        PN1009.5.C65
Communist countries, Literature
  of
    Literary history: PN849.C6+
Communist press: PN4784.C72,
  PN1 14.C6
  United States: PN4888.C593
Communists as critics: PN98.C6
Community newspapers:
  PN4784.C73, PN1 14.C63
  United States: PN4888.C594
Community theater
  United States: PN2267
Commuting in literature
  General
    Collections
      Wit and humor: PN6231.C614
Comorian riddles: PN6377.C65
Comparative literature
  General: PN851+

Competitions
  College theatricals: PN3178.C6
  Journalism: PN4798
  Motion pictures: PN1993.9+
  Oratory: PN4076
Compliments in literature
  General
    Collections
      Quotations
        English: PN6084.C55
Composers in motion pictures:
  PN1995.9.C553
Composition, Literary: PN171.4+
Computer network resources
  Acting: PN2071.C58
  Authorship: PN142.5
  Journalism: PN4729.3
Computer poetry: PN1059.C6
Computer-produced fiction
  General
    Literary history
      Technique: PN3377.5.C57
Computers in literature
  General
    Collections
      Wit and humor: PN6231.E4
Concentration camps in literature
  General
    Literary history: PN56.C663
Concrete poetry
  General
    Collections: PN6110.C77
    Literary history: PN1455
Condensed books
  Collections
    English: PN6013.5
Conduct of life in literature
  General
    Collections
      Quotations
        English: PN6084.C556
      Wit and humor: PN6231.C6142
Confession in literature
  General
    Literary history: PN56.C67
      Medieval: PN682.C58
      Prose: PN3377.5.C6

Conflict of generations in
  literature
  General
    Collections
      Drama: PN6120.C65
Conformity in literature
  General
    Collections
      Wit and humor: PN6231.C6143
Congo (Brazzaville) proverbs:
  PN6519.C62
Congolese proverbs: PN6519.K59
Conscience in literature
  General
    Literary history: PN56.C674
Conservatism: PN1 14.C64
Conservatism in literature
  General
    Collections
      Quotations
        English: PN6084.C56
Conservatism in the press
  United States: PN4888.C598
Consolation in literature
  General
    Collections
      Quotations
        English: PN6084.C57
        German: PN6093.C6
Consumer credit in literature
  General
    Collections
      Wit and humor: PN6231.C6145
Contemporary music stations
  Radio broadcasts:
    PN1991.67.P67
Contentment in literature
  General
    Collections: PN6071.C7
      Quotations
        English: PN6084.C58
Contract bridge in literature
  General
    Collections
      Wit and humor: PN6231.C615

Contracts in literature
  General
    Collections
      Wit and humor: PN6231.C617
Contradiction in literature
  General
    Literary history: PN56.C676
Conundrums
  General
    Collections: PN6366+
Convalescence in literature
  General
    Collections
      Wit and humor: PN6231.C62
Convent theater
  School theatricals: PN3178.C64
Conversation in literature
  General
    Collections
      Maxims: PN6308.C6
Cook, James, in literature
  General
    Literary history: PN57.C64
Cookery in literature
  General
    Collections
      Poetry: PN6110.C78
      Wit and humor: PN6231.C624
Copyreading
  Journalism: PN4784.C75
Corporation reports in literature
  General
    Collections
      Wit and humor: PN6231.C63
Corpulence in literature
  General
    Collections
      Wit and humor: PN6231.C635
Correction articles
  Journalism: PN1 14.C65
Corrugated paperboard in the
  theater: PN2091.C65
Corrupt practices in the
  performing arts: PN1590.C65
Corruption of the press
  United States: PN4888.C6

Cosmogony in literature
  General
    Collections: PN6071.C76
Cosmology in literature
  General
    Literary history: PN56.C68
Cost and standard of living in
  literature
  General
    Collections
      Wit and humor: PN6231.C64
Costume design for the theater:
  PN2067
Costume for the theater: PN2067
Costume in literature
  General
    Literary history: PN56.C684
Costume in motion pictures:
  PN1995.9.C56
Country life in literature
  General
    Collections: PN6071.C8
      Poetry: PN6110.C8
      Wit and humor: PN6231.C65
    Literary history: PN56.C686
Country life in motion pictures:
  PN1995.9.C58
Country newspapers: PN4784.C77,
  PN1 14.C67
  United States: PN4888.C7
Courage in literature
  General
    Collections: PN6071.C815
      Poetry: PN6110.C85
      Quotations
        English: PN6084.C6
Court theater
  Great Britain
    Renaissance theater:
      PN2590.C66
Courtly love in literature
  General
    Literary history
      Medieval: PN682.C6

Courtship in literature
  General
    Collections
      Wit and humor: PN6231.C66
Courtship of animals in
  literature
  General
    Collections
      Wit and humor: PN6231.C67
Cowboys in literature
  General
    Collections
      Aphorisms: PN6278.C6
Cows in literature
  General
    Collections: PN6071.C82
      Wit and humor: PN6231.C24
Crazy Bones (Trademark) in
  literature
  General
    Collections
      Wit and humor: PN6231.C69
Creative ability (Literary,
  artistic, etc.) in literature
  General
    Collections: PN6071.C85
    Literary history: PN56.C69
Credit titles in motion
  pictures: PN1995.9.C65
Cremation in literature
  General
    Collections
      Wit and humor: PN6231.C7
Creole proverbs: PN6519.C8
Crime in literature
  General
    Collections
      Poetry: PN6110.C88
      Wit and humor: PN6231.C73
    Literary history: PN56.C7
    Prose: PN3352.C74
Crime journalism: PN4784.C88,
  PN1 14.C74
  United States: PN4888.C8
Crime writing
  Prose technique: PN3377.5.C75

Criminals in literature
  General
    Collections
      Poetry: PN6110.C88
      Quotations
        English: PN6084.C7
      Wit and humor: PN6231.C73
Criminology in literature
  General
    Literary history: PN56.C72
Critical writing
  Journalism: PN4784.R4
Criticism
  Oratory: PN4096
Criticism in broadcasting:
  PN1990.9.C73
  Television: PN1992.8.C7
Criticism in literature
  General
    Collections
      Wit and humor: PN6231.C75
    Literary history: PN80+
      Drama: PN1707
      Prose: PN3335
Critics, Literary
  Biography: PN149.8+
  Drama: PN1707.9+
Croatia in literature
  General
    Collections
      Wit and humor: PN6231.C78
Croatian proverbs: PN6505.S35
Cross-examination
  Debating: PN4183.C74
Crowds in literature
  General
    Collections: PN6071.C87
    Literary history
      Drama: PN1690
Cruelty in literature
  General
    Literary history
      Drama: PN1650.C78
Cruelty in motion pictures:
  PN1995.9.C7

Crusades in literature
  General
    Collections
      Poetry: PN6110.C9
    Literary history
      Poetry
        Medieval: PN690.C7
Crying in literature
  General
    Literary history: PN56.C74
Cub reporters: PN4784.C9
Cuba in literature
  General
    Literary history: PN56.3.C83
Cuckolds in literature
  General
    Literary history
      Medieval: PN682.C82
Cucurbitaooao in literature
  General
    Literary history: PN56.C83
Culture conflict in motion
  pictures: PN1995.9.C85
Cupid (Roman deity) in literature
  General
    Literary history: PN57.C85
Curiosa
  General
    Literary history: PN605.Z9
Curiosities and wonders in
  literature
  General
    Collections
      Wit and humor: PN6231.C85
Curtains in the theater:
  PN2091.C85
Cyborgs in motion pictures:
  PN1995.9.C9
Cycles in literature
  General
    Poetry: PN1059.C9
Cycling in literature
  General
    Collections: PN6071.C95
      Quotations
        English: PN6084.C95
      Wit and humor: PN6231.C92

Czech proverbs: PN6505.S3
Czech quotations: PN6095.C93
Czechs in literature
  General
    Collections
      Wit and humor: PN6231.C95

D

Dagestan (Russia) in literature
  General
    Literary history: PN56.3.D35
Daghestan proverbs: PN6505.D34
Daily reading, Selections for:
  PN6075+
Dali, Salvador, in literature
  General
    Collections
      Poetry: PN6110.D33
Dance in literature
  General
    Collections: PN6071.D26
      Quotations
        English: PN6084.D34
    Literary history: PN56.D29
Dance parties, Television:
  PN1992.8.D3
Dancers in literature
  General
    Literary history: PN56.5.D32
Dandies in literature
  General
    Collections: PN6071.D28
    Literary history: PN56.5.D34
Danish quotations: PN6095.D3
Danish-American newspapers:
  PN4885.D35
Dathi, King, in literature
  General
    Literary history
      Legends: PN687.D3
Dating in literature
  General
    Collections
      Wit and humor: PN6231.D3

Daughters in literature
  General
    Collections: PN6071.D3
    Quotations
      English: PN6084.D37
David, King of Israel, in
  literature
  General
    Literary history: PN57.D38
    Legends: PN687.D33
Day in literature
  General
    Collections
    Poetry: PN6110.D35
Dead End Kids films:
  PN1995.9.B68
Deadly sins in literature
  General
    Collections: PN6071.D33
    Quotations
      English: PN6084.D39
Deaf in literature
  General
    Collections
    Wit and humor: PN6231.D33
Deaf in motion pictures:
  PN1995.9.D35
Deafness in literature
  General
    Collections: PN6071.D35
    Quotations
      English: PN6084.D394
Death and immortality in
  literature
  General
    Collections: PN6071.D4
    Anecdotes: PN6268.D35
    Poetry: PN6110.D4
    Quotations
      English: PN6084.D4
      French: PN6089.D43
    Thoughts: PN6338.D5
    Wit and humor: PN6231.D35
  Literary history: PN56.D4
    Drama: PN1650.D4
    Juvenile literature:
      PN1009.5.D43

Death and immortality in
  literature
  General
    Literary history
      Legends: PN687.D4
      Medieval: PN682.D4
Death and immortality in motion
  pictures: PN1995.9.D37
Death in television broadcasts:
  PN1992.8.D4
Debate poetry
  General
    Collections: PN6110.D43
Debating: PN4177+
Decadence (Literary movement) in
  literature
  General
    Literary history: PN56.D45
Deception in literature
  General
    Literary history: PN56.D46
Deconstruction: PN98.D43
Dedications in books
  General: PN171.D4
Defecation in literature
  General
    Collections
      Wit and humor: PN6231.D37
Defectors in literature
  General
    Collections
      Wit and humor: PN6231.D38
Delsarte system
  Oratory: PN4157
Dena'ina riddles: PN6377.D45
Dengaku: PN2924.5.D45
Dental journalism: PN4784.D4
Dentistry in literature
  General
    Collections
      Wit and humor: PN6231.D4
Dependency (Psychology) in
  literature
  General
    Literary history: PN56.D47

Depression, Mental, in literature
General
Collections
Wit and humor: PN6231.D43
Descriptive poetry
General
Literary history: PN1411
Desert in literature
General
Collections
Anecdotes: PN6268.D4
Deserts in literature
General
Literary history: PN56.D477
Design in literature
General
Collections
Quotations
English: PNC084.D16
Desire in literature
General
Literary history: PN56.D48
Drama: PN1650.D47
Destruction in literature
General
Collections
Poetry: PN6110.D45
Detective and mystery films:
PN1995.9.D4
Detective and mystery programs
Radio broadcasts: PN1991.8.D47
Television broadcasts:
PN1992.8.D48
Detective and mystery stories
General
Collections: PN6071.D45
Literary history: PN3448.D4
Technique: PN3377.5.D4
Deus ex machina in drama: PN1676
Developing countries
Journalism: PN1 14.D48
Developing countries in
literature
General
Collections: PN6071.D46

Developing countries in
literature
General
Literary history
Juvenile literature:
PN1009.5.D48
Developing countries in motion
pictures: PN1995.9.D44
Developing countries, Literature
of: PN849.U43+
Devil in literature
General
Collections: PN6071.D47
Proverbs: PN6525.D49
Literary history: PN57.D4
Legends: PN687.D47
Medieval: PN682.D48
Devil in motion pictures:
PN1995.9.D46
Dhvani in literature
General
Poetry: PN1059.D45
Dialect in literature
General
Collections
Wit and humor: PN6231.D6
Recitations: PN4305.D6
Dialogue in literature
General
Literary history
Prose: PN3383.D53
Dialogue in motion pictures:
PN1995.9.D49
Dialogues
General
Collections: PN4290+
Literary history: PN1551
Diaries
General: PN4390
Collections
Wit and humor: PN6231.D62
Dictionnaire universal des
littératures: PN41
Didactic literature
General
Collections: PN6071.D5
Poetry: PN6110.D53

Didactic literature
  General
    Literary history
      Poetry: PN1401
Dido, Queen of Carthage, in
  literature
  General
    Literary history: PN57.D5
Dieting in literature
  General
    Collections
      Wit and humor: PN6231.D64
Dietrich von Bern in literature
  General
    Literary history: PN57.D55
Digression (Rhetoric) in
  literature
  General
    Literary history: PN56.D54
Dilettantism
  Literature: PN157
Dimitrov, Georgi, in literature
  General
    Collections: PN6071.D53
Dinner theater
  United States: PN2270.D56
Dinners and dining in literature
  General
    Collections
      Wit and humor: PN6231.D647
Dinners and dining in motion
  pictures: PN1995.9.D52
Dinosaurs in literature
  General
    Collections
      Wit and humor: PN6231.D65
Dinosaurs in motion pictures:
  PN1995.9.D53
Diola proverbs: PN6519.D56
Dionysus (Greek deity) in
  literature
  General
    Literary history: PN57.D57
Diplomacy in literature
  General
    Collections
      Anecdotes: PN6268.D5

Diplomacy in literature
  General
    Collections
      Maxims: PN6308.D5
Disaster reporting: PN4784.D57,
  PN1 14.D58
  United States: PN4888.D57
Disasters in literature
  General
    Collections: PN6071.D56
      Wit and humor: PN6231.D657
Disasters in motion pictures:
  PN1995.9.D55
Disco dancing in literature
  General
    Collections
      Wit and humor: PN6231.D66
Diseases in literature
  General
    Collections: PN6071.D58
    Literary history: PN56.D56
Distributors, Newspaper and
  periodical
  United States: PN4889
District school in literature
  General
    Collections
      Drama: PN6120.D6
Divorce in literature
  General
    Collections
      Wit and humor: PN6231.D662
Divorced people in literature
  General
    Collections
      Wit and humor: PN6231.D662
Do-it-yourself in literature
  General
    Collections
      Wit and humor: PN6231.D67
Doctor Mabuse films:
  PN1995.9.D58
Documentary films: PN1995.9.D6
  Television: PN1992.8.D6
Documentary programs
  Radio broadcasts: PN1991.8.D63

Documentary-style films:
 PN1995.9.D62
Dogri proverbs: PN6519.D6
Dogs in literature
 General
  Collections: PN6071.D6
   Poetry: PN6110.D6
   Quotations
    English: PN6084.D64
    Wit and humor: PN6231.D68
  Literary history: PN56.D6
Dogs in the performing arts:
 PN1590.D63
Dogsledding in literature
 General
  Collections
   Quotations
    English: PN6084.D65
Dolphins in literature
 General
  Collections: PN6071.D64
Domestics in literature
 General
  Collections: PN6071.S414
   Wit and humor: PN6231.S53
Don Juan films: PN1995.9.D63
Don Juan in literature
 General
  Collections
   Drama: PN6120.D7
  Literary history: PN57.D7
   Drama: PN1650.D65
Donkeys and mules in literature
 General
  Collections
   Poetry: PN6110.D7
Donkeys in literature
 General
  Literary history: PN56.D64
Doors in literature
 General
  Literary history: PN56.D65
Doubles in literature
 General
  Literary history: PN56.D67

Dracula in literature
 General
  Literary history
   Legends: PN687.D7
Dracula in motion pictures:
 PN1995.9.D64
Dragons in literature
 General
  Literary history
   Medieval: PN682.D72
Drama
 General
  Collections: PN6110.5+
  Literary history: PN1600+
Drama and political science:
 PN1643
Dramatic representation: PN2000+
Dramatic schools: PN2078.A+
Dravidian proverbs: PN6519.D7
Dreams in literature
 General
  Collections: PN6071.D67
   Poetry: PN6110.D8
  Literary history: PN56.D75
  Poetry
   Medieval: PN690.D73
Dreams in motion pictures:
 PN1995.9.D67
Drifters in motion pictures:
 PN1995.9.D68
Drinking and drinking customs in
 literature
 General
  Collections: PN6071.D7
   Poetry: PN6110.D85
   Quotations
    English: PN6084.D74
    Wit and humor: PN6231.D7
  Literary history: PN56.D8
Drinking of alcoholic beverages
 in television broadcasts:
 PN1992.8.D74
Drive-in theaters in literature
 General
  Collections
   Wit and humor: PN6231.D73

Drug traffic in literature
  General
    Collections
      Wit and humor: PN6231.D77
Drugs in literature
  General
    Collections: PN6071.D77
    Literary history: PN56.D82
Drugs in motion pictures:
  PN1995.9.D78
Drunks in literature
  General
    Collections
      Wit and humor: PN6231.D7
Drury Lane
  General
    Collections: PN6120.P4
Duala proverbs: PN6519.D8
Duct tape in literature
  General
    Collections
      Wit and humor: PN6231.D79
Dueling in literature
  General
    Collections
      Wit and humor: PN6231.D8
    Literary history: PN56.D84
Dusun riddles: PN6377.D76
Dutch quotations: PN6095.D8
Dutch riddles: PN6377.D8
Dwarfs in literature
  General
    Collections
      Anecdotes: PN6268.D8
Dystopias in literature
  General
    Literary history: PN56.D94

E

East Asia in literature
  General
    Literary history: PN56.3.E37
Easter in literature
  General
    Collections: PN6071.E2
     Drama: PN6120.E2

Easter in literature
  General
    Collections
     Poetry: PN6110.E2
     Recitations: PN4305.E2
Eastside Kids films:
  PN1995.9.B68
Eccentric literature
  General
    Authorship: PN171.E3
    Collections: PN6110.E4
    Literary history: PN605.Z9
Eccentrics and eccentricities in
  literature
  General
    Collections
     Quotations
      English: PN6084.E34
     Wit and humor: PN6231.E29
Echo verse: PN1525
Ecocriticism
  Literary criticism: PN98.E36
Economic conditions and drama:
  PN1643
Economic journalism: PN4784.C7
Economics and drama: PN1643
Economics and literature: PN51
Economics and poetry: PN1082
Economics and prose
  Prose: PN3352.E2
Economics in literature
  General
    Collections
     Quotations
      English: PN6084.E36
      German: PN6093.E35
     Wit and humor: PN6231.E295
Economics of the theater:
  PN2293.E35
   English theater: PN2599.5.E25
   French theater: PN2639.5.E35
   German theater: PN2659.5.E35
Ecstasy in literature
  General
    Literary history: PN56.E27

Edison in literature
  General
    Collections
      Wit and humor: PN6231.E3
Editing
  Journalism: PN1 14.E34
  Poetry: PN1059.E35
Editing of books and
  manuscripts: PN162
Editor, The
  Journalism: PN4778
Editorials: PN4784.E28
Education and literature: PN52
Education and prose: PN3352.E38
Education in literature
  General
    Collections
      Proverbs: PN6525.E3
      Quotations
        English: PN6084.E38
Educational journalism:
  PN4784.E3, PN1 14.E38
  United States: PN4888.E3
Educational puppetry: PN1979.E4
Efik proverbs: PN6519.E33
Eginhard and Emma in literature
  General
    Literary history
      Legends: PN687.E4
Egoism in literature
  General
    Collections
      Wit and humor: PN6231.E35
Egypt, Literature of
  Literary history: PN849.E38+
Egyptian proverbs: PN6519.E35
  Ancient: PN6418.5.E35
Ekphrasis in literature
  General
    Literary history: PN56.E45
Electra in literature
  General
    Collections
      Drama: PN6120.E43
    Literary history: PN57.E4
Electric devices in the theater:
  PN2091.E4

Electronic data processing
  Authorship: PN171.D37
  Journalism: PN4784.E5, PN1
    14.D38
Electronic data processing in
  literary criticism: PN98.E4
Electronic data processing in
  literature
  General
    Collections
      Wit and humor: PN6231.E4
Electronic data processing in
  the performing arts:
  PN1590.D37
Electronic information sources
  Authorship citations:
    PN171.F56
Electronic journals: PN4833
  United States: PN4878.1
Electronic news gathering:
  PN4784.E53
Elegies
  General
    Literary history: PN1389
Elephants in literature
  General
    Collections: PN6071.E4
      Wit and humor: PN6231.E5
Elocution: PN4001+
Embarrassment in literature
  General
    Collections: PN6071.E44
Emblems in literature
  General
    Collections: PN6348.5+
    Literary history: PN56.E57
Emigration and immigration in
  literature
  General
    Collections: PN6071.E46
Emigration in motion pictures:
  PN1995.9.E44
Eminescu, Mihail, in literature
  General
    Collections
      Poetry: PN6110.E47

Emma and Eginhard in literature
  General
    Literary history
      Legends: PN687.E4
Emotions in literature
  General
    Collections
      Poetry: PN6110.E5
    Literary history: PN56.E6
    Prose: PN3352.E56
Empathy in literature
  General
    Literary history: PN56.E62
Employees
  Journalism: PN1 14.E6
    United States: PN4888.E58
Employees' magazines
  Journalism: PN4784.E6
Employees' magazines (Journalism)
  United States: PN4888.E6
End of the world in literature
  General
    Collections: PN6071.E5
      Quotations
        English: PN6084.E53
    Literary history: PN56.E63
Engineering in literature
  General
    Collections
      Wit and humor: PN6231.E58
Engineers
  Oratory: PN4192.E53
Englishmen in literature
  General
    Collections
      Anecdotes: PN6268.E8
Enjambement: PN1059.E47
Enlightenment (Buddhism) in
  literature
  General
    Collections
      Wit and humor: PN6231.E63
Entertainers, Blacklisting of
  Performing arts: PN1590.B5
Entertainers in motion pictures:
  PN1995.9.E77

Entertaining in literature
  General
    Collections: PN6071.E56
Entertainment events in
  literature
  General
    Collections
      Wit and humor: PN6231.E64
Enthusiasm
  General
    Literary history: PN56.E635
Entrepreneur in literature
  General
    Collections
      Wit and humor: PN6231.E65
Enumeration in literature
  General
    Poetry: PN1059.E5
Environmental protection
  Journalism: PN1 14.E64
    United States: PN4888.E65
Environmental protection in
  literature
  General
    Collections
      Wit and humor: PN6231.E66
Environmental scenography:
  PN2081.E58
Environmental theater:
  PN2081.E58
Envy in literature
  General
    Collections
      Wit and humor: PN6231.E67
    Literary history: PN56.E64
Epic films: PN1995.9.E79
Epic literature
  General
    Collections: PN6071.E6
    Literary history: PN56.E65
      Medieval: PN694.E6
Epic poetry
  General
    Collections: PN6110.E6
    Literary history: PN1301+
      Medieval: PN689+

Epigrams
  General
    Collections: PN6279+
    Literary history: PN6279.A3+
      Poetry: PN1441
Epilepsy in literature
  General
    Literary history: PN56.E66
Epiphanies in literature
  General
    Literary history: PN56.E67
Epistolary fiction
  General
    Literary history: PN3448.E6
Epistolary style of writing:
  PN235
Epitaphs
  General
    Collections: PN6288.5+
      Wit and humor: PN6231.E69
    Literary history: PN1441
Epithalamia in literature
  General
    Literary history: PN1481
Equipment and supplies in
  journalism: PN4784.E7
Erauso, Catalina de, in
  literature
  General
    Literary history: PN57.E68
Erotic films: PN1995.9.S45
Erotic literature
  General
    Collections: PN6071.E7
      Poetry: PN6110.E65
      Wit and humor: PN6231.E72
    Literary history: PN56.E7
      Fiction: PN3448.E76
      Poetry: PN1412
Erotic stories
  General
    Literary history
      Prose
        Technique: PN3377.5.E76
Errors
  Authorship: PN171.E8

Errors in literature
  General
    Collections
      Wit and humor: PN6231.E74
Eschatology in literature
  General
    Literary history: PN56.E73
Eskimos in motion pictures:
  PN1995.9.E83
Espionage films: PN1995.9.S68
Espionage in literature
  General
    Collections
      Quotations
        English: PN6084.E82
      Wit and humor: PN6231.E75
Essays
  General: PN4500
    Collections: PN6141+
Estonian proverbs: PN6505.E73
Estonian quotations: PN6095.E76
Estonian riddles: PN6377.E76
Estonian-American newspapers:
  PN4885.E87
Eteocles and Polynices in
  literature
  General
    Literary history: PN57.E7
Ethics
  Authorship: PN150
Ethics and journalism: PN1 14.E8
  United States: PN4888.E8
Ethics and literature
  General
    Literary history: PN49
      Drama: PN1647
      Poetry: PN1077
      Prose: PN3347
Ethics and motion pictures:
  PN1995.5
Ethics in literature
  General
    Collections
      Aphorisms: PN6278.E78

Ethnic attitudes in literature
  General
    Literary history
      Juvenile literature:
        PN1009.5.E84
Ethnic broadcasting and programs
  Radio: PN1991.8.E84
  Television: PN1992.8.E84
Ethnic press: PN1 14.E84
  United States: PN4882+
Ethnic wit and humor
  General
    Collections: PN6149.E83
Ethnology in literature
  General
    Collections
      Wit and humor: PN6231.E78
Etiquette in literature
  General
    Collections
      Aphorisms: PN6278.E8
      Quotations
        English: PN6084.E85
      Wit and humor: PN6231.E8
    Literary history: PN56.E74
Etsako proverbs: PN6519.E76
Euphonic poetry: PN1059.E7
Europa in literature
  General
    Literary history: PN57.E8
Europe, Eastern, Literature of
  Literary history: PN849.E9+
Europe in literature
  General
    Collections: PN6071.E78
    Literary history: PN56.3.E85
European Union: PN1 14.E87
Evaluation of motion pictures:
  PN1995.9.E9
Everyman in literature
  General
    Collections
      Drama: PN6120.E9
    Literary history: PN57.E9
Evolution
  Journalism
    United States: PN4888.E94

Evolution (Biology) in literature
  General
    Collections
      Quotations
        English: PN6084.E88
Evolution in literature
  General
    Collections
      Poetry: PN6110.E8
Ewe proverbs: PN6519.E9
Ewondo proverbs: PN6519.E96
Excuses in literature
  General
    Collections
      Wit and humor: PN6231.E87
Executives in literature
  General
    Collections
      Wit and humor: PN6231.E88
Exercise in literature
  General
    Collections
      Wit and humor: PN6231.E9
Exhibitions
  Journalism: PN4720.A+
Exiled authors
  General
    Literary history: PN495
Exiles as authors
  General
    Collections: PN6069.E94
Exiles in literature
  General
    Collections: PN6071.E87
    Literary history: PN56.5.E96
Existentialism in literary
  criticism: PN98.E93
Existentialism in literature
  General
    Collections: PN6071.E9
    Literary history: PN56.E77
Exoticism in literature
  General
    Literary history: PN56.E78
      Medieval: PN682.E88
Exoticism in motion pictures:
  PN1995.9.E95

Expatriates as authors
  General
    Literary history: PN495
Experience in literature
  General
    Collections
      Quotations
        English: PN6084.E9
Experimental films: PN1995.9.E96
Experimental poetry: PN1059.E94
Experimental radio programs:
  PN1991.8.E94
Experimental theater: PN2193.E86
  Great Britain: PN2595.13.E97
Exploitation films:
  PN1995.9.S284
Explorers
  Journalism
    United States: PN4888.E07
Expo 67 in literature
  General
    Collections
      Wit and humor: PN6231.E95
Exposition in literature
  General
    Literary history
      Prose: PN3383.E96
Expressionism
  Theater: PN2193.E87
Expressionism in literature
  General
    Literary history: PN56.E785
Extemporaneous speaking: PN4168
Extortion in literature
  General
    Literary history: PN56.E8
Extra editions
  Journalism: PN1 14.E94
Extras (Actors) in motion
  pictures: PN1995.9.E97
Eyes in literature
  General
    Collections
      Poetry: PN6110.E9
      Quotations
        French: PN6089.E9
    Literary history: PN56.E9

F

Fables
  General
    Collections
      Poetry: PN6110.F2
    Literary history: PN980+
Fabliaux
  General
    Literary history: PN694.F3
Face in motion pictures:
  PN1995.9.F27
Facial expression in literature
  General
    Collections
      Wit and humor: PN6231.F25
Failure in literature
  General
    Collections
      Wit and humor: PN6231.F28
Failure (Psychology) in
  literature
  General
    Literary history: PN56.F27
Fairies in literature
  General
    Collections: PN6071.F15
      Poetry: PN6110.F3
      Wit and humor: PN6231.F283
    Literary history
      Medieval: PN682.F27
Fairy tales
  General
    Collections: PN6071.F15
      Wit and humor: PN6231.F285
    Literary history: PN3437
Fairy tales in motion pictures:
  PN1995.9.F34
Faith in literature
  General
    Collections: PN6071.F17
      Wit and humor: PN6231.F287
Fall of man in literature
  General
    Literary history: PN56.F29
      Medieval: PN682.F3

Fame in literature
 General
  Collections
   Wit and humor: PN6231.F29
  Literary history: PN56.F297
  Poetry: PN1083.F35
Family in literature
 General
  Collections: PN6071.F2
   Anecdotes: PN6268.F35
   Poetry: PN6110.F32
   Quotations
    English: PN6084.F23
   Wit and humor: PN6231.F3
  Literary history: PN56.F3
  Drama
   Tragedies: PN1899.F27
  Juvenile literature:
   PN1009.5.F35
Family in motion pictures:
 PN1995.9.F35
Family in television broadcasts:
 PN1992.8.F33
Family in the press: PN4784.F3
Family violence in literature
 General
  Literary history
   Medieval: PN682.F34
Fang proverbs: PN6519.F36
Fantastic films: PN1995.9.F36
Fantastic literature
 General
  Collections
   Fiction: PN6071.F25
   Poetry: PN6110.F33
  Literary history: PN56.F34
   Fiction: PN3435
   Prose
    Technique: PN3377.5.F34
Fantastic programs
 Television: PN1992.8.F35
Fanzines: PN1 14.F35
Farces
 General
  Collections: PN6120.F3
  Literary history: PN1942+
Farewell letters: PN6140.L3

Farewells in literature
 General
  Collections
   Quotations
    English: PN6084.F25
   Wit and humor: PN6231.F35
Farm life in literature
 General
  Collections
   Poetry: PN6110.F34
Fascism in literature
 General
  Literary history: PN56.F35
Fashion
 Journalism: PN4784.F33, PN1
  14.F37
Fashion in literature
 General
  Collections: PN6071.F27
   Quotations
    English: PN6084.F27
    German: PN6093.F25
Fate and fatalism in literature
 General
  Collections: PN6071.F28
   Quotations
    German: PN6093.F3
  Literary history: PN56.F358
   Romance literatures:
    PN810.F3
Father-search in literature
 General
  Literary history: PN56.F36
Fathers and sons in literature
 General
  Literary history: PN56.F37
Fathers in literature
 General
  Collections: PN6071.F3
   Poetry: PN6110.F36
   Quotations
    English: PN6084.F3
   Wit and humor: PN6231.F37
Fathers' letters: PN6140.F35
Faust in literature
 General
  Collections: PN6071.F33

Faust in literature
General
Collections
Drama: PN6120.F33
Literary history: PN57.F3
Favorite poems
General
Collections: PN6110.F4
Fear in literature
General
Collections
Wit and humor: PN6231.F4
Literary history: PN56.F39
Feast of the Crucifix in
literature
General
Literary history
Legends: PN687.F4
Feature article writing:
PN4784.F37
Feature story writing:
PN4784.F37
Feature writing: PN4784.F37
Federal Theatre Project (United
States): PN2270.F43
Feminine influence in literature
General
Collections
Wit and humor: PN6231.F44
Literary history: PN56.F46
Biography: PN481
Fiction: PN3401
Poetry: PN1091
Feminine influence in motion
pictures: PN1995.9.W6
Feminine influence in theater:
PN1590.W64
Femininity in literature
General
Literary history: PN56.F4
Feminism in motion pictures:
PN1995.9.W6
Feminist films: PN1995.9.W6
Feminist literary criticism:
PN98.W64
Feminist theater: PN1590.W64
Great Britain: PN2595.13.W65

Feminist theater
United States: PN2270.F45
Femmes fatales in literature
General
Literary history: PN56.5.F44
Drama: PN1650.F44
Femmes fatales in motion
pictures: PN1995.9.F44
Fencing on stage: PN2071.F4
Feng shui in literature
General
Collections
Wit and humor: PN6231.F45
Festivals in literature
General
Collections: PN6071.F37
Festivals in the performing
arts: PN1590.F47
Festivals, Marionette:
PN1979.F48
Feuilletons: PN4784.F4
Fiction
General
Collections: PN6010+
Quotations: PN6083
Literary history: PN3311+
Medieval: PN692+
Journalism: PN1 14.F45
United States: PN4888.F5
Fifteen tokens before the last
judgment in literature
General
Literary history
Legends: PN687.F45
Fighting on stage: PN2071.F5
Figures
Literary style: PN227+
Fijian proverbs: PN6519.F54
Filicide in drama: PN1650.F5
Film adaptations: PN1997.85
Films in programming
Television: PN1992.8.F5
Films noirs: PN1995.9.F54
Finance
American theater: PN2293.E35
English theater: PN2599.5.E25
French theater: PN2639.5.E35

Finance
  German theater: PN2659.5.E35
  Journalism: PN4784.F5, PN1
  14.F5
  United States: PN4888.F6
Finance in literature
  General
    Collections
      Wit and humor: PN6231.F47
Finance in the performing arts:
  PN1590.F55
Financial journalism: PN4784.C7
Finnish proverbs: PN6505.F5
Finnish quotations: PN6095.F56
Finnish riddles: PN6377.F5
Finnish-American newspapers:
  PN4885.F55
Fires in literature
  General
    Collections
      Wit and humor: PN6231.F49
Fireworks in theater: PN2091.F54
Fishing in literature
  General
    Collections: PN6071.F47
    Quotations
      English: PN6084.F47
    Wit and humor: PN6231.F5
    Literary history: PN56.F5
Flaneurs in literature
  General
    Literary history: PN56.5.F53
Flashbacks in motion pictures:
  PN1995.9.F56
Flatulence in literature
  General
    Collections
      Wit and humor: PN6231.F55
Fleas in literature
  General
    Literary history: PN56.F53
Flies in literature
  General
    Collections
      Wit and humor: PN6231.F58

Flight attendants in literature
  General
    Collections
      Anecdotes: PN6268.F58
Flight in literature
  General
    Collections: PN6071.F48
    Literary history
      Legends: PN687.F5
Flight in motion pictures:
  PN1995.9.F58
Floire et Blancheflor (Romance)
  General
    Literary history
      Poetry
        Medieval: PN690.F56
Florence (Italy) in literature
  General
    Collections: PN6071.F49
    Literary history: PN56.3.F56
Flowers in literature
  General
    Collections: PN6071.F5
      Poetry: PN6110.F6
    Quotations
      English: PN6084.F5
    Literary history: PN56.F55
Fly fishing in literature
  General
    Collections
      Wit and humor: PN6231.F62
Flying Dutchman in literature
  General
    Literary history: PN57.F6
Flying in theater: PN2091.F58
Folk literature
  General
    Collections
      Drama: PN6120.F6
    Literary history: PN905+
      Poetry: PN1341+
Folk theater
  United States: PN2267
Folklore in literature
  General
    Collections
      Poetry: PN6110.F7

Folklore in literature
  General
    Literary history: PN56.F58
Food
  Journalism: PN4784.F55
Food contamination in the press
  United States: PN4888.F67
Food habits in literature
  General
    Collections
      Wit and humor: PN6231.G35
Food in literature
  General
    Collections: PN6071.F6
      Aphorisms: PN6278.F66
      Maxims: PN6308.F6
      Poetry: PN6110.F73
      Quotations
        English: PN6084.F6
        German: PN6093.F6
      Wit and humor: PN6231.F66
    Literary history: PN56.F59
      Juvenile literature:
        PN1009.5.F66
Food in motion pictures:
  PN1995.9.F65
Fools and jesters in literature
  General
    Collections: PN6071.F64
    Literary history: PN56.5.F64
      Drama: PN1650.F66
Footnotes
  Authorship citations:
    PN171.F56
Forbes magazine
  General
    Collections
      Wit and humor: PN6231.F72
Foregrounding
  Literary style: PN226
Foreign countries in literature
  General
    Literary history
      Juvenile literature:
        PN1009.5.F68
Foreign dialect imitation
  Acting: PN2071.F6

Foreign films: PN1995.9.F67
Foreign language press:
  PN4837.A+, PN1 14.F6+
  United States: PN4884+
Foreign news: PN4784.F6, PN1
  14.F67
  United States: PN4888.F69
Foreign programs
  Television broadcasts:
    PN1992.8.F67
Foreigners in literature
  General
    Collections
      Wit and humor: PN6231.F74
Forensic oratory: PN4171
Forests and trees in literature
  General
    Collections
      Poetry: PN6110.T75
    Literary history: PN56.F64
      Medieval: PN682.F6
Forgeries, Literary: PN171.F6+
Forgiveness in literature
  General
    Collections: PN6071.F65
Formalism in literary criticism:
  PN98.F6
Format radio broadcasting:
  PN1991.66+
Fortuna (Roman deity) in
  literature
  General
    Literary history: PN57.F67
      Legends: PN687.F55
Fortune in literature
  General
    Collections: PN6071.F66
Four daughters of god in
  literature
  General
    Literary history
      Legends: PN687.F6
Four elements (Philosophy) in
  literature
  General
    Literary history
      Medieval: PN682.F64

Fox and the stork
  General
    Literature: PN995.F68
France in literature
  General
    Collections: PN6071.F68
      Wit and humor: PN6231.F743
France in motion pictures:
  PN1995.9.F78
Francis of Assisi, Saint, in
  motion pictures: PN1995.9.F79
Franciscans in literature
  General
    Literary history
      Medieval: PN682.F7
Frankenstein in motion pictures:
  PN1995.9.F8
Free circulation newspapers and
  periodicals: PN4784.F74
Free indirect speech: PN3383.F74
Free newspapers: PN4784.F74
Free periodicals: PN4784.F74
Free thought in literature
  General
    Collections
      Poetry: PN6110.F75
Free verse
  General
    Literary history: PN1059.F7
Freelance journalism: PN4784.F76
Freemasonry
  Journalism: PN1 14.F74
Freemasonry in literature
  General
    Literary history: PN56.F73
French language
  General
    Collections
      Wit and humor: PN6231.F745
French-American newspapers:
  PN4885.F72
Friedrich II, der Grosse, King
  of Prussia, in literature
  General
    Literary history: PN57.F8

Friendship in literature
  General
    Collections: PN6071.F7
    Anecdotes: PN6268.F74
    Aphorisms: PN6278.F7
    Maxims: PN6308.F7
    Poetry: PN6110.F8
    Quotations
      English: PN6084.F8
      German: PN6093.F7
    Thoughts: PN6338.F7
    Wit and humor: PN6231.F748
    Literary history: PN56.F74
      Medieval: PN682.F74
Frisian proverbs: PN6505.F7
Frogs and toads in literature
  General
    Collections: PN6071.F74
      Wit and humor: PN6231.F75
Fruit in literature
  General
    Collections: PN6071.F76
    Quotations
      English: PN6084.F83
    Literary history: PN56.F76
Frustration in literature
  General
    Collections
    Quotations
      English: PN6084.F85
Fugitive verse
  General
    Collections: PN6110.F9
Fulah proverbs: PN6519.F8
Fulah riddles: PN6377.F8
Funeral rites and ceremonies
  Authorship: PN171.O3
Future in literature
  General
    Literary history
      Drama: PN1650.F88
Future life in literature
  General
    Collections: PN6071.F86
    Quotations
      English: PN6084.F89
      German: PN6093.F8

Futurism in literature
  General
    Literary history: PN56.F8
Futurism in motion pictures:
  PN1995.9.F85
Futurism (Literary movement)
  Poetry: PN6110.F95

G

Gaelic (Scottish) proverbs:
  PN6505.C4
Galahad in literature
  General
    Literary history: PN57.G3
Galicia (Poland and Ukraine) in
  literature
  General
    Collections: PN6071.G23
Gallegan proverbs: PN6505.G34
Gambai proverbs: PN6519.G23
Gambling in literature
  General
    Collections: PN6071.G24
      Quotations
        English: PN6084.G32
    Literary history: PN56.G27
Gambling in motion pictures:
  PN1995.9.G26
Ganda proverbs: PN6519.G25
Gandhi, Mohandas Karamchand, in
  literature
  General
    Literary history: PN57.G33
Gangs
  Journalism: PN1 14.G35
Gangster films: PN1995.9.G3
Gardens and gardening in
  literature
  General
    Collections: PN6071.G27
      Poetry: PN6110.G2
      Proverbs: PN6525.G35
      Quotations
        English: PN6084.G33
        German: PN6093.G3
      Wit and humor: PN6231.G3

Gardens and gardening in
  literature
  General
    Literary history: PN56.G3
      Juvenile literature:
        PN1009.5.G37
Garhwali proverbs: PN6519.G27
Garibaldi in literature
  General
    Literary history: PN57.G35
Garrick Club, Cambridge:
  PN2575.G2
Garrick Club, London: PN2575.G3
Gastronomy in literature
  General
    Collections: PN6071.G3
      Wit and humor: PN6231.G35
Gates, Bill, 1955-　, in
  literature
  General
    Collections
      Wit and humor: PN6231.G36
Gawain in literature
  General
    Literary history
      Legends: PN686.G3
Gay actors and actresses:
  PN2286.5
Gay authors
  General
    Literary history: PN491.3
Gay men in literature
  General
    Collections
      Drama: PN6120.G34
Gay theater
  United States: PN2270.G39
Gayo proverbs: PN6519.G3
Gays and broadcasting:
  PN1990.9.H64
Gays in literature
  General
    Collections
      Quotations
        English: PN6084.G35

Geis (tabu) in literature
  General
    Literary history
      Medieval: PN682.G4
Gems in literature
  General
    Collections
      Poetry: PN6110.G3
Gender in literature
  General
    Literary history: PN56.G45
Genealogy in literature
  General
    Collections
      Wit and humor: PN6231.G38
    Literary history: PN56.G46
Generations in literature
  General
    Literary history: PN56.G47
Generosity in literature
  General
    Collections: PN6071.G42
Geneviève of Brabant in
  literature
  General
    Literary history: PN57.G4
      Legends: PN687.G4
Geography in literature
  General
    Collections
      Drama: PN6120.G4
    Literary history: PN56.G48
Geopolitics in motion pictures:
  PN1995.9.G39
Georgia (Transcaucasia) in
  literature
  General
    Literary history: PN56.3.G3
Georgian proverbs: PN6505.G45
German dialect in literature
  General
    Collections
      Wit and humor: PN6231.G4
German language in literature
  General
    Collections
      Wit and humor: PN6231.G42

German literature in American
  magazines: PN4888.G6
German reunification question
  (1949-1990) in motion
  pictures: PN1995.9.G43
German-American newspapers:
  PN4885.G3
Germanic literatures
  General
    Literary history: PN821+
Germans in motion pictures:
  PN1995.9.G45
Germany
  Journalism
    United States: PN4888.G63
Germany in television
  broadcasts: PN1992.8.G47
Gestures
  Acting: PN2071.G4
  Oratory: PN4165
Ghosts in literature
  General
    Collections: PN6071.G45
      Drama: PN6120.G45
      Poetry: PN6110.G5
      Wit and humor: PN6231.G45
    Literary history
      Drama: PN1650.G56
Ghosts in motion pictures:
  PN1995.9.S8
Ghostwriting
  Authorship: PN171.G47
  Journalism: PN4784.G5
Ghouls and ogres in literature
  General
    Collections
      Wit and humor: PN6231.G47
Giants in literature
  General
    Collections
      Poetry: PN6110.G52
    Literary history: PN56.5.G53
Gigaku: PN2924.5.G54
Girl Scouts plays
  General
    Collections
      Drama: PN6120.G5

Girls in literature
  General
    Collections: PN6071.G53
      Poetry: PN6110.G54
      Wit and humor: PN6231.G5
Girls in motion pictures:
  PN1995.9.G57
Glory in literature
  General
    Literary history
      Medieval: PN682.G6
Gluttony in literature
  General
    Collections: PN6071.G55
Gnus in literature
  General
    Collections
      Wit and humor: PN6231.G65
Go-betweens in literature
  General
    Literary history
      Medieval: PN682.G64
Goajiro proverbs: PN6519.G6
Goblins in literature
  General
    Collections
      Wit and humor: PN6231.G66
God in literature
  General
    Collections: PN6071.G57
      Poetry: PN6110.G58
      Proverbs: PN6525.G6
      Quotations
        French: PN6089.G63
        German: PN6093.G6
Goddess religion in literature
  General
    Collections
      Poetry: PN6110.G59
Goddesses in literature
  General
    Literary history
      Medieval: PN682.G65
Godfather films: PN1995.9.G6

Godzilla in literature
  General
    Collections
      Wit and humor: PN6231.G67
Godzilla in motion pictures:
  PN1995.9.G63
Golem in literature
  General
    Collections: PN6071.G6
    Literary history: PN57.G56
Golf in literature
  General
    Collections
      Wit and humor: PN6231.G68
Good and evil in literature
  General
    Literary history: PN56.E75
Good and evil in motion
  pictures: PN1995.9.E93
Good fellowship in literature
  General
    Collections
      Poetry: PN6110.G6
Gorillas in literature
  General
    Collections
      Wit and humor: PN6231.G74
Gothic revival in literature
  General
    Collections: PN6071.G64
Goths in literature
  General
    Literary history: PN56.3.G6
Government and the press:
  PN4735+
Government consultants in
  literature
  General
    Collections
      Wit and humor: PN6231.G76
Government patronage
  Theater: PN2042+
Government press services:
  PN4737
Graces, The, in literature
  General
    Literary history: PN57.G6

Grail in literature
  General
    Literary history: PN56.G67
      Legends: PN686.G7
Grandmothers in literature
  General
    Literary history
    Juvenile literature:
      PN1009.5.G73
Grandparents in literature
  General
    Collections: PN6071.G7
      Anecdotes: PN6268.G7
      Poetry: PN6110.G83
      Quotations
        English: PN6084.G6
      Wit and humor: PN6231.G8
Graphic arts
  Performing arts: PN1590.G73
Graphics
  Television broadcasts:
    PN1992.8.G7
Gratitude in literature
  General
    Collections
      Quotations
        English: PN6084.G63
Gravity in literature
  General
    Collections
      Wit and humor: PN6231.G84
Great Britain in literature
  General
    Collections
      Quotations
        English: PN6084.G66
      Wit and humor: PN6231.G86
Great Britain, Literature of
  Literary history: PN849.G74+
Great men in literature
  General
    Collections
      Quotations
        English: PN6084.G7
Greece in literature
  General
    Literary history: PN56.3.G69

Greek influences in tragedies:
  PN1899.G74
Greek language
  General
    Collections
      Wit and humor: PN6231.G87
Greek (Modern) proverbs:
  PN6505.G7
Greek (Modern) quotations:
  PN6095.G7
Greeting cards
  Authorship: PN171.G74
Grendel in literature
  General
    Literary history: PN57.G75
Grief in literature
  General
    Literary history
      Medieval: PN682.G74
Griselda in literature
  General
    Literary history: PN57.G8
Grotesque in literature
  General
    Literary history: PN56.G7
      Drama: PN1650.G7
      Prose: PN3352.G76
Guarani proverbs: PN6519.G8
Guenevere in literature
  General
    Literary history: PN57.G85
Guignol: PN1979.G84
Guilt in literature
  General
    Literary history: PN56.G87
      Prose: PN3352.G85
Gujarati proverbs: PN6519.G85
Gummy bears in literature
  General
    Collections
      Wit and humor: PN6231.G92
Gun control in literature
  General
    Collections
      Wit and humor: PN6231.G95

Guy of Warwick in literature
  General
    Literary history
      Legends: PN687.G84
Gyges in literature
  General
    Literary history: PN57.G9

H

Hagen in literature
  General
    Literary history
      Legends: PN687.H34
Haiku
  General
    Collections: PN6110.H13
      Wit and humor: PN6231.H28
Hair in literature
  General
    Collections
      Wit and humor: PN6231.H3
Hairy anchorite in literature
  General
    Literary history: PN57.H3
Haitian proverbs: PN6519.H3
Halloween in literature
  General
    Collections
      Drama: PN6120.H3
Hallucinations and illusions in
  literature
  General
    Collections: PN6071.H18
Hamlet in literature
  General
    Literary history: PN57.H32
Hand-to-hand fighting in motion
  pictures: PN1995.9.H3
Happiness in literature
  General
    Collections: PN6071.H2
      Aphorisms: PN6278.H3
      Poetry: PN6110.H14
      Quotations
        English: PN6084.H3
        German: PN6093.H3

Happiness in literature
  General
    Collections
      Thoughts: PN6338.H35
      Wit and humor: PN6231.H35
    Literary history: PN56.H27
Harlequin: PN1988.H3
Harmony (Aesthetics) in
  literature
  General
    Literary history: PN56.H3
Hate mail: PN6140.H38
Hausa proverbs: PN6519.H35
Havana (Cuba) in literature
  General
    Collections: PN6071.H26
Hawaii in motion pictures:
  PN1995.9.H38
Hawaiian proverbs: PN6519.H4
Headlines
  Journalism: PN4784.H4, PN1
    14.H4
Healing in literature
  General
    Literary history: PN56.H35
Health in literature
  General
    Collections
      Wit and humor: PN6231.H38
Health resorts in literature
  General
    Literary history: PN56.H37
Hearing impaired in literature
  Geneal
    Collections
      Wit and humor: PN6231.D33
Heart in literature
  General
    Collections
      Quotations
        English: PN6084.H4
    Literary history: PN56.H374
Heaven in literature
  General
    Collections: PN6071.H37
      Poetry: PN6110.H17
      Wit and humor: PN6231.H42

Heaven in literature
  General
    Literary history
      Legends: PN687.H37
Hebrew quotations: PN6095.H4
Hebrew riddles: PN6377.H4
Heimatfilme: PN1995.9.H4
Heinrich der Löwe in literature
  General
    Literary history
      Legends: PN687.H38
Heldensage: PN684
Helen of Troy in literature
  General
    Literary history: PN57.H4
Hell in literature
  General
    Literary history: PN56.H38
Hellenism in literature
  General
    Literary history: PN56.H4
Helsinki (Finland) in motion
  pictures: PN1995.9.H43
Hengist in literature
  General
    Literary history: PN57.H42
Heralds
  German theater: PN2642.H4
Herbortsage in literature
  General
    Literary history
      Legends: PN687.H4
Hercules in literature
  General
    Literary history: PN57.H43
Hermits in literature
  General
    Literary history
      Medieval: PN682.H47
Hero and Leander in literature
  General
    Literary history: PN57.H44
Hero legends: PN684
Herod I, the Great, King of
  Judea, in literature
  General
    Literary history: PN57.H45

Heroes and heroines in literature
  General
    Collections: PN6071.H4
    Literary history: PN56.5.H45
      Drama: PN1711
      Juvenile literature:
        PN1009.5.H47
      Prose: PN3411
Heroic recitations: PN4305.M3
Heroic romance: PN3448.H4
Heroids
  General
    Literary history: PN1415
Heroism in literature
  General
    Collections
      Poetry: PN6110.H2
Hindi proverbs: PN6519.H55
Hindi quotations: PN6095.H5
Hindi riddles: PN6377.H5
Hindko proverbs: PN6519.H57
Hindustani proverbs: PN6519.H58
Hispanic American theater:
  PN2270.H57
Hispanic Americans
  Journalism
    United States: PN4888.H57
Hispanic Americans in literature
  General
    Collections
      Quotations
        English: PN6084.H47
Hispanic Americans in motion
  pictures: PN1995.9.H47
Hispanic Americans in television
  broadcasts: PN1992.8.H54
Hispanic authors
  General
    Collections
      Fiction: PN6120.92.H56
Historical criticism
  Literary criticism: PN98.H57
Historical drama
  General
    Collections: PN6120.H5
    Literary history: PN1872+

Historical fiction
  General
    Literary history
      Prose
        Technique: PN3377.5.H57
Historical films: PN1995.9.H5
Historical novels
  General
    Literary history: PN3441
Historical poetry
  General
    Collections: PN6110.H3
Historical programs
  Television broadcasts:
    PN1992.8.H56
History and literature: PN50
  Poetry: PN1080
  Prose: PN3343
History and motion pictures:
  PN1995.2
History in literature
  General
    Collections: PN6071.H5
      Wit and humor: PN6231.H47
    Literary history
      Juvenile literature:
        PN1009.5.H57
Hitchhiking in literature
  General
    Collections
      Wit and humor: PN6231.H5
Hitler, Adolf, 1889-1945, in
  motion pictures: PN1995.9.H514
Hmong proverbs: PN6519.H64
Hmong riddles: PN6377.H54
Hô Chí Minh in motion pictures:
  PN1995.9.H52
Hobbies in literature
  General
    Collections
      Wit and humor: PN6231.H53
Hockey in literature
  General
    Collections
      Wit and humor: PN6231.H54

Holidays in literature
  General
    Collections: PN6071.H7
      Drama: PN6120.H7
      Poetry: PN6110.H4
      Thoughts: PN6338.H64
      Wit and humor: PN6231.H547
    Recitations: PN4305.H7
Holocaust, Jewish (1939-1945),
  in literature
  General
    Collections: PN6071.H713
      Drama: PN6120.H73
      Poetry: PN6110.H45
    Literary history: PN56.H55
      Drama: PN1650.H64
        Historical plays:
          PN1879.H65
Holocaust, Jewish (1939-1945),
  in motion pictures:
  PN1995.9.H53
Holocaust, Jewish (1939-1945),
  in television broadcasts:
  PN1992.8.H63
Holy Spirit in literature
  General
    Collections
      Poetry: PN6110.H5
Home economics in literature
  General
    Collections
      Wit and humor: PN6231.H55
Home in literature
  General
    Collections: PN6071.H72
      Anecdotes: PN6268.H6
      Poetry: PN6110.H6
      Quotations
        English: PN6084.H57
    Literary history: PN56.H557
Home in motion pictures:
  PN1995.9.H54
Homeland in literature
  General
    Literary history: PN56.H56

Homophobia
  Journalism
    United States: PN4888.H65
Homosexuality
  Journalism: PN1 14.H55
  Television broadcasts:
    PN1992.8.H64
Homosexuality and broadcasting:
  PN1990.9.H64
Homosexuality in literature
  General
    Collections: PN6071.H724
      Poetry: PN6110.H65
      Wit and humor: PN6231.H57
    Literary history: PN56.H57
      Medieval: PN682.H65
      Prose: PN3352.H65
Homosexuality in motion
  pictures: PN1995.9.H55
Hong Kong in literature
  General
    Collections: PN6071.H725
Honor in literature
  General
    Literary history: PN56.H58
Hopalong Cassidy films:
  PN1995.9.H56
Hope in literature
  General
    Collections
      Maxims: PN6308.H66
      Quotations
        English: PN6084.H62
Horizon in literature
  General
    Literary history: PN56.H59
Horoscopes in literature
  General
    Collections
      Wit and humor: PN6231.H575
Horror films: PN1995.9.H6
Horror stories
  General
    Collections: PN6071.H727
    Literary history: PN56.H6
      Technique: PN3377.5.H67

Horsemanship in literature
  General
    Collections
      Wit and humor: PN6231.H577
Horseracing in literature
  General
    Collections
      Wit and humor: PN6231.H58
Horses and horsemanship in
  literature
  General
    Collections: PN6071.H73
      Poetry: PN6110.H75
    Literary history: PN56.H63
Horses in literature
  General
    Collections
      Aphorisms: PN6278.H67
      Quotations
        English: PN6084.H66
      Wit and humor: PN6231.H59
Hospitality in literature
  General
    Collections
      Anecdotes: PN6268.H76
      Wit and humor: PN6231.H6
    Literary history: PN56.H66
Hotels in literature
  General
    Collections
      Anecdotes: PN6268.H8
      Wit and humor: PN6231.H7
Hours of labor
  Journalism: PN1 14.H58
House buying in literature
  General
    Collections
      Wit and humor: PN6231.H73
House organs
  Journalism: PN4784.H6
Housewives as authors
  General
    Literary history: PN171.H67
Housewives in literature
  General
    Collections
      Wit and humor: PN6231.H74

Hsiang sheng: PN2874.5.H75
Human behavior in literature
  General
    Collections
      Wit and humor: PN6231.H763
Human body in literature
  General
    Collections: PN6110.B75
    Literary history: PN56.B62
Human body in motion pictures:
  PN1995.9.B62
Human body in television
  broadcasts: PN1992.8.B64
Human body in vaudeville:
  PN1969.H85
Human ecology in literature
  General
    Collections: PN6071.H78
Human rights in literature
  General
    Collections: PN6071.H784
Human-animal relationships in
  literature
  General
    Collections
      Wit and humor: PN6231.H76
Humanism in literature
  General
    Collections: PN6071.H79
Humanistic psychology in
  literary criticism: PN98.H85
Humor
  Authorship: PN169
Humor in literature
  General
    Collections
      Drama: PN6120.H8
      Poetry: PN6110.H8
      Quotations
        English: PN6084.H8
        French: PN6089.H85
        German: PN6093.H85
    Literary history: PN56.H83
    Oratory: PN4066
    Recitations: PN4250+
Humorous periodicals: PN1 14.H8
  United States: PN4880

Humorous stories
  General
    Collections: PN6071.H795
Hunde proverbs: PN6519.H85
Hungarian proverbs: PN6505.H8
Hungarian quotations: PN6095.H8
Hunters in literature
  General
    Collections
      Poetry: PN6110.H83
Hunting in literature
  General
    Collections: PN6071.H8
    Epigrams: PN6288.H8
    Poetry: PN6110.H83
    Quotations
      English: PN6084.H84
    Wit and humor: PN6231.H77
    Literary history: PN56.H84
      Medieval: PN682.H8
Hunting in motion pictures:
  PN1995.9.H84
Husbands in literature
  General
    Collections
      Wit and humor: PN6231.H8
Hygiene in literature
  General
    Collections
      Proverbs: PN6525.H9
      Quotations
        English: PN6084.H9
      Wit and humor: PN6231.H94
Hymns and sacred poems
  General
    Literary history: PN1386
Hypnotism in literature
  General
    Literary history: PN1059.H8
Hypnotism in motion pictures:
  PN1995.9.H95
Hypochondria in literature
  General
    Collections
      Wit and humor: PN6231.H96

I

Iambic poetry: PN1059.I17
Ibo proverbs: PN6519.I33
Icarus in literature
  General
    Collections
      Poetry: PN6110.I3
    Literary history: PN57.I3
Icelandic quotations: PN6095.I32
Idealism and literature: PN56.I4
Idealism in literature
  General
    Literary history: PN599
    Drama: PN1633.I3
Identity (Psychology) in
  literature
  General
    Literary history: PN56.I42
Igbo proverbs: PN6519.I33
Ikwere proverbs: PN6519.I35
Illegitimacy in literature
  General
    Literary history
      Prose: PN3352.I53
Illusion in literature
  General
    Literary history: PN56.I43
Illustrated magazines: PN4834
Illustrated periodicals: PN1
  14.I44
Illustrative incidents, stories,
  etc.
  Oratory: PN4193.I5
Imagination in literature
  General
    Literary history: PN56.I45
Imitation
  Literary style: PN223
Imitation in literature
  General
    Literary history: PN166
Imitation of foreign dialects
  Acting: PN2071.F6
Imitation of regional dialects
  Acting: PN2071.F6

Immigration
  Journalism: PN1 14.I55
Immigration in motion pictures:
  PN1995.9.E44
Imperfection in literature
  General
    Literary history: PN56.I46
Imperialism in literature
  General
    Literary history: PN56.I465
Impersonation in literature
  General
    Literary history: PN56.I47
Impersonations
  Acting: PN2071.I47
  English recitations: PN4305.I5
Impersonators in motion
  pictures: PN1995.9.I43
Implication (Logic) in literature
  General
    Literary history: PN56.I48
Impostures, Literary: PN171.F6+
Impotence in literature
  General
    Collections
      Wit and humor: PN6231.I44
Impressionism in literature
  General
    Literary history: PN56.I5
Impressionism in motion
  pictures: PN1995.9.I45
Impromptu theater: PN2071.I5
Improvisation
  Acting: PN2071.I5
Incest in literature
  General
    Collections: PN6071.I5
    Literary history: PN56.I55
      Medieval: PN682.I47
Independent theaters: PN2293.I4
Indexes
  Children's plays: PN1627
  Poetry: PN1022+
    Black: PN1025
  Recitations: PN4321

India in literature
  General
    Literary history: PN56.3.I57
Indian authors
  General
    Quotations: PN6081.4
Indian proverbs: PN6519.I39
Indian riddles: PN6377.I48
Indian theater: PN2270.I53
Indians of North America
  Journalism
    United States: PN4888.I52
Indic proverbs: PN6519.I4
Indic quotations: PN6095.I45
Indigenous peoples in motion
  pictures: PN1995.9.I49
Indirect discourse in literature
  Prose: PN3383.I5
Individualism in literature
  General
    Literary history: PN56.I57
      Medieval: PN682.I5
Individuation in literature
  General
    Literary history: PN56.I57
Indonesian proverbs: PN6519.I5
Indonesian quotations: PN6095.I5
Industrial relations in
  literature
  General
    Collections
      Wit and humor: PN6231.I48
Industry in literature
  General
    Literary history: PN56.I58
Ineffable in literature
  General
    Literary history: PN56.I59
Infants in literature
  General
    Collections: PN6071.I52
      Poetry: PN6110.I52
    Quotations
      English: PN6084.I48
    Wit and humor: PN6231.I5

Influence
  Journalism
    United States: PN4888.I53
Influence (Literary, artistic,
  etc.) in literature
  General
    Literary history: PN56.I593
Influence of radio broadcasts:
  PN1991.6
Influence of television
  broadcasts: PN1992.6
Influence of the theater:
  PN2047+
Information services
  Authorship: PN142+
  Journalism: PN4729.2
Information theory
  Literary criticism: PN98.I54
Inkle and Yarico in literature
  General
    Literary history: PN57.I6
Inner cities in literature
  General
    Collections
      Wit and humor: PN6231.I54
Innocence in literature
  General
    Literary history: PN56.I595
Insane authors: PN171.I6
Insects in literature
  General
    Collections
      Poetry: PN6110.I55
      Wit and humor: PN6231.I56
    Literary history: PN56.I63
Insomnia in literature
  General
    Collections: PN6071.I58
      Poetry: PN6110.I56
Inspiration in literature
  General
    Collections: PN6071.I6
    Literary history: PN46
Insurance in literature
  General
    Collections
      Wit and humor: PN6231.I6

Intellectuals in literature
  General
    Literary history: PN56.5.I57
Intercultural communication in
  motion pictures: PN1995.9.I55
International press: PN4736
International relations in
  motion pictures: PN1995.9.I57
Internet
  Authorship: PN142.5
  Journalism: PN4729.3
Internet in literature
  General
    Collections
      Wit and humor: PN6231.I62
    Literary history: PN56.I64
Interpersonal relations in
  literature
  General
    Collections
      Poetry: PN6110.I57
      Quotations
        English: PN6084.I5
    Literary history
      Prose: PN3352.I56
Interplanetary voyages in
  literature
  General
    Collections: PN6071.I64
Intertextuality in literary
  criticism: PN98.I58
Interviewing
  Authorship: PN171.I66
  Journalism: PN4784.I6
  Radio broadcasts: PN1991.8.I57
  Television broadcasts:
    PN1992.8.I68
Interviews in literature
  General
    Collections
      Wit and humor: PN6231.I63
Introductions in books: PN171.I7
Introductions of speakers:
  PN4305.I7

Invective in literature
  General
    Collections
      Wit and humor: PN6231.I65
Invention
  Literary style: PN221
Inventors and inventions in
  literature
  General
    Collections: PN6071.I67
    Wit and humor: PN6231.I67
Investigative reporting
  United States: PN4888.I56
Iphigenia in literature
  General
    Collections
      Drama: PN6120.I7
    Literary history: PN57.I7
Ireland in literature
  General
    Collection: PN6084.I6
    Collections
      Wit and humor: PN6231.I7
Irish Americans in motion
  pictures: PN1995.9.I67
Irish in literature
  General
    Collections
      Quotations
        English: PN6084.I6
Irish language proverbs:
  PN6505.C5
Irish question in motion
  pictures: PN1995.9.I68
Irish-American newspapers:
  PN4883.5
Iron in literature
  General
    Collections: PN6071.I7
Irony in comedies
  Drama: PN1929.I7
Irony in literature
  General
    History and criticism
      Wit and humor: PN6149.S2
    Literary history: PN56.I65
      Drama: PN1680

Islam
  Journalism: PN1 14.I78
Islamic press: PN4784.R35, PN1
  14.I8
Islands in literature
  General
    Collections: PN6071.I75
      Aphorisms: PN6278.I68
    Literary history: PN56.I7
Islands of the Pacific motion
  pictures: PN1995.9.I7
Israel in motion pictures:
  ˋPN1995.9.I72
Israel, Literature of
  Literary history: PN849.I8+
Istanbul (Turkey) in literature
  General
    Literary history: PN56.3.I74
Italian Americans in literature
  General
    Collections
      Quotations
        English: PN6084.I73
      Wit and humor: PN6231.I85
Italian Americans in motion
  pictures: PN1995.9.I73
Italian language in literature
  General
    Collections
      Wit and humor: PN6231.I84
Italian quotations: PN6095.I7
Italian-American newspapers:
  PN4885.I8
Italian-American theater:
  PN2270.I73
Italians in literature
  General
    Collections
      Wit and humor: PN6231.I85
Italy
  Journalism: PN4784.I82
Italy in literature
  General
    Collections: PN6071.I8
      Wit and humor: PN6231.I86
Itsekiri proverbs: PN6519.I75

Ivory Coast proverbs:
  PN6519.I855

J

Jabo proverbs: PN6519.J15
Jamaican proverbs: PN6519.J2
James Bond films: PN1995.9.J3
Jan III Sobieski, King of
  Poland, in literature
  General
    Literary history: PN57.J35
Japan
  Journalism: PN1 14.J34
Japan in motion pictures:
  PN1995.9.J34
Japanese proverbs: PN6519.J3
Japanese quotations: PN6095.J3
Japanese riddles: PN6377.J3
Japanese theater: PN2920+
Japanese-American newspapers:
  PN4885.J35
Jargon in literature
  General
    Collections
      Wit and humor: PN6231.J3
Javanese proverbs: PN6519.J38
Javanese riddles: PN6377.J38
Jazz in literature
  General
    Collections: PN6071.J28
Jazz in motion pictures:
  PN1995.9.J37
Jazz musicians in literature
  General
    Collections: PN6071.J28
Jealousy in literature
  General
    Literary history: PN56.J43
Jeanne d'Arc in literature
  General
    Literary history: PN57.J4
Jephthah, Judge of Israel, in
  literature
  General
    Literary history: PN57.J44

Jerusalem in literature
General
Collections: PN6071.J38
Literary history: PN56.3.J37
Jesuit theater
College theatricals:
PN3178.J46
Jesus Christ in literature
General
Collections: PN6071.J4
Drama: PN6120.J35
Poetry: PN6110.J4
Literary history: PN57.J47
Jesus Christ in motion pictures:
PN1995.9.J4
Jewelry trade in literature
General
Collections
Wit and humor: PN6231.J4
Jewish authors
General
Collections: PN6067
Poetry: PN6109.5
Jewish boy in literature
General
Literary history
Legends: PN687.J4
Jewish literature
General
Collections
Drama: PN6120.J4
Legends: PN6071.J5
Proverbs: PN6519.J5
Quotations: PN6095.J4
Wit and humor: PN6231.J5
Literary history
Drama: PN3035
Jewish literature in various
languages: PN842
Jewish press: PN5650
Jewish recitations: PN4305.J48
Jewish-Arab relations
General
Motion pictures: PN1995.9.J45
Journalism
United States: PN4888.J48

Jews
Journalism: PN1 14.J48
Jews in literature
General
Collections: PN6071.J6
Anecdotes: PN6268.J4
Poetry: PN6110.J45
Literary history: PN56.3.J4
Drama: PN1650.J48
Prose: PN3418
Jews in motion pictures:
PN1995.9.J46
Jews in television broadcasts:
PN1992.8.J48
Jews in the performing arts:
PN1590.J48
Joan, of Arc, Saint, in
literature
General
Collections
Drama: PN6120.J6
Literary history: PN57.J4
Joan, of Arc, Saint, in motion
pictures: PN1995.9.J57
Job hunting in literature
General
Collections
Wit and humor: PN6231.J59
Job, the Patriarch, in literature
General
Literary history: PN57.J57
Legends: PN687.J62
Jogging in literature
General
Collections
Wit and humor: PN6231.J63
John the Baptist in literature
General
Literary history: PN57.J6
Joseph, the Patrarch, in
literature
General
Literary history: PN57.J68
Journalism: PN4699+
Journalism, Aeronautical:
PN4784.A26

Journalism, Agricultural:
PN4784.A3
Journalism as a profession:
PN4797
Journalism, Automotive:
PN4784.A94
Journalism, Broadcast:
PN4784.B75
Journalism, Dental: PN4784.D4
Journalism, Economic: PN4784.C7
Journalism, Financial: PN4784.C7
Journalism in literature
General
Literary history: PN56.J68
Journalism, Military: PN4784.M5
Journalism, Mining: PN4784.M54
Journalism, Prison: PN4784.P7
Journalism, Religious: PN4784.R3
Journalism, Socialist:
PN4784.S55
Journalism, Sports: PN4784.S6
Journalism, Television:
PN4784.T4
Journalistic criticism:
PN4784.R4
Journalists: PN4699+
Journalists in literature
General
Collections
Wit and humor: PN6231.J68
Journalists in motion pictures:
PN1995.9.J6
Joy in literature
General
Collections
Quotations
English: PN6084.J65
German: PN6093.J6
Joyce, James, in literature
General
Collections
Poetry: PN6110.J69
Judas Iscariot in literature
General
Collections: PN6071.J84
Literary history
Legends: PN687.J8

Judeo-Arabic proverbs:
PN6519.J83
Judeo-Tat proverbs: PN6519.J84
Judging
Debating: PN4183.J83
Judicial error and prose:
PN3352.J9
Judith in literature
General
Literary history: PN57.J8
Jupiter (Roman deity) in
literature
General
Literary history: PN57.J84
Justice, Administration of, in
motion pictures: PN1995.9.J8
Justice in literature
General
Literary history: PN56.J87
Justice in television
broadcasts: PN1992.8.J87
Juvenile belles lettres
General
Recitations: PN4270+
Juvenile delinquency in motion
pictures: PN1995.9.J87
Juvenile fiction
General
Literary history: PN3443
Juvenile periodicals: PN4835,
PN1 14.J8
United States: PN4878

K

Kabardian proverbs: PN6519.K22,
PN6519.K223
Kabuki: PN2924.5.K3
Kaili proverbs: PN6519.K226
Kaisersage in literature
General
Literary history
Legends: PN687.K3
Kalanga proverbs: PN6519.K23
Kamba proverbs: PN6519.K24
Kamishibai: PN1979.K3

Kanagawa-ken (Japan) in motion
  pictures: PN1995.9.K35
Kannada proverbs: PN6519.K25
Kannada quotations: PN6095.K3
Kannada riddles: PN6377.K3
Kansas in literature
  General
    Collections
      Wit and humor: PN6231.K35
Karađorđe Petrović in literature
  General
    Literary history: PN57.K27
Karaim proverbs: PN6519.K27
Karelia in literature
  General
    Literary history: PN56.3.K3
Karelian proverbs: PN6505.K3
Karelian riddles: PN6377.K36
Karl XII, King of Sweden, in
  literature
  General
    Literary history: PN57.K3
Karo-Batak proverbs: PN6519.K28
Kasem proverbs: PN6519.K29
Kashmiri proverbs: PN6519.K3
Kashubian proverbs: PN6505.K34
Kasper (Marionette): PN1979.K34
Kathakali (Dance drama):
  PN2884.5.K36
Kay in literature
  General
    Literary history
      Legends: PN686.K3
Kazakh proverbs: PN6519.K38
Kazakh riddles: PN6377.K39
Kecak: PN2904.5.K43
Kenga proverbs: PN6519.K44
Kenya in literature
  General
    Collections: PN6071.K4
Kikuyu proverbs: PN6519.K5
Kilega proverbs: PN6519.K53
Kim, Il Sung, in literature
  General
    Collections
      Poetry: PN6110.K55

Kim, Il-song, in literature
  General
    Collections
      Poetry: PN6110.K55
Kim, Ir-sen, in literature
  General
    Collections
      Poetry: PN6110.K55
Kimbundu proverbs: PN6519.K55
Kin, Nissei, in literature
  General
    Collections
      Poetry: PN6110.K55
King Kong (Fictitious character)
  in literature
  General
    Collections: PN6071.K44
Kings and rulers
  Theater
    Great Britain: PN2582.K55
Kings and rulers in literature
  General
    Literary history
      Drama: PN1650.K55
Kirghiz proverbs: PN6519.K57
Kissing in literature
  General
    Collections: PN6071.K45
      Quotations
        English: PN6084.K5
        German: PN6093.K5
      Thoughts: PN6338.K58
      Wit and humor: PN6231.K5
    Literary history: PN56.K54
Kissing in motion pictures:
  PN1995.9.K57
Knight, Death and the Devil
  (Painting) in literature
  General
    Collections: PN6071.K5
Knights and knighthood in
  literature
  General
    Literary history: PN56.5.K48
      Fiction: PN3426.K65
      Medieval: PN682.K54

Knives in literature
  General
    Collections
      Wit and humor: PN6231.K54
Knock-knock jokes in literature
  General
    Collections
      Wit and humor: PN6231.K55
Knowledge in literature
  General
    Literary history: PN56.K62
      Prose: PN3352.K56
Komi proverbs: PN6505.K65
Komi riddles: PN6377.K58
Kongolese proverbs: PN6519.K59
Konkani proverbs: PN6519.K593
Korean proverbs: PN6519.K6
Korean quotations: PN6095.K6
Korean riddles: PN6377.K6
Kosciuszko, Tadeusz, in
  literature
  General
    Literary history: PN57.K67
Kosovo, Battle of, 1389, in
  literature
  General
    Literary history: PN56.K66
Kosovo Civil War, 1998-   , in
  literature
  General
    Collections
      Aphorisms: PN6278.K68
Kowaka: PN2924.5.K6
Kowakamai: PN2924.5.K6
Krio proverbs: PN6519.K75
Kuai shu: PN2874.5.K83
Kuaishu: PN2874.5.K83
Kuanyama proverbs: PN6519.K8
Kukwa proverbs: PN6519.K83
Kundrie in literature
  General
    Literary history: PN57.K8
Künstlerroman
  General
    Literary history
      Fiction: PN3448.K85
Kuo proverbs: PN6519.K84

Kurdish proverbs: PN6519.K85
Kusemai: PN2924.5.K6
Kyogen: PN2924.5.K9
Kyrielle: PN1485
Kyūshū Region (Japan) in motion
  pictures: PN1995.9.K95

L

Labor
  Journalism: PN1 14.L3
Labor in literature
  General
    Collections: PN6071.L3
      Drama: PN6120.L3
      Poetry: PN6110.L15
      Wit and humor: PN6231.L32
    Literary history: PN56.L22
      Fiction: PN3426.L3
      Prose: PN3352.L33
Labor in motion pictures:
  PN1995.9.L28
Labor, Portrayal of
  Journalism
    United States: PN4888.L27
Labor press: PN4784.L3
  United States: PN4888.L3
Labor theater: PN3305+
Laboring class authors
  General
    Literary history: PN171.L3
Labyrinths in literature
  General
    Literary history: PN56.L223
Ladakhi proverbs: PN6519.L27
Ladino (Judeo-Spanish) proverbs:
  PN6519.L3
Lakes in literature
  General
    Literary history: PN56.L24
Lambadi proverbs: PN6519.L35
Lameness in literature
  General
    Literary history: PN56.L25
Laments in literature
  General
    Literary history: PN1389

Lampoon in literature
  Collections: PN6149.L35
Lancelot in literature
  General
    Literary history: PN57.L3
      Legends: PN686.L3
Landscape in literature
  General
    Literary history: PN56.L26
Language and broadcasting:
  PN1990.9.L3
  Radio: PN1991.8.L3
  Television: PN1992.8.L35
Language and languages in
  literature
  General
    Literary history: PN56.L27
      Drama: PN1650.L34
Language and literature: PN54
Language and motion pictures:
  PN1995.4
Langue d'oc proverbs: PN6505.L28
Lao proverbs: PN6519.L39
Lapp proverbs: PN6505.L3
Last letters before death:
  PN6140.L3
Last words
  General
    Collections: PN6328.L3
Latin America in motion
  pictures: PN1995.9.L37
Latin lovers in motion pictures:
  PN1995.9.L38
Latvian American theater:
  PN2270.L38
Latvian proverbs: PN6505.L5
Latvian quotations: PN6095.L37
Latvian riddles: PN6377.L4
Latvian-American newspapers:
  PN4885.L37
Laughter in literature
  General
    Literary history: PN56.L3
Laundry in literature
  General
    Collections
      Wit and humor: PN6231.L33

Law and lawyers in literature
  General
    Collections: PN6071.L33
      Anecdotes: PN6268.L4
      Poetry: PN6110.L2
      Wit and humor: PN6231.L4
    Literary history: PN56.L33,
      PN56.5.M4
      Characters: PN56.5.L3
      Fiction: PN3426.L37
      Medieval: PN682.L38
Law and lawyers in motion
  pictures: PN1995.9.J8
Law in television broadcasts:
  PN1992.8.J87
Lazarus in literature
  General
    Collections: PN6071.L35
Laziness in literature
  General
    Collections: PN6071.L37
Leadership in literature
  General
    Collections
      Quotations
        English: PN6084.L15
Leander in literature
  General
    Literary history: PN57.H44
Learning and scholarship in
  literature
  General
    Collections
      Wit and humor: PN6231.L35
Lectures and lecturing
  Oratory: PN4193.L4
Left- and right-handedness in
  literature
  General
    Collections
      Wit and humor: PN6231.L39
Lega proverbs: PN6519.W3
Legal journalism: PN4784.L44,
  PN1 14.L34
Legal novels: PN3448.L4
Legends
  Medieval literature: PN683+

Leisure in literature
General
Collections
Quotations
German: PN6093.L4
Literary history: PN56.L4
Lenin, Vladimir Il'ich, in literature
General
Collections
Poetry: PN6110.L37
Lenin, Vladimir Il'ich, in motion pictures: PN1995.9.L46
Leningrad in literature
General
Literary history: PN56.3.L4
Lenong: PN2904.5.L45
Lesbian theater: PN2270.L47
Lesbianism in literature
General
Literary history: PN56.L45
Lesbianism in motion pictures: PN1995.9.L48
Lesbians in literature
General
Collections: PN6071.L47
Quotations
English: PN6084.L45
Wit and humor: PN6231.L43
Letter writing
General
Collections
Wit and humor: PN6231.L44
Letter writing in literature
General
Collections: PN6071.L48
Letters
General
Collections
Poetry: PN6110.L4
Letters to the editor: PN1 14.L4
United States: PN4888.L47
Libel, Newspaper: PN4741
Liberalism in literature
General
Collections
Wit and humor: PN6231.L47

Liberian proverbs: PN6519.L47
Liberty in literature
General
Collections: PN6071.L5
Poetry: PN6110.L43
Quotations
English: PN6084.L5
Literary history
Romance literatures: PN810.L52
Liberty of the press: PN4735+
Librarians in literature
General
Collections: PN6071.L554
Libraries in literature
General
Collections: PN6071.L554
Literary history: PN56.L48
Libraries in motion pictures: PN1995.9.L49
Library plays
General
Collections: PN6120.L5
Life and literature: PN47
Drama: PN1641
Poetry: PN1075
Prose: PN3341
Life cycle, Human, in literature
General
Literary history: PN56.L52
Life in literature
General
Collections: PN6071.L6
Poetry: PN6110.L5
Wit and humor: PN6231.L48
Literary history
Juvenile literature: PN1009.5.L53
Life skills in literature
General
Collections
Wit and humor: PN6231.L49
Light and darkness in literature
General
Literary history: PN56.L53

Lighthouses in literature
  General
    Collections
      Quotations
        English: PN6084.L54
Lighting
  Television broadcasts:
    PN1992.8.L5
Limbum proverbs: PN6519.L56
Limericks
  General
    Collections: PN6149.L5
      Wit and humor: PN6231.L5
Lincoln, Abraham, in motion
  pictures: PN1995.9.L53
Lincoln, Abraham, in Television
  broadcasts: PN1992.8.L54
Linguists as authors
  General
    Collections
      Poetry: PN6109.95.L54
Lisbon (Portugal) in motion
  pictures: PN1995.9.L55
Lists in literature
  General
    Collections: PN6071.L64
    Literary history: PN56.L54
Literary agents: PN163
  Biography: PN149.8+
Literary composition: PN171.4+
Literary ethics: PN154
Literary extracts: PN6244+
Literary forgeries: PN171.F6+
Literary impostures: PN171.F6+
Literary movements (General):
  PN597
Literary periodicals
  General
    Collections
      Wit and humor: PN6231.L55
Literature
  Journalism: PN1 14.L6
Literature and journalism:
  PN4759
Literature and motion pictures:
  PN1995.3

Literature and radio broadcasts:
  PN1991.8.L5
Literature and sociology: PN51
Literature and television:
  PN1992.655
Lithuania in literature
  General
    Literary history: PN56.3.L56
Lithuanian proverbs: PN6505.L5
Lithuanian riddles: PN6377.L5
Lithuanian-American newspapers:
  PN4885.L54
Little magazines: PN1 14.L62
  United States: PN4878.3
Little Red Riding Hood (Tale) in
  literature
  General
    Literary history
      Juvenile literature:
        PN1009.5.L56
Little theater
  Great Britain: PN2595.3
  United States: PN2267
Living Theater: PN2297.L5
Livonian proverbs: PN6505.L56
Lobsters in literature
  General
    Collections
      Wit and humor: PN6231.L56
Local color in literature
  General
    Literary history: PN56.L55
Local editions
  Journalism: PN4784.L6, PN1
    14.L65
Locations in motion pictures:
  PN1995.67.A1+
Locations in television
  broadcasts: PN1992.78+
Lodge-room recitations:
  PN4305.C6
Lodginghouses in literature
  General
    Collections: PN6071.L66
Logical positivism in literary
  criticism: PN98.L65

London (England) in literature
General
Collections
Quotations
English: PN6084.L56
London (England) in motion
pictures: PN1995.9.L57
Loneliness in literature
General
Collections: PN6071.L68
Literary history: PN56.L56
Lookalikes in literature
General
Collections
Wit and humor: PN6231.L58
Lord Chamberlain's Servants
Great Britain
Renaissance theater:
PN2600.L67
Lord's Supper in literature
General
Collections
Quotations
English: PN6084.L565
Lorelei in literature
General
Literary history: PN57.L65
Loss (Psychology)
General
Collections: PN6071.L69
Loss (Psychology) in literature
General
Collections
Quotations
English: PN6084.L57
Lost articles in literature
General
Collections
Wit and humor: PN6231.L59
Love in literature
General
Collections: PN6071.L7
Anecdotes: PN6268.L7
Aphorisms: PN6278.L6
Epigrams: PN6288.L6
Poetry: PN6110.L6
Proverbs: PN6525.L68

Love in literature
General
Collections
Quotations
English: PN6084.L6
French: PN6089.L6
German: PN6093.L6
Thoughts: PN6338.L6
Wit and humor: PN6231.L6
Literary history: PN56.L6
Medieval: PN682.L68
Poetry: PN1076
Romance literatures:
PN810.L65
Love in motion pictures:
PN1995.9.L6
Love letters
General
Collections: PN6140.L7
Love stories
General
Literary history: PN3448.L67
Technique: PN3377.5.L68
Lovers of Teruel in literature
General
Literary history
Legends: PN687.L68
Low German proverbs: PN6505.L68
Luba-Lulua proverbs: PN6519.L73
Lucazi proverbs: PN6519.L74
Lucretia, Roman matron, in
literature
General
Literary history: PN57.L8
Ludruk: PN2904.5.L83
Lugbara proverbs: PN6519.L76
Lust in literature
General
Collections: PN6071.L86
Luther in literature
General
Literary history: PN57.L9
Lutheran press: PN1 14.L8
Luvale proverbs: PN6519.L8
Luxembourg in literature
General
Literary history: PN849.L88+

Lyric poetry
  General
    Literary history: PN1351+
      Medieval: PN691

M

Macaronic verse: PN1489
Macau in literature
  General
    Collections: PN6071.M12
Macedonian proverbs: PN6505.S37
Machinery in literature
  General
    Literary history: PN56.M2
Machinery in the theater:
  PN2091.M3
Machismo in literature
  General
    Collections
      Wit and humor: PN6231.M15
Madonna, 1958-   , in literature
  General
    Collections
      Wit and humor: PN6231.M16
Madrigals
  General
    Literary history: PN1493
Mafia in literature
  General
    Collections: PN6071.M14
      Wit and humor: PN6231.M163
Mafia in motion pictures:
  PN1995.9.M23
Magazine format television
  programs: PN1992.8.M33
Magazines: PN4832+, PN1 14.P4
Magazines, Employees': PN4784.E6
Magazines, Pulp
  United States: PN4878.5
Maghreb, Literatures of
  Literary history: PN849.A355+
Magi in literature
  General
    Collections: PN6071.M15
      Poetry: PN6110.M23

Magic in literature
  General
    Collections: PN6071.M155
    Literary history: PN56.M23
      Legends
        Arthurian legends:
          PN686.M33
        Medieval: PN682.M34
Magic realism in literature
  General
    Literary history: PN56.M24
Mail-order business in literature
  General
    Collections
      Wit and humor: PN6231.M17
Maine in literature
  General
    Collections
      Wit and humor: PN6231.M18
Majingai proverbs: PN6519.M22
Makasar proverbs: PN6519.M225
Makasar riddles: PN6377.M27
Makeup in motion pictures:
  PN1995.9.M25
Makeup in television:
  PN1992.8.M36
Makeup in the theater: PN2068
Makua proverbs: PN6519.M23
Malagasy proverbs: PN6519.M24
Malapropisms in literature
  General
    Collections
      Wit and humor: PN6231.M19
Malay proverbs: PN6519.M26
Malay riddles: PN6377.M29
Malayalam proverbs: PN6519.M28
Malayalam quotations: PN6095.M3
Malayalam riddles: PN6377.M3
Male authors
  General
    Collections
      Poetry: PN6109.8
Maltese proverbs: PN6505.M34
Mampruli proverbs: PN6519.M29
Man in literature
  General
    Collections: PN6071.M167

Man in literature
  General
    Collections
      Quotations
        German: PN6093.M27
    Literary history: PN56.M25
Man, Primitive, in literature
  General
    Collections: PN6071.M17
Man-woman relationships in
  literature
  General
    Collections
      Quotations
        English: PN6084.M25
    Literary history: PN56.M255
Man-woman relationships in
  motion pictures: PN1995.9.M27
Management
  Journalism: PN4784.M34
Management and prose: PN3352.M3
Management in literature
  General
    Collections
      Wit and humor: PN6231.M2
Management of theaters: PN2053
Manchu proverbs: PN6519.M3
Mandailing proverbs: PN6519.M313
Mandela, Nelson, in literature
  General
    Collections
      Poetry: PN6110.M24
Mandel'shtam, Osip, in literature
  General
    Collections
      Poetry: PN6110.M25
Mandingo proverbs: PN6519.M316
Manipuri proverbs: PN6519.M32
Manners and customs in literature
  General
    Literary history: PN56.M26
Manufactures in literature
  General
    Collections
      Wit and humor: PN6231.M23
Manuscripts, Preparation of:
  PN160

Manzai: PN2924.5.M36
Maori proverbs: PN6519.M35
Maps
  Journalism: PN4784.M36
    United States: PN4888.M37
Maps in literature
  General
    Collections
      Quotations
        English: PN6084.M27
Marat, Jean Paul, in literature
  General
    Literary history: PN57.M24
Marathi proverbs: PN6519.M36
Marathi quotations: PN6095.M35
Marginality, Social, in
  literature
  General
    Literary history: PN56.M27
Marginality, Social, in
  literature
  General
    Literary history
      Prose: PN3352.M34
Mari proverbs: PN6505.M37
Mari riddles: PN6377.M35
Marijuana in literature
  General
    Collections
      Wit and humor: PN6231.M24
Marine fauna in literature
  General
    Collections
      Wit and humor: PN6231.M25
Marketing
  Journalism: PN4784.C6, PN1
  14.C5
    United States: PN4888.C56
Marketing in literature
  General
    Collections
      Wit and humor: PN6231.M26
    Literary history
      Prose fiction: PN3355+
      Technique: PN3355+
    Poetry: PN1059.M3

Marketing in motion pictures:
PN1995.9.M29
Marketing in the performing
arts: PN1590.M27
Marriage in literature
General
Collections: PN6071.M2
Aphorisms: PN6278.M35
Epigrams: PN6288.M3
Maxims: PN6308.M3
Poetry: PN6110.M27
Quotations
English: PN6084.M3
German: PN6093.M3
Wit and humor: PN6231.M3
Literary history: PN56.M28
Medieval: PN682.M37
Marriage in motion pictures:
PN1995.9.M3
Martial arts films: PN1995.9.H3
Martial recitations: PN4305.M3
Marvelous, The, in literature
General
Collections: PN6071.M25
Literary history: PN56.M3
Medieval: PN682.M38
Marx Brothers: PN2297.M3
Mary, Blessed Virgin, Saint, in
literature
General
Collections: PN6071.M27
Poetry: PN6110.M28
Literary history: PN57.M27
Legends: PN687.M37
Mary Magdalene, Saint, in
literature
General
Literary history: PN57.M28
Mary Stuart, Queen of the Scots,
in literature
General
Literary history: PN57.M3
Drama: PN1879.M37
Masai proverbs: PN6519.M37
Masculinity in literature
General
Literary history: PN56.M316

Masculinity in literature
General
Literary history
Juvenile literature:
PN1009.5.M37
Prose: PN3403
Masikoro proverbs: PN6519.M375
Masikoro riddles: PN6377.M37
Masks in literature
General
Literary history: PN56.M318
Masks on stage: PN2071.M37
Masochism in literature
General
Literary history: PN56.M32
Masochism in motion pictures:
PN1995.9.M38
Masquerades in literature
General
Literary history: PN56.M33
Masques
General
Collections: PN6120.M3
Literary history: PN1934
Masses, Treatment of
Drama: PN1690
Masters of ceremonies
Performing arts: PN1590.M3
Matches in literature
General
Collections: PN6071.M28
Materialism in literature
General
Literary history: PN56.M35
Mathematical linguistics in
literature
General
Literary history
Poetry: PN1083.M3
Mathematics
Journalism: PN4784.M37
Mathematics in literature
General
Collections: PN6071.M3
Poetry: PN6110.M29

Matrimonial advertisements in
  literature
  General
    Collections
      Wit and humor: PN6231.M35
Maturation (Psychology) in
  literature
  General
    Collections
      Wit and humor: PN6231.M37
Mauritius, Literature of
  Literary history: PN849.M38+
Maxims: PN6299+
May Day (Labor holiday) in
  literature
  General
    Collections: PN6071.M35
Maya riddles: PN6377.M39
Mbai (Moiooala) proverbc:
  PN6519.M39
Mbund provinces: PN6519.K55
Meaning (Philosophy) in
  literature
  General
    Literary history: PN56.M37
Medea in literature
  General
    Collections
      Drama: PN6120.M4
    Literary history: PN57.M37
      Drama: PN1650.M43
      Legends: PN687.M42
Medical journalism: PN4784.M4,
  PN1 14.M43
  United States: PN4888.M43
Medical personnel
  Oratory: PN4192.M43
Medical personnel in motion
  pictures: PN1995.9.P44
Medici, House of, in motion
  pictures: PN1995.9.M43
Medici, Lorenzino de', in
  literature
  General
    Literary history: PN57.M38

Medicine in literature
  General
    Collections: PN6071.M38
      Anecdotes: PN6268.M4
      Poetry: PN6110.M3
      Quotations
        English: PN6084.M35
      Wit and humor: PN6231.M4
    Literary history: PN56.M38
Medicine in television
  broadcasts: PN1992.8.M43
Medieval drama: PN1751+
Medieval poetry: PN688+
Medieval theater: PN2152+
Meditations
  General
    Collections: PN6146
Mediterranean Region in
  literature
  General
    Literary history: PN56.3.M4
      Medieval: PN682.M42
Mediterranean Region, Literature
  of
  Literary history: PN849.M42+
Medumba proverbs: PN6519.M44
Meetings in literature
  General
    Collections
      Wit and humor: PN6231.M42
Melancholy in literature
  General
    Literary history: PN56.M4
Melodrama
  General
    Literary history: PN1912+
    Motion pictures: PN1995.9.M45
Melusine in literature
  General
    Literary history
      Legends: PN687.M44
Memorabilia
  Motion pictures: PN1995.9.C53
Memorandums in literature
  General
    Collections
      Wit and humor: PN6231.M44

Memorizing, Selections for, in
  literature
  General
    Collections
      Poetry: PN6110.M4
Memory in literature
  General
    Literary history: PN56.M44
    Poetry: PN1083.M4
Men authors
  General
    Literary history
      Prose: PN3403
Men in literature
  General
    Collections: PN6071.M387
      Aphorisms: PN6278.M4
      Epigrams: PN6288.M4
      Quotations
        English: PN6084.M4
      Wit and humor: PN6231.M45
    Literary history: PN56.5.M4
      Drama: PN1650.M44
Men in motion pictures:
  PN1995.9.M46
Menopause in literature
  General
    Collections
      Wit and humor: PN6231.M453
Men's magazines: PN1 14.M45
Menstruation in literature
  General
    Collections: PN6071.M39
Mental health personnel in
  motion pictures: PN1995.9.M462
Mental illness in literature
  General
    Collections: PN6071.M4
    Literary history: PN56.M45
      Drama: PN1650.M45
      Medieval: PN682.M44
Mental illness in motion
  pictures: PN1995.9.M463
Mentally ill in literature
  General
    Collections
      Anecdotes: PN6268.M45

Mentoring in literature
  General
    Literary history: PN56.M48
Merchants in literature
  General
    Collections: PN6071.M45
    Literary history: PN56.5.M46
Mérida (Spain) in literature
  General
    Literary history: PN56.3.M45
Merlin in literature
  General
    Collections: PN6071.M46
    Literary history: PN57.M4
  Literary history
    Legends: PN686.M4
Merope, wife of Cresphontes, in
  literature
  General
    Literary history: PN57.M44
Mesmerism in literature
  General
    Literary history: PN56.M52
Metals in stage setting:
  PN2091.M48
Metamorphosis in literature
  General
    Literary history: PN56.M53
Metaphor in literature
  General
    Literary history
      Prose: PN3383.M48
    Literary style: PN228.M4
    Poetry: PN1059.M4
Metaphor in motion pictures:
  PN1995.9.M472
Method acting: PN2062
Mexican American theater:
  PN2270.M48
Mexican Americans
  Journalism
    United States: PN4888.H57
Mexican Americans in motion
  pictures: PN1995.9.M49
Mexican-American Border region
  in motion pictures:
  PN1995.9.M48

Mexico in literature
General
Collections: PN6071.M49
Literary history: PN56.3.M47
Mexico in motion pictures:
PN1995.9.M5
Mice in literature
General
Collections
Poetry: PN6110.M43
Wit and humor: PN6231.M46
Microcosm and macrocosm in
literature
General
Literary history
Medieval: PN682.M53
Microphone technique
Radio broadcasts: PN1991.8.M5
Midas in literature
General
Literary history: PN57.M53
Middle age in literature
General
Collections
Wit and humor: PN6231.M47
Middle Ages in literature
General
Collections
Wit and humor: PN6231.M48
Literary history: PN56.M534
Juvenile literature:
PN1009.5.M54
Middle Ages in motion pictures:
PN1995.9.M52
Middle classes in literature
General
Literary history: PN56.M535
Middle-finger gesture in
literature
General
Collections
Wit and humor: PN6231.O26
Military art and science in
literature
General
Collections
Anecdotes: PN6268.M48

Military art and science in
literature
General
Collections
Aphorisms: PN6278.M54
Military in literature
General
Collections
Poetry: PN6110.M45
Wit and humor: PN6231.M5
Military journalism: PN4784.M5,
PN1 14.M5
United States: PN4888.M54
Military religious orders in
literature
General
Literary history
Medieval: PN682.M57
Military service
Oratory: PN4193.M5
Milk in literature
General
Collections
Proverbs: PN6525.M55
Millennium in literature
General
Collections
Wit and humor: PN6231.M52
Milon d'Angers in literature
General
Literary history
Legends: PN687.M54
Mimes: PN1942+
Mimesis in literature
General
Literary history: PN56.M536
Miming: PN2071.G4
Minangkabau proverbs: PN6519.M54
Miners in literature
General
Collections
Anecdotes: PN6268.M5
Wit and humor: PN6231.M55
Literary history: PN56.5.M5
Miners in motion pictures:
PN1995.9.M54
Minianka proverbs: PN6519.M55

Miniature dolls in literature
  General
    Literary history: PN56.M5363
Miniature newspapers: PN4839
Mining journalism: PN4784.M54
Minnesota in literature
  General
    Collections
      Wit and humor: PN6231.M57
Minorities
  Journalism: PN1 14.M53
Minorities and broadcasting:
  PN1990.9.M56
Minorities in motion pictures:
  PN1995.9.M56
Minorities in television
  broadcasts: PN1992.8.M54
Minorities in the press
  United States: PN4888.M56
Minority authors
  General
    Collections
      Poetry: PN6109.95.M55
    Literary history
      Biography: PN491.5
Minority press
  United States: PN4882+
Minstrel shows: PN1969.M5
Minstrels
  Medieval German theater:
  PN2648.M55
Miracle plays
  General
    Collections: PN6120.M5
    Literary history: PN1761
Miracles in literature
  General
    Collections: PN6071.M54
    Literary history: PN56.M3
Mirrors in literature
  General
    Literary history: PN56.M537
Misanthropy in literature
  General
    Collections
      Wit and humor: PN6231.M59

Misogyny in literature
  General
    Literary history: PN56.M538
Moba proverbs: PN6519.M57
Mock trials in literature
  General
    Collections
      Drama: PN6120.M7
Mock-heroic literature
  General
    Collections
      Wit and humor: PN6149.M55
Models of theaters: PN2091.M6
Modernism in literature
  General
    Literary history: PN56.M54
Moldavian proverbs: PN6505.M64
Monasticism in literature
  General
    Collections
      Wit and humor: PN6231.M65
Money in literature
  General
    Collections: PN6071.M55
      Anecdotes: PN6268.M6
      Maxims: PN6308.M6
      Quotations
        English: PN6084.M56
      Wit and humor: PN6231.M66
    Literary history: PN56.M547
      Drama: PN1650.M65
      Juvenile literature:
        PN1009.5.M64
Mongo proverbs: PN6519.M58
Mongolian proverbs: PN6519.M6
Monk and the bird's song in
  literature
  General
    Literary history
      Legends: PN687.M58
Monkeys in literature
  General
    Collections
      Quotations
        English: PN6084.M57

Monodrama
  General
    Literary history: PN1936
Monologues
  General
    Collections: PN4305.M6
    Literary history: PN1530
Monsters in literature
  General
    Collections
      Wit and humor: PN6231.M665
    Literary history: PN56.M55
      Medieval: PN682.M65
Monsters in motion pictures:
  PN1995.9.M6
Montenegrin proverbs: PN6505.S6
Moon in literature
  General
    Collections: PN6071.M6
      Poetry: PN6110.M6
      Wit and humor: PN6231.M67
    Literary history: PN56.M58
Moon Pies in literature
  General
    Collections
      Wit and humor: PN6231.M672
Moral and ethical aspects of
  literary criticism: PN98.M67
Moral and ethical aspects of
  literature
  General
    Literary history
      Juvenile literature:
        PN1009.5.M67
Moral and religious aspects of
  radio broadcasts: PN1991.6
Moral and religious aspects of
  television broadcasts:
  PN1992.6
Morality plays
  General
    Literary history: PN1771
Moré proverbs: PN6519.M64
More, Sir Thomas, in literature
  General
    Literary history
      Drama: PN1879.M67

Mormon Church in literature
  General
    Collections
      Wit and humor: PN6231.M675
Mormons in literature
  General
    Collections
      Wit and humor: PN6231.M675
Mother's Day in literature
  General
    Collections
      Drama: PN6120.M75
Mothers in literature
  General
    Collections: PN6071.M7
      Anecdotes: PN6268.M65
      Poetry: PN6110.M64
      Quotations
        English: PN6084.M6
        German: PN6093.M6
      Wit and humor: PN6231.M68
    Literary history: PN56.5.M67
      Poetry: PN1083.M64
Mothers in motion pictures:
  PN1995.9.M63
Mothers in television
  broadcasts: PN1992.8.M58
Mothers' sayings
  General
    Collections: PN6328.M67
Mothers-in-law in literature
  General
    Collections
      Wit and humor: PN6231.M682
Motion picture cartoons
  Television broadcasts:
    PN1992.8.M6
Motion picture collecting:
  PN1995.9.C53
Motion picture industry in
  motion pictures: PN1995.9.M65
Motion picture journalism:
  PN4784.M6, PN1 14.M68
  United States: PN4888.M6
Motion picture remakes:
  PN1995.9.R45

Motion picture trailers:
PN1995.9.T685
Motion pictures: PN1993+
Motion pictures and children:
PN1995.9.C45
Motion pictures and history:
PN1995.2
Motion pictures and language:
PN1995.4
Motion pictures and literature:
PN1995.3
Motion pictures and television:
PN1992.63
Motion pictures and the arts:
PN1995.25
Motion pictures as a profession:
PN1995.9.P75
Motion pictures in literature
General
Collections: PN6071.M73
Wit and humor: PN6231.M7
Motor vehicles in motion
pictures: PN1995.9.A85
Motorcycles in motion pictures:
PN1995.9.M66
Motorcycling in literature
General
Collections
Wit and humor: PN6231.M744
Mottoes in literature
General
Literary history: PN6309+
Mountain whites (Southern
States) in motion pictures:
PN1995.9.M67
Mountains and mountaineering in
literature
General
Collections: PN6071.M738
Poetry: PN6110.M65
Wit and humor: PN6231.M75
Literary history: PN56.M7
Mountains in motion pictures:
PN1995.9.M68
Mourning customs in tragedies:
PN1899.M68

Movement (Posture)
Acting: PN2071.M6
Television: PN1992.8.P4
Multiculturalism in literature
General
Collections
Quotations
English: PN6084.M75
Literary history: PN56.M8
Multilingualism
Authorship: PN171.M93
Multilingualism in literature
General
Poetry: PN1059.M8
Mummies in literature
General
Collections: PN6071.M77
Mummies in motion pictures:
PN1995.9.M83
Mumming plays
General
Collections: PN6120.M8
Munchausen in literature
General
Literary history: PN57.M77
Mundari proverbs: PN6519.M85
Mungaka proverbs: PN6519.M87
Municipal theaters
United States: PN2268
Murder in literature
General
Literary history: PN56.M85
Prose: PN3352.M87
Murphy's law in literature
General
Collections
Wit and humor: PN6231.M82
Museums and exhibitions
Literature
General: PN34
Motion pictures: PN1993.4
Performing arts: PN1590.M87
Museums, Marionette: PN1979.M87
Music and acting: PN2071.M87
Music in literature
General
Collections: PN6071.M8

Music in literature
  General
    Collections
      Poetry: PN6110.M7
      Quotations
        English: PN6084.M8
      Wit and humor: PN6231.M85
    Literary history: PN56.M87
    Recitations: PN4305.M8
Music in television broadcasts:
  PN1992.8.M87
Music radio stations
  Radio broadcasts:
    PN1991.67.P67
Music videos
  History: PN1992.8.M87
Musical films: PN1995.9.M86
Muslim press: PN4784.R35
Muslims in literature
  General
    Literary history: PN56.5.M87
Mustache in literature
  General
    Collections
      Wit and humor: PN6231.M87
Mustapha und Zeangir in
  literature
  General
    Literary history: PN57.M8
Mysteries
  Drama
    General
      Collections: PN6120.M9
      Literary history
        Medieval: PN1761
Mysticism in literature
  General
    Poetry: PN1059.M92
Myth in literature
  General
    Literary history: PN56.M94
    Poetry: PN1077
Myth in motion pictures:
  PN1995.9.M96

Mythology in literature
  General
    Collections
      Poetry: PN6110.M8
    Literary history: PN56.M95
    Prose: PN3351
Mythology in motion pictures:
  PN1995.9.M97

N

Nahuatl riddles: PN6377.N24
Names in literature
  General
    Collections
      Poetry: PN6110.N15
      Wit and humor: PN6231.N24
    Literary history: PN56.N16
Names, Personal, in literature
  General
    Literary history
      Juvenile literature:
        PN1009.5.N34
Naniwabushi: PN2924.5.N36
Naples (Italy) in motion
  pictures: PN1995.9.N3
Napoleon I, Emperor of the
  French, in motion pictures:
  PN1995.9.N32
Napoleon I in literature
  General
    Literary history: PN57.N3
Narcissus in literature
  General
    Literary history: PN57.N33
Narcotics in literature
  General
    Literary history: PN56.N18
Narration
  Literary style: PN212
Narration in literature
  General
    Collections
      Poetry: PN6110.N17
    Literary history
      Prose: PN3383.N35

Nasreddin Hoca (Legendary
  character) in literature
  General
    Collections
      Wit and humor: PN6231.N27
National characteristics,
  American, in motion pictures:
  PN1995.9.N34
National characteristics,
  Australian, in motion
  pictures: PN1995.9.N35
National characteristics,
  British, in motion pictures:
  PN1995.9.N352
National characteristics,
  German, in motion pictures:
  PN1995.9.N354
National characteristics in
  literature
  General
    Collections: PN6071.N28
      Wit and humor: PN6231.N3
National characteristics in
  motion pictures: PN1995.9.N33
National heroic epics
  General
    Literary history: PN1323
National socialism in literature
  General
    Collections
      Wit and humor: PN6231.N35
    Literary history
      Drama: PN1633.N16
      Juvenile literature:
        PN1009.5.N36
National socialism in motion
  pictures: PN1995.9.N36
National songs
  General
    Collections
      Poetry: PN6110.N19
National theater
  Great Britain: PN2582.N3
Nationalism in literature
  General
    Literary history: PN56.N19

Naturalism in literature
  General
    Literary history: PN56.R3
      Drama: PN1633.N2
Nature and literature
  General
    Literary history: PN48
    Poetry: PN1065
Nature films: PN1995.9.N38
Nature in literature
  General
    Collections: PN6071.N3
      Poetry: PN6110.N2
      Quotations
        English: PN6084.N2
        German: PN6093.N3
    Literary history
      Medieval: PN682.N3
      Recitations: PN4305.N3
Nautanki: PN2884.5.N38
Navarre (Spain) in literature
  General
    Literary history
      Romance literatures:
        PN810.N37
Navy newspapers
  United States: PN4888.M54
Ndebele (Zimbabwe) proverbs:
  PN6519.N38
Ndonga proverbs: PN6519.N385
Ndonga riddles: PN6377.N3
Ndumu proverbs: PN6519.N387
Near Eastern proverbs:
  PN6519.N39
Nebraska in literature
  General
    Collections
      Wit and humor: PN6231.N4
Negritude in literature
  General
    Literary history: PN56.N36
Neighbors in literature
  General
    Collections
      Wit and humor: PN6231.N53
Nepali proverbs: PN6519.N4
Nepali quotations: PN6095.N4

Neruda, Pablo, in literature
  General
    Collections
      Poetry: PN6110.N35
Neuroses in literature
  General
    Collections
      Wit and humor: PN6231.N55
    Literary history: PN56.N4
Neurotics in literature
  General
    Collections
      Wit and humor: PN6231.N55
New Age movement in literature
  General
    Collections
      Wit and humor: PN6231.N556
New Criticism
  Literary criticism: PN98 N4
New Deal, 1933-1939, in motion
  pictures: PN1995.9.N47
New England in literature
  General
    Collections
      Wit and humor: PN6231.N557
New Jersey in literature
  General
    Collections
      Wit and humor: PN6231.N558
New literates
  Journalism: PN4784.N4
New York (N.Y.) in literature
  General
    Collections
      Quotations
        English: PN6084.N38
      Wit and humor: PN6231.N559
New York (N.Y.) in motion
  pictures: PN1995.9.N49
Newari proverbs: PN6519.N5
Newfoundland in literature
  General
    Collections
      Wit and humor: PN6231.N56
News agencies: PN4714
News audiences
  Journalism: PN4784.N48

News broadcasts
  Radio: PN4784.R2
  Television: PN4784.T4
News, Foreign: PN4784.F6
Newsbreaks in literature
  General
    Collections
      Wit and humor: PN6231.N6
Newsletters: PN4784.N5
  Journalism
    United States: PN4888.N48
Newspaper and periodical
  distributors
  United States: PN4889
Newspaper libel: PN4741
Newspapers in literature
  General
    Collections
      Wit and humor: PN6231.N63
Newspapers, Indian: PN4883
Ngaju proverbs: PN6519.N52
Nias proverbs: PN6519.N53
Nicaragua
  Journalism
    United States: PN4888.N53
Nicodemus in literature
  General
    Literary history
      Legends: PN687.N5
Nigerian proverbs: PN6519.N55
Night in literature
  General
    Collections: PN6071.N5
      Poetry: PN6110.N46
    Quotations
      English: PN6084.N5
    Literary history: PN56.N5
Nightingales in literature
  General
    Literary history
      Medieval: PN682.N54
Nightmare on Elm Street films:
  PN1995.9.N53
Nihilism in literature
  General
    Collections: PN6071.N53

Nihilism in literature
  General
    Collections
      Quotations
        English: PN6084.N53
    Literary history: PN56.N55
Nihilism (Philosophy) in motion
  pictures: PN1995.9.N55
Niskavuori films: PN1995.9.N57
Nixon, Richard M. (Richard
  Milhous), in motion pictures:
  PN1995.9.N59
No as a literary motif
  General
    Literary history: PN56.N6
Nō theater: PN2924.5.N6
Nobel Prize winners as authors
  General
    Collections: PN6069.N63
Nobility in literature
  General
    Collections
      Wit and humor: PN6231.N67
Nobility of character
  General
    Literary history: PN56.N63
Nomaante proverbs: PN6519.N58
Nomads in literature
  General
    Collections: PN6071.N57
Nōmai: PN2924.5.N65
Nonbroadcast video recordings:
  PN1992.93+
Nonprofit theater: PN2293.N67
Nonsense in literature
  General
    Collections
      Poetry: PN6110.N6
Nonsense literature
  General
    Collections
      Wit and humor: PN6231.N68
Nonsense rhymes: PN1525
Nonsense verse
  General
    Literary history: PN1525

Nonverbal communication in
  literature
  General
    Literary history
      Medieval: PN682.N65
Nonverbal communication in
  television broadcasts:
  PN1992.8.N65
North Dakota in literature
  General
    Collections
      Wit and humor: PN6231.N69
Northeastern States in literature
  General
    Collections
      Wit and humor: PN6231.N693
Northern Sotho proverbs:
  PN6519.N6
Norwegian quotations: PN6095.N6
Norwegian-American dialect in
  literature
  General
    Collections
      Wit and humor: PN6231.N7
Norwegian-American newspapers:
  PN4885.N6
Noses in literature
  General
    Collections: PN6071.N6
      Wit and humor: PN6231.N72
    Literary history: PN56.N67
Nostalgia in literature
  General
    Collections
      Wit and humor: PN6231.N73
Nostalgia in motion pictures:
  PN1995.9.N67
Notetaking
  Journalism: PN4784.N6
Nothingness in literature
  General
    Literary history: PN56.N69
Novel, The: PN3365
Nuclear warfare and prose:
  PN3352.N83

Nuclear warfare in literature
  General
    Literary history: PN56.N83
Nudism in literature
  General
    Collections
      Wit and humor: PN6231.N9
Nudity in literature
  General
    Literary history
      Medieval: PN682.N84
Nudity in motion pictures:
  PN1995.9.N92
Numbers in literature
  General
    Literary history: PN56.N86
      Medieval: PN682.N86
Nuns in literature
  General
    Literary history
      Fiction: PN3426.N85
      Medieval: PN682.N87
Nurses in television broadcasts:
  PN1992.8.N87
Nursing in literature
  General
    Collections: PN6071.N87
Nyaneka proverbs: PN6519.N9
Nyanja proverbs: PN6519.N93
Nzima proverbs: PN6519.N95

O

Obesity in literature
  General
    Collections
      Wit and humor: PN6231.O23
Obituaries in literature
  General
    Collections
      Wit and humor: PN6231.O25
Objectivity
  Journalism: PN4784.O24, PN1
  14.O24
    United States: PN4888.O25

Obscene gestures in literature
  General
    Collections
      Wit and humor: PN6231.O26
Obsequies
  Authorship: PN171.O3
Occasional addresses
  English recitations: PN4305.O4
Occasional speeches: PN4193.O4
Occasional verse
  General
    Literary history: PN1443
Occasions in literature
  General
    Collections
      Poetry: PN6110.O3
      Quotations
        English: PN6084.O3
Occult sciences in literature
  General
    Collections: PN6071.O22
    Literary history: PN56.O33
Occultism in literature
  General
    Literary history: PN56.O33
Occultism in motion pictures:
  PN1995.9.O28
Occupations in literature
  General
    Collections
      Wit and humor: PN6231.P74
Occupations in television
  broadcasts: PN1992.8.O27
Ocean in literature
  General
    Collections
      Quotations
        English: PN6084.O35
Ocean travel in literature
  General
    Collections
      Wit and humor: PN6231.O27
    Literary history
      Romance literatures:
        PN810.O35
Oceania, Literature of
  Literary history: PN849.O26+

Odes
  General
    Literary history: PN1371
Odysseus in literature
  General
    Collections: PN6071.O49
    Literary history: PN57.O3
Oedipus in literature
  General
    Collections
      Drama: PN6120.O3
    Literary history: PN57.O35
Ogier le Danois in literature
  General
    Literary history: PN57.O4
Old age in literature
  General
    Collections: PN6071.O5
      Anecdotes: PN6268.O4
      Poetry: PN6110.O4
      Quotations
        English: PN6084.O5
        German: PN6093.O4
    Literary history: PN56.O4
      Juvenile literature:
        PN1009.5.O43
      Medieval: PN682.O43
Older people in amateur theater:
  PN3160.A34
Ombudsmen
  Journalism: PN4784.O6
One-act plays
  General
    Collections: PN6120.O5
    Literary history: PN1865
Online dramas: PN1992.924+
Online journalism: PN4784.O62
Ontario in literature
  General
    Collections
      Wit and humor: PN6231.O58
Op-ed pages
  United States: PN4888.O73
Open letters
  Journalism: PN4784.O64
Open stage: PN2081.O6

Open-air meetings
  Oratory: PN4193.O7
Open-air theater
  Germany: PN2642.O6
  United States: PN2269
Openings (Rhetoric)
  General
    Collections
      Quotations
        English: PN6084.O63
Opera in motion pictures:
  PN1995.9.O64
Optimism in literature
  General
    Collections: PN6071.O7
      Poetry: PN6110.H14
      Thoughts: PN6338.O6
Oracles in literature
  General
    Literary history: PN56.O63
Oratory
  General
    Collections: PN6121+
    Literary history: PN4001+,
      PN4001+
    Television broadcasts:
      PN1992.8.P83
Ordeal in literature
  General
    Literary history
      Medieval: PN682.O7
Order in literature
  General
    Literary history: PN56.O66
Orestes in literature
  General
    Collections
      Drama: PN6120.O7
Organ (Musical instrument) in
  literature
  General
    Collections: PN6071.O72
Organizational behavior
  Motion pictures: PN1995.9.O75
  Television broadcasts:
    PN1992.8.O72

Orient in literature
  General
    Literary history
      Medieval: PN682.O75
Oriental influences
  Performing arts: PN1590.O7
Oriental proverbs: PN6511
Oriental quotations: PN6095.O7
Originality in literature
  General
    Literary history: PN56.O67
Oriya proverbs: PN6519.O7
Oriya quotations: PN6095.O74
Oriya riddles: PN6377.O75
Orlando in literature
  General
    Literary history: PN57.R6
Oromo proverbs: PN6519.O75
Orpheus in literature
  General
    Collections: PN6071.O74
    Literary history: PN57.O65
      Legends: PN687.O7
Ossetic proverbs: PN6519.O85
Ossetic riddles: PN6377.O78
Oswald, Saint, King of
  Northumbria, in literature
  General
    Literary history: PN57.O7
Otherworld in literature
  General
    Literary history: PN56.O7
Otoshibanashi: PN2924.5.R34
Our Gang films: PN1995.9.O8
Outdoor journalism: PN4784.O9
Outdoor life in literature
  General
    Collections: PN6071.O87
    Literary history
      Prose: PN3377.5.O9
Outdoor recreation in literature
  General
    Collections
      Wit and humor: PN6231.O96
Outdoor theater: PN2219.O8

Outer space in literature
  General
    Collections
      Wit and humor: PN6231.S645
Outhouses in literature
  General
    Collections
      Wit and humor: PN6231.O97
Outlaws in literature
  General
    Literary history
      Medieval: PN682.O87
Outlaws in motion pictures:
  PN1995.9.O84
Outsiders in literature
  General
    Literary history: PN56.5.O95
Owls in literature
  General
    Collections
    Quotations
      English: PN6084.O93
Ownership
  Journalism: PN1 14.O9
    United States: PN4888.O85
Oxymoron in literature
  General
    Collections
      Wit and humor: PN6231.O98

P

Pacific Islands in motion
  pictures: PN1995.9.I7
Pageants: PN3203+
Paimpont Forest in literature
  General
    Literary history
      Legends: PN686.B68
Pain in literature
  General
    Collections
      Poetry: PN6110.P2
Painting in literature
  Collections
    Quotations
      English: PN6084.A8

Palinode
  General
    Literary history: PN1496
Palmer Institute: PN143
Pan (Deity) in literature
  General
    Literary history: PN57.P25
Pandava: PN2884.5.P36
Pandora in literature
  General
    Literary history: PN57.P255
Panics in theaters: PN2091.P3
Panjabi proverbs: PN6519.P3
Pantomimes
  General
    Collections
      Drama: PN6120.P3+,
        PN6120.P3
    Literary history: PN1985+
Pantoum: PN1497
Panza, Sancho, in literature
  General
    Literary history: PN57.P27
Papiamento proverbs: PN6519.P36
Papiamento quotations:
  PN6095.P27
Parables
  General
    Collections: PN6071.P27
    Literary history: PN56.P23
Paradise in literature
  General
    Literary history: PN56.P25
      Medieval: PN682.P27
Paradoxes
  General
    Collections: PN6361+
    Literary style: PN228.P2
Paragraph writing
  Journalism: PN4784.P2
Paranoia in literature
  General
    Collections
      Wit and humor: PN6231.P16

Parasites (Social sciences) in
  literature
  General
    Literary history: PN56.5.P35
Parent and child in literature
  General
    Collections: PN6071.P28
    Poetry: PN6110.P25
    Literary history
      Medieval: PN682.P28
Parents in literature
  General
    Collections
      Wit and humor: PN6231.P2
Parents' sayings
  General
    Collections: PN6328.P3
Paris (Greek mythology) in
  literature
  General
    Literary history
      Legends: PN687.P27
Paris in literature: PN3352.P3
  General
    Collections: PN6071.P29
Paris in motion pictures:
  PN1995.9.P3
Parliamentary oratory: PN4193.P6
Parodies
  General
    Collections
      Poetry: PN6110.P3
      Wit and humor: PN6231.P3
Parody
  General
    Prose: PN3383.P37
    Wit and humor: PN6149.P3
Parody in literature
  General
    Literary history: PN56.P26
Parsifal in literature
  General
    Literary history: PN57.P3
      Legends: PN686.P4

Passersby in literature
General
Literary history:
PN56.5.P37, PN56.5.P4
Passion plays in literature
General
Literary history: PN1761
Passion plays in motion
pictures: PN1995.9.P34
Pasticcios: PN1475
Pastoral drama
General
Literary history: PN1883
Pastoral literature
General
Literary history: PN56.P3
Fiction: PN3448.P38
Poetry: PN1421
Pastorals in literature
General
Collections
Poetry: PN6110.C8
Paternity in literature
General
Literary history: PN56.P32
Pathetic recitations: PN4305.P3
Patience in literature
General
Collections
Quotations
English: PN6084.P3
Patriotism in literature
General
Collections: PN6071.P3
Anecdotes: PN6268.P3
Aphorisms: PN6278.P3
Drama: PN6120.H5
Quotations
English: PN6084.P4
German: PN6093.P3
Literary history
Poetry: PN1080
Recitations: PN4240+
Patrons in literature
General
Literary history
Medieval: PN682.P3

Peace in literature
General
Collections: PN6071.P34
Drama: PN6120.P5
Poetry: PN6110.P4
Quotations
English: PN6084.P45
German: PN6093.P43
Literary history: PN56.P35
Peanuts in literature
General
Collections
Wit and humor: PN6231.P33
Peasantry in literature
General
Literary history
Medieval: PN682.P35
Peasants in literature
General
Literary history
Fiction: PN3426.P4
Peasants in motion pictures:
PN1995.9.P36
Pedro I, el Cruel, King of
Castile and Leon, in literature
General
Literary history: PN57.P4
Penelope (Greek mythology) in
literature
General
Literary history: PN57.P43
Peng peng hsi (Folk dramas):
PN2874.5.P56
Penguins in literature
General
Collections
Wit and humor: PN6231.P34
Penis in literature
General
Collections
Wit and humor: PN6231.P344
Pensions
Authors: PN171.P4
Penthouse theater: PN2081.A7

People with disabilities in
literature
General
Literary history: PN56.5.H35
People with disabilities in
motion pictures: PN1995.9.H34
People with disabilities in
television broadcasts:
PN1992.8.H36
People with disabilities in the
performing arts: PN1590.H36
People with mental disabilities
in literature
General
Literary history: PN56.5.M44
Fiction: PN3426.P46
Perceval in literature
General
Literary history
Legends: PN686.M4,
PN686.P4, PN686.T7
Performing arts: PN1560+
Performing arts and children:
PN1590.C45
Performing arts and television:
PN1992.66
Periodical press, The: PN4699+
Periodicals
Authorship citations:
PN171.F56
Journalism: PN1 14.P4
Periodization in literature
General
Literary history: PN56.P374
Peronism in motion pictures:
PN1995.9.P38
Persephone (Greek deity) in
literature
General
Literary history: PN57.P45
Persian proverbs: PN6519.P5
Persian quotations: PN6095.P35
Persian riddles: PN6377.P47
Personal appearance
Television: PN1992.8.P4

Personal space in literature
General
Literary history: PN56.P377
Personality tests in literature
General
Collections
Wit and humor: PN6231.P35
Personals in literature
General
Collections
Wit and humor: PN6231.P36
Personification in literature
General
Literary history: PN56.P38
Poetry: PN1059.P47
Personnel management
Journalism: PN4784.P4
United States: PN4888.P45
Personnel management in
literature
General
Collections
Wit and humor: PN6231.P37
Pessimism in literature
General
Literary history: PN56.P4
Peter, Saint, apostle, in
literature
General
Collections
Wit and humor: PN6231.P39
Petroleum in literature
General
Collections
Wit and humor: PN6231.P4
Pets in literature
General
Collections
Wit and humor: PN6231.P42
Phaedra in literature
General
Literary history: PN57.P48
Drama: PN1650.P45
Phaeton in literature
General
Literary history: PN57.P485

Pharmacy in literature
  General
    Collections
      Wit and humor: PN6231.P43
Philemon and Baucis in literature
  General
    Literary history: PN57.P487
Philip II, King of Spain, in
  literature
  General
    Literary history: PN57.P4875
Philippine proverbs: PN6519.P55
Philippine quotations: PN6095.P4
Philippine riddles: PN6377.P49
Philoctetes in literature
  General
    Literary history: PN57.P488
Philosophy and literature
  General
    Collections
      Wit and humor: PN6149.P5
    Literary history: PN49
      Drama: PN1631+
      Oratory: PN4061
      Poetry: PN1077
      Prose: PN3329+
Philosophy in literature
  General
    Collections
      Wit and humor: PN6231.P47
Philosophy in motion pictures:
  PN1995.9.P42
Philosophy of the theater:
  PN2039+
Phobias in literature
  General
    Collections
      Quotations
        English: PN6084.P52
Photographers in literature
  General
    Collections: PN6071.P42
Photography in literature
  General
    Collections
      Thoughts: PN6338.P45
      Wit and humor: PN6231.P5

Photography in literature
  General
    Literary history: PN56.P46
Physicians as authors
  General: PN492
Physicians in literature
  General
    Collections: PN6071.P45
    Literary history: PN56.5.P56
Piarist theater
  College theatricals:
    PN3178.P52
Picaresque novels
  General
    Collections: PN6071.P5
Picasso, Pablo, in motion
  pictures: PN1995.9.P48
Pictorial art and drama: PN1637
Pictorial journalism: PN4704.P5
Pidgin English proverbs:
  PN6519.P6
Pierrot in literature
  General
    Literary history: PN57.P49
Pilgrims and pilgrimages in
  literature
  General
    Literary history
      Medieval: PN682.P5
Pilot programs
  Television broadcasts:
    PN1992.8.P54
P'ing ch'iang pang tzu hsi (Folk
  dramas): PN2874.5.P56
P'ing hsi (Folk dramas):
  PN2874.5.P56
P'ing hua: PN2874.5.P58
Ping ju (Folk dramas):
  PN2874.5.P56
Ping shu: PN2874.5.P58
Pinggiang bangzixi (Folk
  dramas): PN2874.5.P56
Pinghua: PN2874.5.P58
Pingju (Folk dramas):
  PN2874.5.P56
Pingshu: PN2874.5.P58

Pingxi (Folk dramas):
  PN2874.5.P56
Piper of Hamelin in literature
  General
    Literary history: PN57.P5
Pirates in motion pictures:
  PN1995.9.P49
Piscatory literature
  General
    Literary history: PN56.F5
Places in literature
  Drama technique: PN1672.9
  General
    Collections
      Poetry: PN6110.P6+
    Quotations
      English: PN6084.P55
Plagiarism
  General
    Literary history: PN167+
Plague in literature
  General
    Literary history: PN56.P5
Planet of the Apes films:
  PN1995.9.P495
Planning
  Theater: PN2293.P53
Plants in literature
  General
    Collections
      Poetry: PN6110.P72
      Wit and humor: PN6231.P55
    Literary history: PN56.P52
Play in literature
  General
    Literary history: PN56.P53
Play within a play
  General
    Literary history: PN1692
Playbills
  British theater: PN2582.P54
  French theater: PN2622.P53
  German theater: PN2642.P5
Playbills in motion pictures:
  PN1995.9.P5
Plays
  Motion pictures: PN1997+

Plays, Children's, Presentation
  of: PN3157+
Plays-in-progress
  United States: PN2270.P58
Pleasure in literature
  General
    Literary history: PN56.P534
Plots in literature
  General
    Literary history: PN1683
    Prose: PN3378
Plots in motion pictures:
  PN1997.8
Plumbing in literature
  General
    Collections
      Wit and humor: PN6231.P58
Poetic justice in literature
  General
    Literary history
      Drama: PN1675
Poetic license: PN1059.P7
Poetics: PN1039+
Poetry
  Collections
    General: PN6099+
  Literary history
    General: PN1010+
    Medieval: PN688+
  Oral interpretation: PN4151
  Oratory: PN4193.P5
  Quotations: PN6082
  Radio broadcasts: PN1991.8.P6
Poetry and political science:
  PN1081
Poetry and social progress:
  PN1081
Poetry by women
  Indexes: PN1024
Poetry interpretation: PN4151
Poetry readings: PN4151
Point of view in literature
  General
    Literary history
      Prose: PN3383.P64
Poland and the press: PN1 14.P54

Poles in literature
General
Collections
Wit and humor: PN6231.P588
Police and the press: PN1 14.P58
Police films: PN1995.9.P57
Police in literature
General
Collections
Wit and humor: PN6231.P59
Polichinelle: PN1979.P9
Polish American theater:
PN2270.P64
Polish jokes: PN6231.P588
Polish proverbs: PN6505.S4
Polish quotations: PN6095.P6
Polish Revolution, 1830-1832, in
literature
General
Literary history: PN56.P54
Polish riddles: PN6377.P67
Polish-American newspapers:
PN4885.P7
Political aspects of journalism
United States: PN4888.P6
Political aspects of juvenile
literature: PN1009.5.P64
Political aspects of television
broadcasts: PN1992.6
Political aspects of the
performing arts: PN1590.P64
Political literature
General
Collections
Poetry: PN6110.P728
Satire: PN6149.P64
Literary history
Fiction: PN3448.P6
Political oratory: PN4193.P6
Political plays
General
Collections: PN6120.P64
Political science and drama:
PN1643
Political science and literature
General
Literary history: PN51

Political science and literature
General
Literary history
Drama: PN1643
Poetry: PN1081
Political science and poetry:
PN1081
Political science in literature
General
Collections: PN6071.P57
Aphorisms: PN6278.P64
Quotations
English: PN6084.P6
French: PN6089.P6
Political style of writing:
PN239.P64
Politics
Journalism: PN1 14.P6
Politics in literary criticism:
PN98.P64
Politics in literature
General
Collections
Anecdotes: PN6268.P6
Epigrams: PN6288.P6
Wit and humor: PN6231.P6
Journalism: PN4751
Politics in motion pictures:
PN1995.9.P6
Polynices in literature
General
Literary history: PN57.E7
Polyphemus in literature
General
Literary history: PN57.P64
Pool (Game) in literature
General
Collections: PN6071.P575
Popes in literature
General
Collections
Wit and humor: PN6231.P63
Literary history: PN56.5.P66
Popular culture in literature
General
Literary history: PN56.P547

Popular literature
  General
    Literary history: PN56.P55
Popular music stations
  Radio broadcasts:
    PN1991.67.P67
Popular theater for community
  development: PN3305+
Populist films: PN1995.9.P64
Portmanteau words in literature
  General
    Collections
      Wit and humor: PN6231.P64
Portuguese quotations: PN6095.P7
Portuguese riddles: PN6377.P7
Posters
  French theater: PN2622.P53
  General
    Collections
      Wit and humor: PN6231.P645
  German theater: PN2642.P5
Posters in motion pictures:
  PN1995.9.P5
Postmodernism in literary
  criticism: PN98.P67
Potatoes in literature
  General
    Collections
      Poetry: PN6110.P73
Pottery in literature
  General
    Collections: PN6071.P58
Poverty in literature
  General
    Collections: PN6071.P6
      Wit and humor: PN6231.P65
Power in literature
  General
    Collections
      Aphorisms: PN6278.P68
Practical jokes in literature
  General
    Collections
      Wit and humor: PN6231.P67

Prague (Czech Republic) in
  literature
  General
    Collections: PN6071.P617
Prefaces in books
  General: PN171.P7
Pregnancy in literature
  General
    Collections: PN6071.P62
    Quotations
      English: PN6084.P73
    Wit and humor: PN6231.P68
Prehistoric animals in motion
  pictures: PN1995.9.P67
Prejudice in literature
  General
    Collections: PN6071.P63
Premenstrual syndrome in
  literature
  General
    Collections
      Wit and humor: PN6231.P686
Preppies in literature
  General
    Collections
      Wit and humor: PN6231.P69
Presentation of children's
  plays: PN3157+
Presidents in literature
  General
    Collections
      Wit and humor: PN6231.P693
Presley, Lisa Marie, 1968-   ,
  in literature
  General
    Collections
      Wit and humor: PN6231.P696
Press agents
  Performing arts: PN1590.P7
Press and the government:
  PN4735+
Press conferences
  Journalism: PN4784.P69
  Oratory: PN4193.P73
Press councils: PN4715, PN4846
Press, International: PN4736
Press, Liberty of the: PN4735+

Press, The, in literature
General
Collections: PN6071.P65
Prices
Journalism: PN1 14.P65
Prices of theater tickets:
PN2582.T5
Pride in literature
General
Literary history: PN56.P6
Primitivism in literature
General
Literary history: PN56.P7
Printers and printing in
literature
General
Collections
Poetry: PN6110.T8
Wit and humor: PN6231.P7
Literary history: PN56.5.P7
Prison films: PN1995.9.P68
Prison journalism: PN4784.P7,
PN1 14.P67
United States: PN4888.P75
Prisoners as authors
General
Collections: PN6069.P7
Literary history: PN494
Prisoners in literature
General
Literary history
Drama: PN1650.P74
Prisons and prisoners in
literature
General
Collections: PN6071.P68
Poetry: PN6110.P8
Prisons in literature
General
Literary history: PN56.P72
Drama: PN1650.P74
Prizes
Journalism: PN4798
Literature: PN171.P75

Probability in literature
General
Literary history
Prose: PN3352.P67
Procrastination in literature
General
Collections
Wit and humor: PN6231.P73
Production and direction
Broadcasting: PN1990.9.P76
College theatricals: PN3178.P7
Motion pictures: PN1995.9.P7
Nonbroadcast video recordings:
PN1992.94
Performing arts: PN1590.P74
Theater: PN2053
Professional ethics for actors:
PN2056
Professions in literature
General
Collections
Wit and humor: PN6231.P74
Professors in literature
General
Collections
Wit and humor: PN6231.S3
Program ratings
Television broadcasts:
PN1992.8.R3
Programs in the performing arts:
PN1590.P75
Programs, Television:
PN1992.77.A1+
Progressivism in literature
General
Literary history: PN56.P74
Prohibition in literature
General
Collections
Wit and humor: PN6231.P75
Proletariat theater: PN3305+
Prologues and epilogues
General
Literary history: PN171.P8
Prometheus in literature
General
Collections: PN6071.P695

Prometheus in literature
  General
    Literary history: PN57.P73
      Drama: PN1650.P76
Propaganda
  Journalism: PN1 14.P7
Prophecies in literature
  General
    Literary history: PN56.P744
Proposals of marriage in
  literature
  General
    Collections: PN6071.P7
Props, Stage
  Motion pictures: PN1995.9.S69
Prose poems
  General
    Collections: PN6110.P82
    Literary history: PN1059.P76
Proserpine in literature
  General
    Literary history: PN57.P45
Prostitutes in literature
  General
    Literary history
      Fiction: PN3426.P75
Prostitutes in motion pictures:
  PN1995.9.P76
Prostitution
  Journalism: PN1 14.P73
Prostitution in literature
  General
    Collections: PN6071.P75
    Literary history: PN56.5.P74
Protest poetry
  General
    Collections: PN6110.P83
Protestant press: PN1 14.P74
Provençal proverbs: PN6505.P6
Proverbs
  General
    Collections: PN6400+
    Literary history: PN56.P75
Provincetown Players: PN2297.P7
Prussia, East, in literature
  General
    Collections: PN6071.P77

Prussia in motion pictures:
  PN1995.9.P77
Psyche (Greek deity) in
  literature
  General
    Literary history: PN57.P77
Psychiatrists in motion
  pictures: PN1995.9.M462
Psychiatry in literature
  General
    Literary history: PN56.P9
Psychiatry in motion pictures:
  PN1995.9.P78
Psychoanalysis in literature
  General
    Collections
      Wit and humor: PN6231.P78
    Literary history: PN56.P92
      Poetry: PN1083.P74
Psychoanalysis in motion
  pictures: PN1995.9.P783
Psychoanalytic approach to
  literary criticism: PN98.P75
Psychological aspects of acting:
  PN2071.P78
Psychological aspects of
  authorship: PN171.P83
Psychological aspects of
  juvenile literature:
  PN1009.5.P78
Psychological aspects of the
  performing arts: PN1590.P76
Psychological fiction
  General
    Literary history: PN3448.P8
Psychologists in literature
  General
    Literary history: PN56.5.P8
Psychology in literature
  General
    Collections: PN6071.P8
      Wit and humor: PN6231.P785
    Literary history: PN56.P93
      Prose: PN3352.P7
Psychopaths in motion pictures:
  PN1995.9.P785

Psychotherapists in motion
  pictures: PN1995.9.M462
Public administration in
  literature
  General
    Collections
      Wit and humor: PN6231.P79
Public health in literature
  General
    Literary history: PN56.P95
Public officers in literature
  General
    Collections
      Aphorisms: PN6278.P8
Public opinion
  Journalism: PN1 14.P82
    United States: PN4888.P82
Public relations
  Motion pictures: PN1006.0.P70
  Theater: PN2053.5
Public service programs
  Broadcasting: PN1990.9.P82
    Radio: PN1991.8.P83
    Television: PN1992.8.P8
Publicity
  Journalism: PN4784.P8
Publishing
  Periodicals and newspapers:
    PN4734+
Puerto Ricans
  Journalism
    United States: PN4888.H57
Puerto Rico in motion pictures:
  PN1995.9.P793
Pulp magazines
  United States: PN4878.5
Pulpit oratory and elocution:
  PN4173
Punch and Judy shows: PN1979.P9
Punchinello: PN1979.P9
  Literary history: PN57.P79
Punishment in literature
  General
    Literary history: PN56.P97
Puns in literature
  General
    Collections: PN6149.P85

Puns in literature
  General
    Collections
      Wit and humor: PN6231.P8
Puppet films: PN1995.9.P8
Puppet plays
  General
    Collections: PN6071.P9
  Television broadcasts:
    PN1992.8.P86
Puppet theater
  General
    Literary history: PN1972+
Puppets
  General
    Literary history: PN56.P975
  Television broadcasts:
    PN1992.8.P86
Pushto proverbs: PN6519.P8
Pushto quotations: PN6095.P8
Pygmalion (Greek mythology) in
  literature
  General
    Collections: PN6071.P95
Pygmalion in literature
  General
    Literary history: PN57.P86
Pyramus and Thisbe in literature
  General
    Literary history: PN57.P9

Q

Quakers in literature
  General
    Collections
      Poetry: PN6110.Q3
Quarreling in literature
  General
    Collections
      Quotations
        English: PN6084.Q3
Quatrains
  General: PN1499
    Collections: PN6110.Q33
Quechua proverbs: PN6519.Q45
Quechua riddles: PN6377.Q42

Queens in literature
  General
    Collections
      Quotations
        English: PN6084.Q4
    Literary history
      Medieval: PN682.Q44
Queensland in motion pictures:
  PN1995.9.Q36
Quests in literature
  General
    Collections: PN6071.Q47
    Literary history
      Prose: PN3352.Q37
Quiet life in literature
  General
    Collections
      Poetry: PN6110.Q8
Quilting in literature
  General
    Collections
      Quotations
        English: PN6084.Q54
Quiz programs
  Radio broadcasts: PN1991.8.Q58
  Television broadcasts:
    PN1992.8.Q5
Quotation
  Journalism: PN4784.Q6
Quotations: PN6080+
  Authorship: PN171.Q6

R

Rabbits in literature
  General
    Collections: PN6071.R2
      Wit and humor: PN6231.R23
Race in literature
  General
    Literary history: PN56.R16
Race problems
  Journalism: PN1 14.R28
Race problems in literature
  General
    Collections: PN6071.R23
      Wit and humor: PN6231.R25

Race problems in literature
  General
    Literary history: PN56.R18
    Juvenile literature:
      PN1009.5.R32
Racism
  Journalism: PN1 14.R29
  United States: PN4888.R3
Radicalism in literature
  General
    Collections: PN6071.R25
Radio and poetry: PN1991.8.P6
Radio announcing: PN1991.8.A6
Radio book review programs:
  PN1991.8.B66
Radio broadcasts: PN1991+
Radio comedy shows: PN1991.8.C65
Radio journalism: PN4784.R2,
  PN1 14.R3
  United States: PN4888.R33
Radio news: PN4784.R2
Radio plays
  General
    Collections: PN6120.R2
    Literary history: PN1991.73
    Recitations in English:
      PN4305.R3
Radio programs, Experimental:
  PN1991.8.E94
Radio stories
  General
    Collections: PN6071.R27
Raeto-Romance proverbs:
  PN6505.R33
Railroads in literature
  General
    Collections: PN6071.R3
      Poetry: PN6110.R2
      Wit and humor: PN6231.R3
    Literary history: PN56.R22
      Prose: PN3352.R34
Railroads in motion pictures:
  PN1995.9.R25
Rain forests in literature
  General
    Collections: PN6071.R35
Rajasthani proverbs: PN6519.R35

Rajasthani riddles: PN6377.R34
Rakugo: PN2924.5.R34
Rama (Hindu deity) in literature
  General
    Literary history: PN57.R35
Ranch life in literature
  General
    Collections
      Wit and humor: PN6231.R35
Randai: PN2904.5.R35
Rape in literature
  General
    Literary history: PN56.R24
Rape in motion pictures:
  PN1995.9.R27
Rape in television broadcasts:
  PN1992.8.R26
Rasas
  General
    Literary history
      Poetry: PN1059.R37
Ratings
  Television broadcasts:
    PN1992.8.R3
Rats in literature
  General
    Literary history: PN56.R27
Ravenna (Italy) in literature
  General
    Collections: PN6071.R37
Readability: PN204
Reader-oriented literary
  criticism: PN98.R38
Reader-response literary
  criticism: PN98.R38
Readers (Books) in literature
  General
    Collections
      Wit and humor: PN6231.R36
Readers' opinions, etc.
  Journalism
    United States: PN4888.L47
Readers' theater: PN2081.R4
Readership
  Literary history
    General
      Poetry: PN1059.R4

Readership surveys
  Journalism: PN4784.R27, PN1
    14.R43
  United States: PN4888.R37
Reading in literature
  General
    Collections
      Quotations
        English: PN6084.B65
Realism and literature: PN601
Realism in literary criticism:
  PN98.R4
Realism in literature
  General
    Literary history: PN56.R3
    Prose fiction: PN3340
Realism in motion pictures:
  PN1995.9.R3
Realism in television
  broadcasts: PN1992.8.R4
Reality in literature
  General
    Literary history: PN56.R32
      Medieval: PN682.R37
Reality programs
  Television broadcasts:
    PN1992.8.R43
Rebels (Social psychology) in
  motion pictures: PN1995.9.A47
Reception aesthetics
  Literary criticism: PN98.R38
Recitations in English: PN4199+
Recognition in literature
  General
    Literary history: PN56.R33
Reconciliation in literature
  General
    Literary history: PN56.R34
Redheads in literature
  General
    Collections
      Wit and humor: PN6231.R37
Rednecks in literature
  General
    Collections
      Wit and humor: PN6231.R38

Reformers in literature
  General
    Collections
      Thoughts: PN6338.R4
Refuge in literature
  General
    Literary history: PN56.R35
Refugees in motion pictures:
  PN1995.9.R34
Regeneration in motion pictures:
  PN1995.9.R35
Regional dialect imitation
  Acting: PN2071.F6
Regional journalism:
  PN4784.R29, PN1 14.R44
Regional periodicals
  United States: PN4878.7
Regionalism in literature
  General
    Literary history
      Prose: PN3352.R43
Regulation of the theater:
  PN2042+
Rehearsals
  Acting: PN2071.R45
Reincarnation in literature
  General
    Collections: PN6071.R39
Reinoldlegende in literature
  General
    Literary history
      Legends: PN687.R4
Rejection in literature
  General
    Collections
      Wit and humor: PN6231.R39
Relaxation in literature
  General
    Collections
      Quotations
        German: PN6093.R27
      Wit and humor: PN6231.R397
Religion and journalism: PN4756
Religion and literary criticism:
  PN98.R44

Religion and literature
  General
    Literary history: PN49
      Drama: PN1647
      Poetry: PN1077
      Prose: PN3351
Religion in literature
  General
    Collections: PN6071.R4
      Anecdotes: PN6268.R4
      Poetry: PN6110.R4
      Wit and humor: PN6231.R4
    Literary history
      Medieval: PN682.R4
Religion in motion pictures:
  PN1995.9.R4
Religious drama
  General
    Collections: PN6120.R4
    Literary history: PN1880
Religious journalism:
  PN4784.R3, PN1 14.R45
  United States: PN4888.R44
Religious orders in literature
  General
    Collections
      Wit and humor: PN6231.M65
Religious quotations
  General
    Collections
      English: PN6084.R3
      German: PN6093.R3
Religious recitations: PN4230+
Remakes, Motion picture:
  PN1995.9.R45
Renaissance literature
  General
    Literary history: PN715+
      Drama: PN1785+
        The theater: PN2171+
          Great Britain: PN2589+
      Poetry: PN1180+
Rendille proverbs: PN6519.R46
Renga
  General
    Collections
      Poetry: PN6110.R42

Repertory theater
  Great Britain: PN2595.3
Repetition in literature
  General
    Literary history: PN56.R45
      Prose: PN3383.R46
Reportage literature
  General
    Literary history
      Prose
        Technique: PN3377.5.R45
Reporters and reporting:
  PN4781, PN1 14.R5
Research
  Journalism: PN4784.R38
    United States: PN4888.R45
  Literature
    General: PN73
Research institutes. PN2070.A
Rest in literature
  General
    Collections
      Quotations
        German: PN6093.R4
Restaurants in literature
  General
    Collections
      Wit and humor: PN6231.R43
Resurrection in literature
  General
    Literary history: PN56.R47
Retirement in literature
  General
    Collections
      Wit and humor: PN6231.R44
Revenge in literature
  General
    Collections: PN6071.R42
      Wit and humor: PN6231.R45
    Literary history: PN56.R48
Reviewing of books: PN98.B7
Reviews
  Journalism: PN4784.R4, PN1
    14.R55
Revolutionary literature
  General
    Collections: PN6071.R43

Revolutionary literature
  General
    Collections
      Poetry: PN6110.R48
    Literary history
      Poetry: PN1083.R47
      Prose
        Technique: PN3377.5.R48
Revolutions in literature
  General
    Collections
      Drama: PN6120.R47
Revues
  Drama
    General
      Collections: PN6120.R5
Reynard the Fox in literature
  General
    Literary history: PN57.R18
      Poetry
        Medieval: PN690.R5
Rhyme
  Poetry: PN1059.R5
Rhythm in literature
  General
    Literary history
      Drama: PN1693
      Poetry: PN1059.R53
Riddles
  General
    Collections: PN6366+
Rites and ceremonies in
  literature
  General
    Collections
      Wit and humor: PN6231.R56
Rites and ceremonies in motion
  pictures: PN1995.9.R56
Rivers in literature
  General
    Collections: PN6071.R5
Road films: PN1995.9.R63
Roasts
  Oratory: PN4193.R63

Roberval, Marguerite de, in
  literature
  General
    Literary history: PN57.R57
Robin in motion pictures:
  PN1995.9.R65
Robinsonades: PN3432
Robots in literature
  General
    Literary history
      Drama: PN1650.R63
Roca, Julio Argentino, in
  literature
  General
    Literary history
      Poetry: PN1083.R63
Rock music in literature
  General
    Collections
      Quotations
        English: PN6084.R62
      Wit and humor: PN6231.R59
Rock musical films: PN1995.9.M86
Rock videos
  History: PN1992.8.M87
Rodrick in literature
  General
    Literary history
      Legends: PN687.R6
Roguery, Romances of: PN3428+
Rogues and vagabonds in
  literature
  General
    Collections: PN6071.R55
      Poetry: PN6110.V3
    Literary history: PN56.5.R63
Roland in literature
  General
    Literary history: PN57.R6
Roman charity in literature
  General
    Literary history: PN56.R58
Romance in literature
  General
    Literary history: PN56.R6

Romance literatures
  General
    Literary history: PN801+
Romances of chivalry
  General
    Literary history: PN1326,
      PN1329
Romanian proverbs: PN6505.R7
Romanian quotations: PN6095.R6
Romanian riddles: PN6377.R7
Romanies in literature
  General
    Collections: PN6071.G5
    Literary history: PN56.3.R58
      Romance literatures:
        PN810.G86
Romanies in motion pictures:
  PN1995.9.R67
Romantic epics
  General
    Literary history: PN1326
Romanticism
  General
    Literary history
      Drama: PN1633.R65
Romanticism in literature
  General
    Literary history: PN56.R7
      Prose: PN3340
Rome in literature
  General
    Collections: PN6071.R57
    Literary history: PN56.3.R6
Rome in motion pictures:
  PN1995.9.R68
Rondeau: PN1501
Rondel: PN1504
Roommates in literature
  General
    Collections
      Wit and humor: PN6231.R62
Rooms in literature
  General
    Literary history: PN56.R73
Roses in literature
  General
    Collections: PN6071.R58

Roses in literature
  General
    Collections
      Poetry: PN6110.R6
    Literary history: PN56.R75
Rotterdam in literature
  General
    Collections: PN6071.R6
Roundelay: PN1507
Ruanda proverbs: PN6519.R8
Ruanda riddles: PN6377.R8
Rubik's Cube in literature
  General
    Collections
      Wit and humor: PN6231.R78
Rugby in literature
  General
    Collections
      Wit and humor. PN0231.R79
Rugs, Hooked, in literature
  General
    Collections
      Wit and humor: PN6231.R8
Ruins in literature
  General
    Literary history: PN56.R87
Rundi proverbs: PN6519.R84
Running in literature
  General
    Collections
      Wit and humor: PN6231.R85
Rural churches in literature
  General
    Collections
      Wit and humor: PN6231.R87
Rural journalism: PN4784.C77,
  PN1 14.C67
Russia in literature
  General
    Collections: PN6071.R8
Russian proverbs: PN6505.S5
Russian quotations: PN6095.R8
Russian Revolution, 1917-1921 in
  literature
  General
    Collections: PN6071.R83
Russian riddles: PN6377.R9

Russo-Turkish War, 1877-1878, in
  literature
  General
    Literary history: PN56.R93
Ruthenian proverbs: PN6505.S76
Ruthenian-American newspapers:
  PN4885.U4
Ryukyu proverbs: PN6519.R98

S

Sabaot proverbs: PN6519.S23
Sacred quotations
  General
    Collections
      English: PN6084.S2
Sadism in motion pictures:
  PN1995.9.S23
Safety plays
  General
    Collections: PN6120.S3
Sailing in literature
  General
    Collections
      Poetry: PN6110.S22
      Quotations
        English: PN6084.S26
Saint Patrick's purgatory in
  literature
  General
    Literary history
      Legends: PN687.P3
Saint Petersburg (Russia) in
  literature
  General
    Collections: PN6071.S16
Saint Valentine's Day in
  literature
  General
    Collections
      Wit and humor: PN6231.S16
      Recitations: PN4305.S3
Saints in literature
  General
    Collections
      Poetry: PN6110.S23

Saints in literature
General
Literary history
Prose: PN3426.S24
Saladin, Sultan of Egypt and
Syria, in literature
General
Literary history: PN57.S27
Salesmen in literature
General
Collections
Wit and humor: PN6231.S17
Salome in literature
General
Literary history: PN57.S3
Salutations in literature
General
Collections
Poetry: PN6110.S25
Salvation in literature
General
Literary history: PN56.S34
Sami (European people) in motion
pictures: PN1995.9.S237
Samoan proverbs: PN6519.S3
Samson, Judge of Israel, in
literature
General
Literary history: PN57.S33
Samurai films: PN1995.9.S24
Sancho Panza in literature
General
Literary history: PN57.P27
Sanskrit proverbs: PN6418.5.S3
Sanskrit quotations: PN6095.S3
Sanskrit riddles: PN6377.S25
Santa Claus in literature
General
Collections: PN6071.S19
Sappho in literature
General
Literary history: PN57.S335
Sardinian proverbs: PN6505.S15
Sarugaku: PN2924.5.S3
Satanism in literature
General
Collections: PN6071.S2

Satire
Authorship: PN169
Oratory: PN4066
Satire in literature
General
Collections: PN6146.2+
Poetry: PN6110.S27
Wit and humor: PN6231.S2
History and criticism
Wit and humor: PN6149.S2
Literary history: PN1435
Saturn (Roman deity) in
literature
General
Literary history: PN57.S34
Saul, King of Israel, in
literature
General
Literary history: PN57.S35
Sausages in literature
General
Collections
Wit and humor: PN6231.S22
Sayings: PN6319+
Scandinavia in literature
General
Literary history: PN849.S25+
Scandinavian-American
newspapers: PN4885.S2
Scandinavians in literature
General
Collections
Wit and humor: PN6231.S25
Scapegoat in literature
General
Collections: PN6071.S23
Scenarios
Motion pictures: PN1997+
Scenarios (Motion pictures)
Scenario writing: PN1996
Scheherazade in literature
General
Literary history: PN57.S42
Scholarly periodicals
Journalism: PN1 14.S34
School administrators
Oratory: PN4192.S35

School days in literature
  General
    Collections
      Poetry: PN6110.S3
School exercises
  English recitations: PN4305.S4
School prose
  General
    Collections: PN6071.S27
    Literary history: PN3352.S3
School verse
  General
    Collections: PN6110.S35
Schools in literature
  General
    Collections
      Wit and humor: PN6231.S3
Schools in motion pictures:
  PN1995.9.S253
Schools of journalism
  United States: PN4791.A+
Science
  General
    Literary history: PN3352.S34
Science and literature: PN55
Science fiction
  General
    Collections: PN6071.S33
      Quotations
        English: PN6084.S34
      Wit and humor: PN6231.S42
    Literary history: PN3433+
      Technique: PN3377.5.S3
    Radio broadcasts: PN1991.8.S34
    Television broadcasts:
      PN1992.8.S35
Science fiction films:
  PN1995.9.S26
Science fiction plays: PN1950
Science films: PN1995.9.S265
Science in literature
  General
    Collections: PN6071.S3
      Poetry: PN6110.S37
      Thoughts: PN6338.S4,
        PN6338.T7
      Wit and humor: PN6231.S4

Science in literature
  General
    Literary history
      Drama: PN1650.S34
      Poetry: PN1083.S43
Scientific journalism: PN1
  14.S35
Scientists
  Oratory: PN4192.S39
Scientists in literature
  General
    Literary history: PN56.5.S35
Scooby-Doo television programs:
  PN1992.8.S36
Scotland in literature
  General
    Collections
      Quotations
        English: PN6084.S38
Scotland in motion pictures:
  PN1995.9.S27
Scots humor
  General
    Collections
      Wit and humor: PN6231.S45
Scots in literature
  General
    Collections
      Quotations
        English: PN6084.S38
Scrapbooks, Literary: PN245
Script writing
  Broadcasting: PN1990.9.A88
    Television: PN1991.7+,
      PN1992.7
Scuba diving in literature
  General
    Collections
      Wit and humor: PN6231.S46
Sea and sailors in literature
  General
    Collections: PN6071.S4
      Anecdotes: PN6268.S4
      Poetry: PN6110.S4
      Wit and humor: PN6231.S15
Sea and sailors in motion
  pictures: PN1995.9.S28

Sea in literature
  General
    Collections
      Proverbs: PN6525.S36
    Literary history: PN56.S4
Seasons in literature
  General
    Collections: PN6071.S4114
      Poetry: PN6110.S5
Secrecy in literature
  General
    Literary history: PN56.S43
Secretaries in literature
  General
    Collections
      Wit and humor: PN6231.S48
Securities fraud in the press
  United States: PN4888.S43
Seduction in literature
  General
    Literary history: PN56.S45
      Medieval: PN682.S32
Segregation in literature
  General
    Collections
      Wit and humor: PN6231.S485
Selections for daily reading:
  PN6075+
Self in literature
  General
    Collections
      Poetry: PN6110.S513
    Literary history
      Medieval: PN682.S34
      Prose: PN3352.S44
Self-care, Health, in literature
  General
    Collections
      Wit and humor: PN6231.S489
Self-defense in literature
  General
    Collections
      Wit and humor: PN6231.S49
Self-interest in literature
  General
    Collections
      Wit and humor: PN6231.S493

Self-knowledge in literature
  General
    Literary history: PN56.S46
Self-realization in literature
  General
    Collections: PN6071.S412
      Quotations
        English: PN6084.S45
Semiotic approach to literature:
  PN98.S46
Senari proverbs: PN6519.S36
Sensationalism
  Journalism: PN4784.S4, PN1
    14.S45
  United States: PN4888.S46
  Television broadcasts:
    PN1992.8.S37
Sensationalism in motion
  pictures: PN1995.9.S284
Senses and sensation in
  literature
  General
    Literary history: PN56.S47
      Romance literatures:
        PN810.S44
Sentimental novel: PN3448.S46
Sentimentality in literature
  General
    Literary history: PN56.S475
Separation (Psychology) in
  literature
  General
    Collections
      Wit and humor: PN6231.S495
Sequels
  General
    Collections
      Wit and humor: PN6231.S497
    Fiction: PN3448.S47
  Motion pictures: PN1995.9.S29
  Radio broadcasts: PN1991.8.S4
  Television broadcasts:
    PN1992.8.S4
Serbian proverbs: PN6505.S6
Serbo-Croatian quotations:
  PN6095.S4

Serbo-Croatian riddles:
PN6377.S4
Serer proverbs: PN6519.S38
Serial murderers in motion
pictures: PN1995.9.S297
Sermons (Burlesques)
General
Collections
Wit and humor: PN6231.S5
Serra, Junípero, in literature
General
Collections
Poetry: PN6110.S515
Servants' epitaphs: PN6298.S4
Sestina: PN1511
Seth (Biblical character) in
literature
General
Literary history
Legends: PN687.S3
Setting in literature
Drama technique: PN1672.9
General
Literary history: PN56.S48
Prose: PN3383.S42
Seven against Thebes (Greek
mythology) in literature
General
Literary history
Legends: PN687.S37
Seven Sages in literature
General
Literary history
Legends: PN687.S43
Seven sleepers in literature
General
Literary history
Legends: PN687.S5
Seven (The number) in literature
General
Literary history: PN56.S49
Sex crimes in the press: PN1
14.S47
United States: PN4888.S49
Sex differences
Authorship: PN171.S45

Sex differences in literature
General
Collections
Wit and humor: PN6231.S542
Literary history: PN56.S52
Sex in literature
General
Collections: PN6071.S416
Anecdotes: PN6268.S47
Proverbs: PN6525.S4
Quotations
English: PN6084.S49
French: PN6089.S4
German: PN6093.S4
Wit and humor: PN6149.S37,
PN6231.S54
Literary history: PN56.S5
Prose: PN3352.S48
Sex in motion pictures:
PN1995.9.S45
Sex in radio broadcasts:
PN1991.8.S44
Sex role
Television broadcasts:
PN1992.8.S44
Sex role in literature
General
Literary history
Drama: PN1650.S48
Juvenile literature:
PN1009.5.S48
Sex role in motion pictures:
PN1995.9.S47
Sexism in literature
General
Collections
Quotations
English: PN6084.S493
Literary history
Juvenile literature:
PN1009.5.S48
Sexual deviation in literature
General
Literary history: PN56.S53
Medieval: PN682.S38

Shades and shadow in literature
  General
    Literary history: PN56.S536
Shadow pantomimes: PN6120.S5
Shadow plays: PN1979.S5
Shaggy dog stories
  General
    Collections: PN6149.S4
Shakespeare, William, in
  literature
  General
    Collections
      Poetry: PN6110.S517
Shamanism in literature
  General
    Literary history
      Drama: PN1650.S52
Shamanism in motion pictures:
  PN1995.9.S48
Shantung Kuai shu: PN2874.5.K83
Sharks in literature
  General
    Collections
      Wit and humor: PN6231.S545
Sheep in literature
  General
    Collections: PN6071.S418
      Wit and humor: PN6231.S546
Sherlock Holmes films:
  PN1995.9.S5
Shi proverbs: PN6519.S43
Shipwrecks in literature
  General
    Literary history: PN56.S54
Shona proverbs: PN6519.S45
Shona riddles: PN6377.S42
Shoppers (Publications):
  PN4784.F74
Shopping in literature
  General
    Collections
      Wit and humor: PN6231.S5467
Short men in literature
  General
    Collections
      Wit and humor: PN6231.S547
Show business: PN1560+

Showboats: PN2293.S4
Sibille, Queen, in literature
  General
    Literary history
      Legends: PN687.S56
Sibyls in literature
  General
    Literary history: PN56.5.S54
Sicily (Italy) in literature
  General
    Literary history: PN56.3.S53
Sicily (Italy) in motion
  pictures: PN1995.9.S54
Sick in literature
  General
    Collections
      Wit and humor: PN6231.S548
Sick, Poems for the
  General
    Collections: PN6110.S52
Sickness in literature
  General
    Literary history
      Prose: PN3352.S5
Siebengebirge in literature
  General
    Collections: PN6071.S42
Siegfried in literature
  General
    Literary history: PN57.S5
Silence in literature
  General
    Collections
      Quotations
        German: PN6093.S5
      Literary history: PN56.S55
Silent films: PN1995.75
Silent pictures: PN1995.75
Simelungun proverbs: PN6519.S48
Simile in literature
  General
    Collections
      Quotations
        English: PN6084.S5
    Literary style: PN228.S5

Simpson, O.J., in literature
General
Collections
Wit and humor: PN6231.S5483
Sinbad, the philosopher, in
literature
General
Literary history
Legends: PN687.S6
Sincerity in literature
General
Literary history: PN56.S57
Sindhi proverbs: PN6519.S49
Sindhi riddles: PN6377.S45
Single parents in literature
General
Collections
Wit and humor: PN6231.S5484
Single women in literature
General
Collections
Wit and humor: PN6231.S5485
Sinhalese proverbs: PN6519.S5
Sinhalese quotations: PN6095.S44
Sins in literature
General
Collections
Quotations
French: PN6089.S5
Literary history: PN56.S56
Siraiki proverbs: PN6519.S55
Sirens (Mythology) in literature
General
Literary history: PN56.S574
Sisters in literature
General
Collections: PN6071.S425
Anecdotes: PN6268.S55
Aphorisms: PN6278.S55
Quotations
English: PN6084.S56
Wit and humor: PN6231.S5486
Sisters in motion pictures:
PN1995.9.S55
Skepticism in literature
General
Literary history: PN56.S576

Skiing in literature
General
Collections
Wit and humor: PN6231.S549
Skits
Drama
General
Collections: PN6120.S8
Sky in literature
General
Collections: PN6071.S43
Poetry: PN6110.S525
Slasher films: PN1995.9.S554
Slavery in literature
General
Collections
Poetry: PN6110.S53
Slavery in motion pictures:
PN1995.9.S557
Slavic proverbs: PN6505.S2+
Slavic-American newspapers:
PN4885.S45
Sleep in literature
General
Collections: PN6071.S45
Poetry: PN6110.S55
Literary history: PN56.S577
Sleeping Beauty in literature
General
Literary history: PN57.S54
Sleeping customs in literature
General
Collections
Wit and humor: PN6231.S55
Slovak proverbs: PN6505.S7
Slovak riddles: PN6377.S49
Slovak Uprising, 1944, in
literature
General
Collections: PN6071.S47
Slovak-American newspapers:
PN4885.S47
Slovakia in motion picture:
PN1995.9.S56

Slovenes in literature
  General
    Collections
      Wit and humor: PN6231.S555
Slovenian proverbs: PN6505.S75
Slovenian quotations: PN6095.S46
Slovenian riddles: PN6377.S5
Slovenian-American newspapers:
  PN4885.S5
Slums in literature
  General
    Collections
      Poetry: PN6110.S556
Small town journalism: PN4784.S5
Smiles in literature
  General
    Collections
      Quotations
        English: PN6084.S58
Smoking in literature
  General
    Collections
      Wit and humor: PN6231.S56
  Literary history: PN56.S58
Smoking in motion pictures:
  PN1995.9.S58
Snakes in literature
  General
    Collections: PN6071.S49
      Wit and humor: PN6231.S6
Snobs and snobbishness in
  literature
  General
    Collections
      Wit and humor: PN6231.S625
  Literary history: PN56.S6
Snow in literature
  General
    Collections: PN6071.S5
Snowboarding in literature
  General
    Collections
      Wit and humor: PN6231.S627
Soap bubbles in literature
  General
    Collections
      Wit and humor: PN6231.S63

Soccer in literature
  General
    Collections
      Wit and humor: PN6231.S632
Social aspects
  Acting: PN2071.S63
  Journalism
    United States: PN4888.S6
  Motion pictures: PN1995.9.S6
Social aspects of journalism:
  PN1 14.S6
Social aspects of wit and humor:
  PN6149.S62
Social classes in literature
  General
    Literary history: PN56.S64
      Juvenile literature:
        PN1009.5.S62
Social conditions in literature
  General
    Collections
      Poetry: PN6110.S56
Social conditions of authors:
  PN149.8+
Social conflict in literature
  General
    Literary history: PN56.S65
Social ideals, forces, etc., in
  literature
  General
    Literary history: PN51
Social justice in literature
  General
    Collections
      Poetry: PN6110.S56
Social life and customs in
  literature
  General
    Literary history
      Medieval: PN682.S7
Social marginality in literature
  General
    Literary history: PN56.M27
Social problems in literature
  Drama
    Comedies: PN1929.S6

Social problems in literature
  General
    Collections
      Quotations
        English: PN6084.S62
    Literary history: PN56.S65
Social problems in motion
  pictures: PN1995.9.S62
Social progress and poetry:
  PN1081
Social service in literature
  General
    Collections
      Maxims: PN6308.S58
Social structure in literature
  General
    Literary history: PN56.S654
Socialism in literature
  General
    Collections: PN6071.S52
      Poetry: PN6110.S57
Socialist journalism:
  PN4784.S55, PN1 14.S63
Socialist realism in literature
  General
    Literary history: PN56.S66
Socialist realism in motion
  pictures: PN1995.9.S63
Socialization in literature
  General
    Literary history
      Juvenile literature:
        PN1009.5.S625
Societies, Literary
  General: PN20+
Sociological approach to
  literary criticism: PN98.S6
Sociological novel: PN3448.S6
Sociology and literature: PN51
  Drama: PN1643
  Prose: PN3344
Sociology in literature
  General
    Collections: PN6071.S53
      Wit and humor: PN6231.S633

Socks in literature
  General
    Collections
      Wit and humor: PN6231.S634
Socrates in literature
  General
    Literary history: PN57.S57
Sohrab and Rustum in literature
  General
    Literary history: PN57.S6
Soldiers' epitaphs: PN6298.S64
Soldiers in literature
  General
    Collections: PN6071.S55
      Anecdotes: PN6268.S6
      Wit and humor: PN6231.M5
Solitude in literature
  General
    Collections: PN6071.S56
      Poetry: PN6110.S58
      Quotations
        English: PN6084.S65
    Literary history: PN56.S665
Somali proverbs: PN6519.S58
Song pantomimes: PN6120.S7
Song-writing
  Poetry: PN1059.S7
Songs in literature
  General
    Literary history
      Poetry: PN1381+
Sonnets
  General
    Collections: PN6110.S6
    Literary history: PN1514
Sons in literature
  General
    Collections: PN6071.S57
      Quotations
        English: PN6084.S67
Sorbian proverbs: PN6505.S77
Soul mates in literature
  General
    Literary history: PN56.S666
Sound effects in radio
  broadcasts: PN1991.8.S69

Sound effects in the theater:
  PN2091.S6
Sound motion pictures: PN1995.7
South Africa in literature
  General
    Collections
      Wit and humor: PN6231.S638
South Africa in motion pictures:
  PN1995.9.S655
Southern states in literature
  General
    Collections
      Quotations
        English: PN6084.S7
Southern States in literature
  General
    Collections
      Wit and humor: PN6231.S64
Southern States in motion
  pictures: PN1995.9.S66
Soviet Union in literature
  General
    Collections: PN6071.R8
      Proverbs: PN6505.S5
      Wit and humor: PN6231.S643
    Literary history: PN56.3.S67
Soviet Union in motion pictures:
  PN1995.9.S665
Soviet Union, Literature of
  Literary history: PN849.R9+
Space flight to the moon in
  literature
  General
    Collections: PN6071.S58
Space in literature
  General
    Literary history: PN56.S667
      Prose: PN3383.S67
Space travel in literature
  General
    Collections
      Wit and humor: PN6231.S645
    Literary history: PN56.V6
Spacebridges
  Television broadcasts:
    PN1992.8.S62

Spain in literature
  General
    Literary history: PN56.3.S7
Spain, Literature of
  Literary history: PN849.S6+
Spanish Civil War in literature
  General
    Collections: PN6071.S6
    Literary history: PN56.S67
    Poetry: PN1083.S63
Spanish language in literature
  General
    Collections
      Wit and humor: PN6231.S646
Spanish quotations: PN6095.S5
Spanish-American newspapers:
  PN4885.S75
Special effects
  Theater
    Great Britain: PN2582.S64
Special programs
  Television broadcasts:
    PN1992.8.S64
Specialization
  Journalism: PN4784.S58
Specials
  Television broadcasts:
    PN1992.8.S64
Speech
  Acting: PN2071.S65
Speed in literature
  General
    Literary history: PN56.S69
Spelling in literature
  General
    Collections
      Wit and humor: PN6231.S647
Spies in literature
  General
    Collections: PN6071.S64
Spirit possession in literature
  General
    Literary history: PN56.S697
Spiritual life in literature
  General
    Collections: PN6071.S615

Spirituality in literature
  General
    Literary history: PN56.S7
Sponsorship of performing arts:
  PN1590.S7
Spoonerisms in literature
  General
    Collections
      Wit and humor: PN6231.S649
Sports in literature
  General
    Collections: PN6071.S62
      Maxims: PN6308.S6
      Poetry: PN6110.S65
      Quotations
        English: PN6084.S72
      Wit and humor: PN6231.S65
    Literary history: PN56.S73
      Juvenile literature:
        PN1009.5.S67
Sports in motion pictures:
  PN1995.9.S67
Sports journalism: PN4784.S6,
  PN1 14.S65
Spring in literature
  General
    Collections: PN6071.S63
      Poetry: PN6110.S7
      Quotations
        English: PN6084.S73
Spy films: PN1995.9.S68
Spy stories
  General
    Collections: PN6071.S64
    Literary history: PN3448.S66
Spy television programs:
  PN1992.8.S67
Sranan proverbs: PN6519.S67
Stage and journalism: PN4765
Stage English: PN2071.S65
Stage lighting in the theater:
  PN2091.E4
Stage models: PN2091.M6
Stage props
  Motion pictures: PN1995.9.S69
Stage rigging: PN2091.M3

Stage setting and scenery
  Motion pictures: PN1995.9.S4
  Television broadcasts:
    PN1992.8.S7
  Theater: PN2091.S8
    College theatricals:
      PN3178.S8
Stalin, Joseph, in literature
  General
    Literary history: PN57.S82
Stand-up comedy: PN1969.C65
Standards
  Journalism
    United States: PN4888.S67
Stanislavsky method of acting:
  PN2062
Stanza: PN1059.S83
Star Trek films: PN1995.9.S694
Star Trek television programs:
  PN1992.8.S74
Star Wars films: PN1995.9.S695
Stars in literature
  General
    Collections: PN6071.S67
      Poetry: PN6110.S75
    Literary history: PN56.S735
State and the press: PN4735+
State and the theater: PN2042+
Statisticians in literature
  General
    Collections: PN6071.S68
Stenography in literature
  General
    Collections
      Poetry: PN6110.S8
Stills in motion pictures:
  PN1995.9.S696
Stimulants
  Effect on voice: PN4163.S8
Stock ownership in literature
  General
    Collections
      Wit and humor: PN6231.S73
Stonemasons in literature
  General
    Collections
      Anecdotes: PN6268.S7

Stories
  Journalism: PN4784.S7
Storytelling in literature
  General
    Literary history
      Prose: PN3352.S74
Strangers in literature
  General
    Literary history: PN56.5.S75
      Medieval: PN682.S75
Strasberg method of acting:
  PN2062
Stream of consciousness fiction
  General
    Literary history
      Technique: PN3377.5.S77
Street scenes in literature
  General
    Collections: PN6071.S7
Stress in literature
  General
    Collections
      Anecdotes: PN6268.S73
Stress management in literature
  General
    Collections
      Wit and humor: PN6231.S75
Strikes and lockouts
  Journalism: PN1 14.S75
String correspondents
  Journalism: PN4784.S73
Stringers
  Journalism: PN4784.S73
Striptease: PN1949.S7
Striptease in literature
  General
    Literary history: PN56.S736
Strong men in motion pictures:
  PN1995.9.S697
Strophe: PN1059.S83
Structuralism in literary
  criticism: PN98.S7
Student television: PN1992.8.S78
Students in literature
  General
    Collections: PN6071.S75
    Literary history: PN56.5.S78

Students' sayings
  General
    Collections: PN6328.S78
Stunt men in motion pictures:
  PN1995.9.S7
Stunts
  Drama
    General
      Collections: PN6120.S8
Stupidity in literature
  General
    Literary history: PN56.S737
Style in literature
  General
    Literary history
      Prose: PN3383.S79
Subconsciousness in literature
  General
    Literary history: PN56.S74
Subjectivity in literature
  General
    Literary history: PN56.S7414
Subjects for articles
  Journalism: PN4784.S75
Substance abuse in literature
  General
    Collections: PN6071.S78
Subtenants in literature
  General
    Collections
      Wit and humor: PN6231.S79
Subtext in literature
  General
    Literary history
      Drama: PN1681
Suburban life in literature
  General
    Collections
      Wit and humor: PN6231.S8
Suburbs in motion pictures:
  PN1995.9.S74
Subversive activities in
  literature
  General
    Collections: PN6071.S79

Subways in literature
  General
    Collections
      Wit and humor: PN6231.S82
Subways in motion pictures:
  PN1995.9.S75
Success in literature
  General
    Collections: PN6071.S8
      Quotations
        English: PN6084.S78
      Wit and humor: PN6231.S83
Sudanese proverbs: PN6519.S8
Suffering in literature
  General
    Collections
      Quotations
        English: PN6084.S79
    Literary history: PN56.S742
Sufi tales: PN6071.S85
  Wit and humor: PN6231.S86
Suicide in literature
  General
    Collections: PN6071.S87
      Wit and humor: PN6231.S876
    Literary history: PN56.S744
Sukuma proverbs: PN6519.S83
Sumerian proverbs: PN6418.5.S8
Summer in literature
  General
    Collections
      Poetry: PN6110.S85
Summer theater
  United States: PN2269
Sun in literature
  General
    Collections: PN6071.S88
      Poetry: PN6110.S87
Sundanese proverbs: PN6519.S85
Sundanese riddles: PN6377.S85
Sunday in literature
  General
    Literary history: PN56.S747
Sung, Kim Il, in literature
  General
    Collections
      Poetry: PN6110.K55

Sunshine in literature
  General
    Collections
      Quotations
        English: PN6084.S8
Superficiality in literature
  General
    Literary history: PN56.S75
Superhero films: PN1992.8.S76,
  PN1995.9.S76
Superman films: PN1995.9.S77
Superman, The, in literature
  General
    Literary history: PN57.S94
Supernatural
  Journalism
    United States: PN4888.S77
Supernatural in literature
  General
    Collections: PN6071.S9
      Poetry: PN6110.S9
      Wit and humor: PN6231.S877
    Literary history: PN56.S8
Supernatural in motion pictures:
  PN1995.9.S8
Superstition in literature
  General
    Collections
      Wit and humor: PN6231.S88
Supervisors
  Oratory: PN4192.S94
Supervisors in literature
  General
    Collections
      Quotations
        English: PN6084.S84
Supplements
  Journalism
    United States: PN4888.S8
Suriname, Literature of
  Literary history: PN849.S75+
Surrealism in literature
  General
    Collections
      Wit and humor: PN6231.S883
    Literary history: PN56.S87
      Poetry: PN1059.S88

Surrealism in motion pictures:
PN1995.9.S85
Survival skills in literature
General
Collections
Wit and humor: PN6231.S886
Suspense in drama: PN1687
Suspense in literature
General
Collections: PN6071.S92
Literary history: PN56.S88
Suspense in motion pictures:
PN1995.9.S87
Svan proverbs: PN6519.S87
Swahili proverbs: PN6519.S9
Swan-knight in literature
General
Literary history
Legends: PN687.S8
Swans in literature
General
Collections
Poetry: PN6110.S92
Swearing in literature
General
Collections: PN6071.S93
Swedish quotations: PN6095.S8
Swedish-American newspapers:
PN4885.S8
Sweeping and dusting in
literature
General
Collections
Wit and humor: PN6231.S89
Swindlers and swindling in
literature
General
Literary history
Prose: PN3352.S94
Swine in literature
General
Collections: PN6071.S94
Poetry: PN6110.S93
Wit and humor: PN6231.S895
Literary history
Medieval: PN682.S94

Switzerland, Literature of
Literary history: PN849.S9+
Symbolism in literature
General
Collections: PN6071.S96
Literary history: PN56.S9
Drama: PN1633.S9
Poetry: PN1059.S94
Sympathy in literature
General
Literary history: PN56.S94
Syndicate writing: PN4784.S8
Syndicates
Journalism
United States: PN4888.S9
Theater: PN2291
Synecdoche
Literary style: PN228.S95
Syntax in literature
General
Poetry: PN1059.S96
Systems in literature
General
Collections
Wit and humor: PN6231.S93

T

Tableaux
General
Collections: PN6120.T3
Literary history: PN3203+
Recitations in English:
PN4305.T3
Tabloid newspapers: PN4784.T23
United States: PN4888.T3
Tackiness in literature
General
Collections
Wit and humor: PN6231.T15
Tag-Nung proverbs: PN6519.T36
Tagalog proverbs: PN6519.T2
Tagalog riddles: PN6377.T23
Tajik proverbs: PN6519.T28
Tajik riddles: PN6377.T24
Talk shows
Broadcasting: PN1990.9.T34

Talk shows
  Broadcasting
    Radio broadcasts:
      PN1991.8.T35
    Television broadcasts:
      PN1992.8.T3
Talk shows in literature
  General
    Collections
      Wit and humor: PN6231.T17
Tamashek proverbs: PN6519.T29
Tamazight riddles: PN6377.T246
Tamil proverbs: PN6519.T3
Tamil quotations: PN6095.T3
Tamil riddles: PN6377.T25
Tamu proverbs: PN6519.T32
Tangier (Morocco) in literature
  General
    Collections: PN6071.T25
Tannhäuser in literature
  General
    Literary history: PN57.T3
Tanzanian proverbs: PN6519.T33
Tarzan in motion pictures:
  PN1995.9.T3
Tatar proverbs: PN6519.T35
Taverns in literature
  General
    Collections
      Anecdotes: PN6268.H8
Taxation in literature
  General
    Collections
      Wit and humor: PN6231.T2
Taxicabs in literature
  General
    Collections
      Anecdotes: PN6268.T3
      Wit and humor: PN6231.T23
Tay-Nung riddles: PN6377.T32
Tea in literature
  General
    Literary history: PN56.T34
Teachers
  Oratory: PN4192.T43

Teachers in literature
  General
    Collections: PN6071.T3
    Wit and humor: PN6231.S3
Teachers in motion pictures:
  PN1995.9.T4
Technical journalism:
  PN4784.T3, PN1 14.T37
Technique
  Authorship: PN171.4+
Technique in literature
  General
    Literary history
      Drama: PN1660+
      Prose: PN3355+
Technique in the performing
  arts: PN1590.T43
Technocracy in literature
  General
    Collections
      Wit and humor: PN6231.T3
Technology in literature
  General
    Collections
      Poetry: PN6110.T4
    Literary history: PN56.T37
    Juvenile literature:
      PN1009.5.T43
    Poetry: PN1083.T42
Teddy bears in literature
  General
    Collections
      Wit and humor: PN6231.T35
Teeth in literature
  General
    Literary history: PN56.T4
Telchines (Greek mythology) in
  literature
  General
    Literary history: PN56.T44
Telegrams in literature
  General
    Collections
      Wit and humor: PN6231.T4

Telephone in literature
  General
    Collections
      Wit and humor: PN6231.T5
Telephone in motion pictures:
  PN1995.9.T45
Television broadcasts
  Communication: PN1992+
  Television drama: PN1992.65
Television in literature
  General
    Collections
      Wit and humor: PN6231.T53
Television journalism:
  PN4784.T4, PN1 14.T4
  United States: PN4888.T4
Television plays
  General
    Collections: PN6120.T4
Television program guides
  Journalism: PN1 14.T43
Telugu proverbs: PN6519.T4
Telugu quotations: PN6095.T4
Telugu riddles: PN6377.T4
Tennis in literature
  General
    Collections
      Wit and humor: PN6231.T55
Terror and wonder in literature
  General
    Collections
      Poetry: PN6110.T5
Terrorism
  Journalism: PN4784.T45, PN1
  14.T46
Terrorism in literature
  General
    Literary history
      Drama: PN1650.T47
      Prose: PN3352.T35
Texans in literature
  General
    Collections
      Wit and humor: PN6231.T56

Texas in literature
  English
    Collections
      Wit and humor: PN6231.T56
Texas in motion pictures:
  PN1995.9.T47
Textile fabrics in literature
  General
    Collections: PN6071.T35
Textile industry in literature
  General
    Collections: PN6071.T35
Thai proverbs: PN6519.T45
Thai quotations: PN6095.T5
Thais in literature
  General
    Literary history: PN57.T5
Thanksgiving in literature
  General
    Collections
      Drama: PN6120.T5
      Poetry: PN6110.T6
      Recitations: PN4305.T5
Theater, Dinner
  United States: PN2270.D56
Theater, Environmental:
  PN2081.E58
Theater, Hispanic American:
  PN2270.H57
Theater in literature
  General
    Collections: PN6071.T4
      Poetry: PN6110.T63
    Quotations
      English: PN6084.T48
      German: PN6093.T5
    Wit and humor: PN6231.T57
    Literary history
      Prose: PN3352.T45
Theater management: PN2053
  College theatricals:
    PN3178.T68
Theater, Nonprofit: PN2293.N67
Theater rehearsals in literature
  General
    Literary history
      Drama: PN1650.T5

Theaters, Independent: PN2293.I4
Theatrical troupes: PN2297.A2+
Theatrical troupes and companies
  England: PN2599.5.T54
  France: PN2639.5.T54
  Germany: PN2659.5.T47
Theatrical trusts: PN2293.T8
Themes in motion pictures:
  PN1997.8
Theology in literature
  General
    Collections
      Wit and humor: PN6231.T6
Theophilus in literature
  General
    Literary history
      Legends: PN687.T5
Theory of literature: PN45+
Thorapoutics in literature
  General
    Collections
      Wit and humor: PN6231.T63
Thisbe in literature
  General
    Literary history: PN57.P9
Thonga proverbs: PN6519.T74
Three Stooges films: PN1995.9.T5
Thumri (Dance drama):
  PN2884.5.T45
Tibetan proverbs: PN6519.T55
Ticket prices
  Theater
    Great Britain: PN2582.T5
Tickets
  Performing arts: PN1590.T53
Time in literature
  General
    Collections: PN6071.T5
      Aphorisms: PN6278.T5
      Quotations
        English: PN6084.T5
      Wit and humor: PN6231.T64
    Literary history: PN56.T5
      Drama: PN1650.T56
      Juvenile literature:
        PN1009.5.T55
      Medieval: PN682.T55

Time in literature
  General
    Literary history
      Prose: PN3352.T5
Time in motion pictures:
  PN1995.9.T55
Time management
  Journalism
    United States: PN4888.T55
Time, the weekly news-magazine,
  in literature
  General
    Collections
      Wit and humor: PN6231.T642
Timur, the Great, in literature
  General
    Literary history: PN57.T65
Titanic (Steamship) in literature
  General
    Collections: PN6071.T55
Titles, Credit, in motion
  pictures: PN1995.9.C65
Titles of books
  General: PN171.T5
    Collections
      Wit and humor: PN6231.T65
Titles of motion pictures:
  PN1995.9.T57
Titles of poems: PN1059.T5
Toasts in literature
  General
    Collections
      Miscellaneous: PN6340+
Toba-Batak proverbs: PN6519.T57
Tobacco chewing in literature
  General
    Collections
      Wit and humor: PN6231.T656
Tobote proverbs: PN6519.T58
Toilets in literature
  General
    Collections
      Wit and humor: PN6231.W3
Tokyo in motion pictures:
  PN1995.9.T64
Tony awards: PN2270.A93

Top forty stations
  Radio broadcasts:
    PN1991.67.P67
Toposforschung
  Literary criticism: PN98.T6
Toraja proverbs: PN6519.T62
Toronto (Ontario) in literature
  General
    Collections
      Wit and humor: PN6231.T66
Torture in literature
  General
    Literary history: PN56.T62
Totalitarianism in literature
  General
    Literary history: PN56.T64
Tourist trade in literature
  General
    Collections
      Wit and humor: PN6231.T67
Tower of Babel in literature
  General
    Literary history: PN56.B23
Toy theaters: PN1979.T6
Toys in literature
  General
    Collections
      Quotations
        English: PN6084.T68
      Wit and humor: PN6231.T673
Tractors in literature
  General
    Collections
      Wit and humor: PN6231.T677
Traffic regulations in literature
  General
    Collections
      Wit and humor: PN6231.T68
Tragedy in literature
  General
    Literary history
      Drama: PN1892+
Tragic, The, in literature
  General
    Literary history: PN56.T68
      Juvenile literature:
        PN1009.5.T7

Tragic, The, in literature
  General
    Literary history
      Medieval: PN682.T68
Tragicomedy in literature
  General
    Literary history: PN1902+
Trailers, Motion picture:
  PN1995.9.T685
Tramps in literature
  General
    Collections
      Wit and humor: PN6231.T69
Transatlantic speech
  Acting: PN2071.S65
Translating and translations
  General
    Collections
      Foreign classics into
        English: PN6019+
    Literary history
      Poetry: PN1059.T7
Translating and translations in
  literature
  General
    Literary history
      Juvenile literature:
        PN1009.5.T75
Transportation in literature
  General
    Collections
      Wit and humor: PN6231.T694
Trapalhões films: PN1995.9.T72
Travel
  Television broadcasts:
    PN1992.8.T75
Travel in literature
  General
    Collections: PN6071.T7
      Quotations
        English: PN6084.T7
        German: PN6093.T7
    Literary history: PN56.T7
      Medieval: PN682.T7

Traveling in literature
  General
    Collections
      Anecdotes: PN6268.T7
      Poetry: PN6110.T7
      Wit and humor: PN6231.T7
Traveling theater
  England: PN2599.5.T73
    Renaissance: PN2590.T7
  France: PN2639.5.T73
Trees in literature
  General
    Collections: PN6071.T74
    Quotations
      English: PN6084.T75
Trephining in literature
  General
    Literary history: PN56.T73
Trials in motion pictures:
  PN1995.9.T75
Tricksters in literature
  General
    Collections: PN6071.T746
    Literary history: PN56.5.T74
Triolet: PN1517
Tristan and Isolde in literature
  General
    Literary history: PN57.T8
Tristan in literature
  General
    Collections: PN6071.T75
    Literary history
      Legends: PN686.T7
      Poetry
        Medieval: PN690.T7
Trojan War in literature
  General
    Literary history: PN56.T76
Trolls in literature
  General
    Collections
      Wit and humor: PN6231.T73
Troubadours in literature
  General
    Literary history
      Medieval: PN682.T76
Troupes, Theatrical: PN2297.A2+

Truck drivers in literature
  General
    Collections
      Anecdotes: PN6268.T77
True crime programs
  Broadcasting
    Television broadcasts:
      PN1992.8.T78
Trust in literature
  General
    Literary history: PN56.T77
Trusts, Theatrical: PN2293.T8
Truthfulness and falsehood in
  literature
  General
    Collections
      Wit and humor: PN6231.T74
    Literary history: PN56.T78
Tshi proverbs: PN6519.T7
Tsonga proverbs: PN6519.T74
Tswana proverbs: PN6519.T75
Tuberculosis in literature
  General
    Collections: PN6071.T82
    Literary history: PN56.T82
Tugen proverbs: PN6519.T76
Tulu proverbs: PN6519.T77
Turkey in literature
  General
    Literary history: PN56.3.T87
Turkic proverbs: PN6519.T78
Turkish proverbs: PN6519.T79
Turkish quotations: PN6095.T8
Turkish riddles: PN6377.T8
Turkmen proverbs: PN6519.T8
Turks in motion pictures:
  PN1995.9.T87
Tusia riddles: PN6377.T87
Tuvinian proverbs: PN6519.T84
Twelfth-night in literature
  General
    Collections
      Drama: PN6120.T8

Twenty-first century in
  literature
  General
    Collections
      Quotations
        English: PN6084.T83
      Wit and humor: PN6231.T76
Twins in literature
  General
    Literary history: PN56.5.T85
      Drama: PN1650.T84
Typewriting in literature
  General
    Collections
      Wit and humor: PN6231.T78
Typographical humor in literature
  General
    Collections
      Wit and humor: PN6231.T8
Typography in literature
  General
    Collections
      Poetry: PN6110.T8
Tzu ti shu: PN2874.5.K83

U

Udmurt proverbs: PN6505.U34
Udmurt riddles: PN6377.U26
Ugliness in literature
  General
    Literary history
      Medieval: PN682.U4
Uighur proverbs: PN6519.U5
Ukrainian proverbs: PN6505.S76
Ukrainian quotations: PN6095.U5
Ukrainian riddles: PN6377.U4
Ukrainian-American newspapers:
  PN4885.U4
Ukrainians in motion pictures:
  PN1995.9.U45
Ulysses in literature
  General
    Literary history: PN57.O3
Umbundu proverbs: PN6519.U54

Uncles in literature
  General
    Collections
      Aphorisms: PN6278.U52
Underdeveloped areas in
  literature
  General
    Literary history
      Juvenile literature:
        PN1009.5.U53
Underground films: PN1995.9.E96
Underground literature
  Journalism: PN1 14.U5
Underground movements in motion
  pictures: PN1995.9.U6
Underground press: PN4784.U53,
  PN1 14.U53
    United States: PN4888.U5
Underwear in literature
  General
    Collections
      Wit and humor: PN6231.U52
Undine in literature
  General
    Literary history: PN57.U5
Uneducated poets
  General
    Literary history: PN1097
Unicorns in literature
  General
    Collections
      Wit and humor: PN6231.U54
    Literary history
      Medieval: PN682.U5
Unidentified flying objects in
  motion pictures: PN1995.9.U62
Unification Church authors
  General
    Collections
      Poetry: PN6109.95.U55
Union representatives
  Oratory: PN4192.U54
United Nations in literature
  General
    Collections
      Drama: PN6120.U5

United States in literature
  General
    Collections
      Quotations
        English: PN6084.U53
    Literary history: PN56.3.U5
United States in motion
  pictures: PN1995.9.U64
United States, Literature of
  Literary history: PN849.U5+
Unities
  Drama technique: PN1672+
Universities and colleges in
  literature
  General
    Literary history: PN56.U54
University magazines
  United States: PN4881
Upper classes in literature
  General
    Collections
      Wit and humor: PN6231.U64
Urdu proverbs: PN6519.U7
Urdu quotations: PN6095.U7
Urdu riddles: PN6377.U7
Utopian literature: PN3448.U7
Utopias in literature
  General
    Collections: PN6071.U85
    Literary history: PN56.U8
      Juvenile literature:
        PN1009.5.U85
      Medieval: PN682.U75
Uzbek proverbs: PN6519.U9
Uzbek riddles: PN6377.U9

V

Vacations in literature
  General
    Collections
      Wit and humor: PN6231.V2
Valentine and Orson in literature
  General
    Literary history
      Legends: PN687.V3

Valentine verses
  General
    Collections: PN6110.V35
Valentines in literature
  General
    Collections
      Quotations
        English: PN6084.V3
Valley girls in literature
  General
    Collections
      Wit and humor: PN6231.V25
Values in literature
  General
    Literary history: PN56.V28
Vampires in literature
  General
    Collections: PN6071.V3
      Poetry: PN6110.V37
      Quotations
        English: PN6084.V35
      Wit and humor: PN6231.V27
    Literary history: PN56.V3
      Drama: PN1650.V34
Vampires in motion pictures:
  PN1995.9.V3
Varieties
  Drama: PN1962+
Variety shows
  Television: PN1992.8.V3
Vaudeville: PN1962+
  Drama
    General
      Collections: PN6120.V3
Vegetables in literature
  General
    Collections
      Quotations
        English: PN6084.V44
Veils in literature
  General
    Literary history: PN56.V44
Venality in literature
  General
    Literary history
      Medieval: PN682.V4

Veneto (Italy) in motion
pictures: PN1995.9.V4
Venice (Italy) in literature
General
Collections: PN6071.V4
Wit and humor: PN6231.V4
Literary history: PN56.3.V4
Ventriloquism in literature
General
Collections
Drama: PN6120.V4
Venus (Goddess) in literature
General
Literary history: PN57.V4
Verisimilitude in literature
General
Literary history
Prose: PN3352.P67
Vermont in literature
General
Collections
Wit and humor: PN6231.V46
Vers de société
General
Collections: PN6110.V4
Literary history: PN1451
Veterans in motion pictures:
PN1995.9.V44
Veterinary medicine in literature
General
Collections
Wit and humor: PN6231.V48
Video adaptations: PN1997.85
Videocassettes: PN1992.93+
Videodiscs: PN1992.93+
Videotapes: PN1992.93+
Vienna. Universität in
literature
General
Literary history: PN56.V5
Vietnamese Conflict in literature
General
Collections: PN6071.V46
Drama: PN6120.V48
Poetry: PN6110.V53
Literary history
Drama: PN1650.V53

Vietnamese proverbs: PN6519.V5
Vietnamese quotations:
PN6095.V53
Vietnamese riddles: PN6377.V53
Vietnamese-American newspapers:
PN4885.V53
Vikings in literature
General
Collections
Wit and humor: PN6231.V53
Villains in literature
General
Literary history: PN56.5.V5
Villains in motion pictures:
PN1995.9.V47
Villanelles
General
Literary history: PN1521
Violence
Journalism: PN1 14.V56
Television broadcasts:
PN1992.8.V55
Violence in literature
General
Collections: PN6071.V5
Literary history: PN56.V53
Drama: PN1650.V55
Juvenile literature:
PN1009.5.V54
Medieval: PN682.V55
Violence in motion pictures:
PN1995.9.V5
Virelai: PN1523
Virginity in literature
General
Literary history
Medieval: PN682.V56
Virtues in literature
General
Collections
Poetry: PN6110.V54
Visions in literature
General
Literary history
Medieval: PN682.V57

Visual literature
  General
    Literary history: PN56.V54
Visual perception in literature
  General
    Collections
      Quotations
        English: PN6084.V58
    Literary history: PN56.V543
      Medieval: PN682.V59
Visual poetry
  General
    Collections: PN6110.V56
    Literary history: PN1455
Vocabulary in literature
  General
    Collections
      Wit and humor: PN6231.W64
Vocational guidance
  Broadcasting: PN1990.55
  Oratory: PN4098
Voice culture
  Oratory: PN4197
Voice in literature
  General
    Literary history: PN56.V55
Voice-overs
  Motion pictures: PN1995.9.V63
  Television broadcasts:
    PN1992.8.A6
Vomiting in literature
  General
    Collections
      Wit and humor: PN6231.V65
Voodooism in motion pictures:
  PN1995.9.V66
Vortex-motion in literature
  General
    Literary history: PN56.V57
Votic proverbs: PN6505.V63
Votic riddles: PN6377.V66
Voyages, Imaginary, in literature
  General
    Literary history: PN56.V59

Voyages, Interplanetary, in
  literature
  General
    Literary history: PN56.V6

W

Wade in literature
  General
    Literary history
      Legends: PN687.W2
Wages
  Journalism: PN1 14.W25
  United States: PN4888.W34
Waiters in literature
  General
    Collections
      Wit and humor: PN6231.W27
Waldman, Hans, in literature
  General
    Literary history: PN57.W25
Wales in literature
  General
    Collections
      Quotations
        English: PN6084.W3
      Wit and humor: PN6178.W44
Walking in literature
  General
    Collections: PN6071.W3
      Quotations
        English: PN6084.W32
    Literary history
      Prose: PN3352.W34
Walthari, of Aquitaine, in
  literature
  General
    Collections: PN6071.W32
    Literary history: PN57.W257
      Legends: PN687.W26
Wandering Jew in literature
  General
    Literary history: PN57.W3
      Legends: PN687.W3
War correspondents: PN4823

War in literature
  General
    Collections: PN6071.W35
      Aphorisms: PN6278.W35
      Poetry: PN6110.W28
      Quotations
        English: PN6084.W35
        French: PN6089.W3
    Literary history: PN56.W3
    Drama: PN1650.W3
      Comedies: PN1929.W35
    Fiction: PN3448.W3
    Juvenile literature:
      PN1009.5.W35
    Medieval: PN682.W35
    Poetry: PN1083.W37
    Prose: PN3377.5.W37
War in motion pictures:
  PN1995.9.W3
War in the press: PN4784.W37
Warega proverbs: PN6519.W3
Warning labels in literature
  General
    Collections
      Wit and humor: PN6231.W29
WASPs (Persons) in literature
  General
    Collections
      Wit and humor: PN6231.W17
Water closets in literature
  General
    Collections
      Wit and humor: PN6231.W3
Water in literature
  General
    Collections: PN6071.W37
      Poetry: PN6110.W3
    Literary history: PN56.W34
    Legends
      Arthurian legends:
        PN686.W37
    Medieval: PN682.W37
Water spirits in literature
  General
    Literary history: PN56.W37

Watering-places in literature
  General
    Literary history: PN56.H37
Wax works in literature
  General
    Collections
      Drama: PN6120.W3
Wayang: PN1979.S5
Wayang orang (Dance drama):
  PN2904.5.W38
Wayang wong (Dance drama):
  PN2904.5.W38
WD-40 (Trademark) in literature
  General
    Collections
      Wit and humor: PN6231.W35
Wealth in literature
  General
    Literary history: PN56.W4
Weather in literature
  General
    Collections
      Maxims: PN6308.W4
      Proverbs: PN6525.W4
    Literary history: PN56.W43
Weddings
  Television broadcasts:
    PN1992.8.W36
Weddings in literature
  General
    Collections: PN6071.W4
      Poetry: PN6110.W4
      Wit and humor: PN6231.W37
    Recitations: PN4305.W44
Weddings in motion pictures:
  PN1995.9.M3
Welsh-American newspapers:
  PN4885.W44
Wendic proverbs: PN6505.S77
Werewolves in literature
  General
    Collections: PN6071.W47
    Literary history: PN56.W45
Werewolves in motion pictures:
  PN1995.9.W38

West Indians in literature
General
Collections
Anecdotes: PN6268.W4
West Indies, Literature of
Literary history: PN849.C3+
West (U.S.) in literature
General
Collections
Quotations
English: PN6084.W39
Wit and humor: PN6231.W4
Western films: PN1995.9.W4
Western stories
General
Literary history: PN3448.W4
Technique: PN3377.5.W47
Westerns
Radio broadcasts: PN1991.8.W47
Television broadcasts:
PN1992.8.W4
Whales in literature
General
Collections
Wit and humor: PN6231.W44
White collar workers in
literature
General
Literary history: PN56.5.W46
White Russian proverbs:
PN6505.S78+
Whites in literature
General
Collections
Wit and humor: PN6231.W444
Whites in motion pictures:
PN1995.9.W45
Widow of Ephesus in literature
General
Literary history: PN57.W5
Wild huntsman in literature
General
Literary history: PN57.W55
Wild men in literature
General
Literary history: PN56.5.W5

Wilderness areas in literature
General
Collections
Quotations
English: PN6084.W47
Windows in literature
General
Collections: PN6071.W56
Literary history: PN56.W47
Winds in literature
General
Literary history: PN56.W49
Windsurfing in literature
General
Collections
Wit and humor: PN6231.W45
Wine in literature
General
Collections: PN6071.W57
Drama: PN6120.W5
Quotations
English: PN6084.W5
German: PN6093.W5
Wit and humor: PN6231.W46
Literary history: PN56.W5
Winter in literature
General
Collections: PN6071.W6
Wisdom in literature
General
Literary history: PN56.W54
Wishes in literature
General
Collections
Quotations
English: PN6084.W53
Wit and humor: PN6231.W48
Wit and humor
General
Collections: PN6146.2+
Witches in literature
General
Literary history: PN56.5.W56
Wives in literature
General
Collections
Anecdotes: PN6268.W5

Wives in literature
  General
    Collections
      Quotations
        English: PN6084.W55
        Wit and humor: PN6231.W5
Wobe proverbs: PN6519.W62
Woisika riddles: PN6377.W64
Women
  Literary critics: PN98.W64
  Oratory: PN4192.W65
  Radio broadcasts: PN1991.8.W65
  Theater
    France: PN2622.W65
    Great Britain: PN2582.W65
    United States
      Biography: PN2286.8
Women and broadcasting:
  PN1990.9.W64
Women and literature
  General
    Literary history
      Poetry: PN1091
Women authors
  General
    Collections: PN6069.W65
      Drama: PN6119.8
      Fiction: PN6120.92.W65
      Poetry: PN6109.9
    Literary history: PN471+
    Prose: PN3401
    Quotations
      English: PN6081.5
Women in amateur theater:
  PN3160.W64
Women in journalism: PN4784.W7
Women in literature
  General
    Collections: PN6071.W7
    Anecdotes: PN6268.W6
    Aphorisms: PN6278.W6
    Drama: PN6120.W6
    Epigrams: PN6288.W6
    Maxims: PN6308.W6
    Poetry: PN6110.W6
    Quotations
      English: PN6084.W6

Women in literature
  General
    Collections
      Quotations
        French: PN6089.W6
        German: PN6093.W6
        Thoughts: PN6338.W6
        Wit and humor: PN6231.W6
    Literary history: PN56.5.W64
    Drama: PN1650.W65
    Fiction: PN3426.W65
    Legends: PN686.W65
    Medieval: PN682.W6
    Romance literatures:
      PN810.W6
Women in motion pictures:
  PN1995.9.W6
Women in television broadcasts:
  PN1992.8.W65
Women in the performing arts:
  PN1590.W64
Women in the theater
  German theater: PN2642.W65
Women murderers in motion
  pictures: PN1995.9.W65
Women, Portrayal of
  Journalism
    United States: PN4888.W65
Women travelers in literature
  General
    Collections: PN6071.W72
Women's magazines
  United States: PN4879
Women's periodicals: PN4835.5
Women's theater
  Great Britain: PN2595.13.W65
Words in literature
  General
    Collections
      Quotations
        English: PN6084.W65
      Wit and humor: PN6231.W64
Work in literature
  General
    Collections: PN6071.W74
    Aphorisms: PN6278.W63
    Poetry: PN6110.W7

Work in literature
  General
    Collections
      Quotations: PN6084.W67
      Wit and humor: PN6231.W644
    Literary history: PN56.W65
Workaholics in literature
  General
    Collections
      Wit and humor: PN6231.W645
Workers' theaters: PN3305+
Working class
  Journalism
    United States: PN4888.L27
Working class in literature
  General
    Collections: PN6071.L3
      Wit and humor: PN6231.L32
    Literary history
      Fiction: PN3426.L3
      Prose: PN3352.L33
Working class in motion
  pictures: PN1995.9.L28
World records in literature
  General
    Collections
      Wit and humor: PN6231.W646
World War I in literature
  General
    Collections: PN6071.E8
World War II in literature
  General
    Collections: PN6071.W75
Worldliness in literature
  General
    Literary history: PN56.W67
Worry in literature
  General
    Collections
      Wit and humor: PN6231.W648
Worship programs in literature
  General
    Collections
      Wit and humor: PN6231.W65

Wrestling in literature
  General
    Collections
      Wit and humor: PN6231.W73
Writer's block: PN171.W74

X

Xiang sheng: PN2874.5.H75
Xosa proverbs: PN6519.X6

Y

Yaka (Zaire and Angola)
  proverbs: PN6519.Y19
Yaksagana (Dance drama):
  PN2884.5.Y35
Yakut proverbs: PN6519.Y2
Yakut riddles: PN6377.Y34
Yarico and Inkle in literature
  General
    Literary history: PN57.I6
Yay proverbs: PN6519.Y25
Yiddish films: PN1995.9.Y54
Yiddish riddles: PN6377.Y5
Yiddish-American newspapers:
  PN4885.Y5
Yombe proverbs: PN6519.Y55
York (Pa.) in literature
  General
    Collections
      Wit and humor: PN6231.Y67
Yoruba proverbs: PN6519.Y6
Young adult fiction
  General
    Literary history: PN3443
Youth in literature
  General
    Collections
      Quotations
        English: PN6084.Y6
      Wit and humor: PN6231.A26
    Literary history: PN56.5.Y67
Youth in motion pictures:
  PN1995.9.Y6
Youth in television broadcasts:
  PN1992.8.Y68

Ywain in literature
  General
    Literary history
      Legends: PN686.Y8

Z

Zambian proverbs: PN6519.Z27
Zapotec proverbs: PN6519.Z3
Zarma proverbs: PN6519.Z35
Zeangir in literature
  General
    Literary history: PN57.M8
Zen Buddhism in literature
  General
    Literary history: PN56.Z44
Zen poetry
  General
    Collections: PN6110.Z45
Zionism in literature
  General
    Literary history: PN56.Z55
Zombie films: PN1995.9.Z63
Zombies in literature
  General
    Collections
      Wit and humor: PN6231.Z65
Zorro films: PN1995.9.Z67
Zulu proverbs: PN6519.Z8
Zurich in literature
  General
    Collections: PN6071.Z8